UNDER NEW MANAGEMENT

Port Growth and Emerging Coastal Management Programs

D1073672

UNDER NEW MANAGEMENT

Port Growth and Emerging Coastal Management Programs

Marc Hershman
Robert Goodwin
Andrew Ruotsala
Maureen McCrea
Yehuda Hayuth

A WASHINGTON SEA GRANT PUBLICATION
Distributed by University of Washington Press
Seattle and London

This research was carried out by the Coastal Resources
Program of the Institute for Marine Studies, University of
Washington, between July 1976 and December 1977, under grant
04-7-158-44021 from the National Oceanic and Atmospheric
Administration (NOAA) to the Washington Sea Grant Program. Funds
were provided by the Information and Technical Assistance group of
the federal Office of Coastal Zone Management, NOAA, U.S.
Department of Commerce.

Library of Congress Cataloging in Publication Data

Main entry under title:

Under new management.

  "WSG 78-4"
  Bibliography: p.
  1. Harbors—United States. 2. Coastal zone manage-
ment—United States. I. Hershman, Marc, 1942-
HE553.U52 387.1'0973 78-66066
ISBN 0-295-95659-3.

CONTENTS

Foreword   vii
Preface   ix
Acknowledgments   xi

1 **TRENDS IN PORT DEVELOPMENT AND COASTAL MANAGEMENT PROGRAM DEVELOPMENT**   1
   Study Methods and Definitions   4
   Related Studies   7

2 **PORT DEVELOPMENT**   9
   Port Authorities   9
   Demand for Port Services   17
   Federal Port Programs   22
   Land and Water Regulation   23

3 **COASTAL ZONE MANAGEMENT PROGRAMS**   30
   State Coastal Program Development   31
   Federal Review and Approval   46
   Program Implementation and Administration   47
   Aspects of Coastal Management Programs Added by 1976 Amendments   48
   Summary   49

4 **LAND- AND WATER-USE PROBLEMS AND EMERGING POLICIES**   51
   Management of Landfill   52
   Management of Dredging and Dredged Materials Disposal   57
   Air and Water Quality Degradation   61
   Mitigation and Compensation for Environmental Damage   63
   Public Access and Aesthetics   66
   Siting Hazardous Facilities   70
   Small-craft Harbor Facilities   73
   Allocation of Waterfront Land   75
   Streamlining Environmental Permit Procedures   83
   Future Use of Obsolete Waterfront Facilities   90

5 **PORT PARTICIPATION IN COASTAL MANAGEMENT PROGRAMS**   93
   Participation and Information Exchange During Program Development   93
   Port Participation in Implementing Coastal Management Programs   104
   Mechanisms to Address Multijurisdictional Port-related Problems in the Coastal Zone   109
   Summary   112

6 **RECOMMENDATIONS AND CONCLUSIONS**   113
   Effects of Coastal Management Programs on Port Development   114
   National Interests, Port Development, and Coastal Management Programs   114
   Ports and the Definition of the Coastal Zone   115
   Port Participation in Coastal Management Programs   116
   Development of Regional Land- and Water-Use Allocation Plans   118
   Resolving Permit Delay Problems   120

vi

Information Exchange and Technical Assistance 121
Redevelopment of Obsolete Port Facilities 122
Mitigating the Adverse Effects of Dredging, Dredged Material, Disposal, and Landfill 124
Capital Improvement Projects to Enhance the Coastal Environment 125

7 CASE STUDIES 128
Port of Milwaukee/Wisconsin Coastal Management Program 128
Delaware River and Bay Region 138
South Jersey Port Corporation/New Jersey Coastal Management Program 140
Philadelphia Port Corporation/Pennsylvania Coastal Management Program 146
Georgia Ports Authority/Coastal Management Program 150
Port of Brownsville/Texas Coastal Management Program 158
Port of Los Angeles/California Coastal Managemen Program 166
Port of Grays Harbor/Washington Coastal Management Program 176

ENDNOTES 186
BIBLIOGRAPHY 197
INDEX 208

FOREWORD

This study and report on the interaction between U.S. port development and coastal management program development deals with the quite recent and still emerging areas of conflict involving port interests and those individuals and groups dedicated to coastal zone protection and noncommercial uses of our limited shoreline resources. As is the case in so many of these confrontations between advocates of economic development and environmental preservation and protection, solutions to the problems created by competing interests are not easily obtained. This report contains a positive approach to methods that can be used to solve problems which have arisen and will continue to do so. The authors believe a balance can, and inevitably must, be found in order to avoid costly and unnecessary delays in the management of our coastal resources.

From the viewpoint of the port industry—which considers itself a vital national asset in handling the nation's foreign and domestic commerce and its national security requirements—it is vitally necessary to modernize, expand, and upgrade its facilities. Nothing illustrates this point more clearly than the so-called "container revolution" that has created a spectacular change in the ocean shipping lanes in the past two decades. U.S. ports have expended billions of dollars in this relatively short period of time to re-equip themselves with giant shipside container cranes and related shoreside handling equipment, and to acquire substantial additional lands. Dredging of channels and harbor areas to accommodate the deeper-draft vessels now transporting the nation's waterborne commerce is another prime example of the requirements of today's ports and harbors.

Within the last decade particularly, a whole new range of competing uses has developed in urban port areas. The original concept of deep-water port areas being committed almost irrevocably to commercial port development has changed substantially. We find strenuous advocates for allocation of the scarce urban coastal regions for parks, bikeways, trailways, fishing piers, green spaces, aquariums, marinas, viewing areas, and other uses providing a wide range of public amenities. In the Seattle area, examples of this change can be found in the City of Seattle's waterfront park and aquarium and the Port of Seattle's 4000-lineal-foot Myrtle Edwards Park, which includes a bikeway and a trailway utilizing a beautiful stretch of shoreside area running past the huge ships loading grain at the port's new Pier 86 elevator.

With the new interest in environmental enhancement and public-sector recreational uses, there is definitely a need for better planning in harbor areas and better coordination of the many governmental agencies regulating coastal uses. Some sort of balance must be found among competing uses. It is necessary in the public interest to minimize the confrontations between the various local public agencies dealing with these problems. Several years ago, for instance, the Seattle City Council, in carrying out its responsibility for zoning of the various areas of the city's shorelines, spot-zoned (to conservancy natural) a valuable Port of Seattle property on the lower reach of the Duwamish Waterway, in an area historically committed to urban development. After an extended period of claims and counterclaims and a threat by the port to sue the city for damages, the city council reversed its earlier action. It is this type of strident activity which must be avoided.

Coastal management is a new government program that attempts to be comprehensive in planning and regulating shoreline use. In Washington State, we have had about five years' experience with shorelines management. It has provided policies and a procedure for addressing the competing-use problems. In my view it has been a useful program, given the divergent community views about the proper use of Seattle's shoreline.

This book provides a national perspective on how port authorities and coastal management programs are dealing with one another. It also recommends some future direction in these relationships. It will be useful to the maritime commerce and transportation industry and to coastal planners in state and local government.

It is believed that this book will provide a valuable contribution to resolving some of the major points of controversy in this important field.

J. Eldon Opheim
General Manager (Retired)
Port of Seattle

August 1978
Seattle, Washington

PREFACE

This study was motivated by a number of important factors. Port growth in recent years has caused considerable social conflicts. Ports consume a large amount of coastal area because of construction of new piers and terminals and development of new channels. Many people perceive these changes as significant environmental and social impacts and have opposed port development projects. The result has been delay and uncertainty on the part of all coastal users.

Yet, a dilemma exists because ports must have space along shorelines (they are water dependent) and they must deepen channels and construct piers to service the new ships, or marine trade will go elsewhere. Thus, we must either choose to allow one use of shorelines to ascend in time over others, or find a method to accommodate all users.

Assuming that we try to accommodate everyone, how do we do it in a way that will satisfy most people? A traditional response is to call for a better system of planning where those representing diverse views jointly develop goals, policies, and a decision-making framework. Coastal management programs now being developed and implemented throughout the country follow this model closely. But are they helping to resolve the social conflicts that surround port growth in coastal areas? This question was foremost in our minds when we decided to undertake this research.

Certain practical, immediate concerns motivated this study as well. In 1975 and 1976 some port officials expressed publicly their belief that coastal management programs would result only in more permit requirements and thus further delay and uncertainty in port development. They saw no benefits to the port industry because, in their view, coastal management programs were favoring environmental protection goals. These industry comments did not appear to be true in some locations. In Washington State for example, port development is considered a priority use of shorelines. It seemed fruitful, therefore, to examine more systematically how coastal management programs were addressing port development issues.

Another factor motivating the study was a survey conducted by the federal Office of Coastal Zone Management in the summer of 1975. That survey asked coastal managers throughout the country to rank the problems and issues of greatest concern to them. Port development problems ranked very high and coastal managers were asking for more information about the port development process and experience in dealing with port related land- and water-use issues.

Finally, we felt that the time had come to stop talking about how to develop coastal management programs and to start talking about what

coastal management programs were doing in the field. Ultimately, some-
one in government or the public is going to ask what benefits society has
received from the public funds expended on coastal planning and management. To address that question fairly and credibly, information is
needed about the performance of the programs. This task is large, and it
seemed reasonable to start the inquiry with one important user in the
coastal zone—ports and marine trade. We hope that the progress of
coastal management programs will be assessed further so that government, industry and the public will have the information necessary to improve upon coastal management efforts.

MJH
October 1978

ACKNOWLEDGMENTS

A number of groups and individuals were particularly helpful to this effort. In particular, the project would have been impossible to complete without the participation of our Technical Advisory Panel composed of nationally prominent experts in port development and coastal management. Special thanks are due all members of that panel, but the contributions of six were especially significant: Dick Schultz, executive director of the American Association of Port Authorities; Joe Moseley, III, executive director of the Texas Coastal and Marine Council (at the time of this study) and a member of the national Coastal Zone Management Advisory Committee; Eldon Opheim, affiliate professor of marine studies at the University of Washington and retired general manager of the Port of Seattle; Eric Schenker, professor of economics at the University of Wisconsin; Peter Wise, director of the Illinois coastal management program; and John Clark, Senior Associate, The Conservation Foundation.

We are also grateful to Douglas Fleming, associate professor of geography and adjunct professor of marine studies, University of Washington, and to Michele Tetley, Paul Stang, and Dick Gardner, Office of Coastal Zone Management, for their support and assistance throughout this project.

Our thanks go also to the following staff members of the Coastal Resources Program in the Institute for Marine Studies, University of Washington: Doug Ancona, presently attorney with NOAA General Counsel in Seattle, who managed the administrative aspects of the project during its first year; Saskia Schott, research literature analyst and librarian, who provided substantial bibliographic support; and Doris Olsen, secretary, who weathered the paper storm and typed numerous drafts.

The authors wish especially to thank the entire staff of the Washington Sea Grant Communications Program for their skill and patience in editing and for providing assistance in graphics, layout, and manuscript preparation.

Finally, many officials of case study port authorities and coastal management agencies extended their hospitality and precious time to the authors during their visits. Their assistance was invaluable and is greatly appreciated.

Although many individuals reviewed early drafts of this report and provided valuable advice and guidance, the findings, conclusions, and recommendations contained in this report are solely those of the authors.

Freighter with tug assist entering the Duwamish River waterway, Port of Seattle.
(Photo courtesy of Port of Seattle)

1 TRENDS IN PORT DEVELOPMENT AND COASTAL MANAGEMENT PROGRAM DEVELOPMENT

The coastal zone of the United States is the region in which most of the nation's growth and development has taken place in the 20th century. It is here that more than 50 percent of the population now lives and where the country's largest urban centers are found. The great industrial, commercial, and transportation networks are concentrated here, as well as increasing numbers of second home developments, public shorefront parks, and marinas for recreational boaters and commercial and sports fishermen. Further, the natural environment of the coastal zone is rich in scenic beauty, and coastal estuaries and wetlands support an ecosystem abundant in wildlife.

Ports are traditional users of the coastal zone. This country's birth and growth can be traced to the major coast and inland ports where ships brought settlers and goods, and exported raw materials and manufactured items. Until recent years ports have operated virtually free of government regulations. Even today, competition between ports is vigorous, each trying to gain additional trade and commerce for the region being served.

But now, when port authorities propose major developments—such as new channels, expanded terminals, landfills, and turning basins—they frequently encounter opposition from recreational and environmental interests, from fish and wildlife interests, and sometimes even from other commercial and industrial developers. As a result, port development in recent years has been slowed in some areas, and in other areas new public interest features (public access and mitigation) have significantly increased development costs. Furthermore, some cities and communities have encouraged recreational and commercial developments, rather than expanded port facilities, and some federal and state agencies have found that the value of fish and wildlife resources outweighs potential benefits of new port facilities.

In addition to the problem of changing values, ports are going through a period of rapid technological change. Traditional break-bulk general cargoes are being replaced by containerized shipments of general cargo and specialized bulk commodity handling and shipping techniques. These changes necessitate altering shorefront facilities to provide deeper channels, greater backup and storage space, and marginal wharves rather than traditional small finger piers. But to modernize a port, a port authority must abandon or sell obsolete facilities, remodel existing facilities, develop new facilities (sometimes in new locations), and promote federal navigation improvement projects. Development activities like landfill and dredging often compete directly with other waterfront uses, particularly recreational development and environmental enhancement.

In 1972, Congress passed the Coastal Zone Management Act to enhance state and local capabilities for managing land and water uses in the coastal zone. The act calls for the development of state coastal management programs which give full consideration to aesthetic, ecological, historical, and cultural values, as well as to economic values. As an initial

Smaller ships relied on steam-power and muscle to handle cargo around the turn of the century. Photo shows lumber loading operations at Port Blakeley, Bainbridge Island, Washington. (Photo courtesy Arney A. Rodal of Bainbridge Photography)

step, state programs are expected to analyze competing coastal land and water uses and to develop procedures for deciding permissible and priority uses in particular areas in accordance with environmental impact or resource capacity assessments. State coastal managers are also expected to consult and coordinate with existing governmental units at all levels and to involve these agencies in the coastal management program whenever feasible.

Since the act was passed, most coastal and Great Lakes states have begun developing coastal management programs, and some programs have been approved.* Other states and territories are at varying stages of program development. Specific policies about coastal development are being debated, and in many cases existing state and local laws and agencies will augment their land use, resource management, and environmental activities to form the basis for coastal management programs.

*As of September 1978 the following programs have been approved: Oregon, Washington, California and the San Francisco Bay region, North Carolina, Maryland, Massachusetts, Maine, Michigan, Wisconsin, Hawaii, Rhode Island, the Island of Culebra, Puerto Rico, and the nonindustrialized coastal segment of New Jersey.

Port authorities and coastal management programs are extremely important to one another. Ports that must develop new facilities because of changing technology are vitally concerned that emerging coastal program policies recognize their needs and provide for them. The port industry is highly competitive, and officials realize that coastal management policies that hinder port development will upset competitive balances.

Coastal management programs are concerned with new port facilities and may address aspects of site selection, facility design, and facility needs in order to protect environmental and public access values. They must plan for transportation and economic development interests, especially water-dependent uses, and must balance port development needs with other competing coastal uses. When many uses conflict it may be necessary to allocate land and water uses along the shoreline.

To allocate coastal space for port activities, port space needs must first be determined. But this is extremely difficult to do. It involves predicting future trade and commerce in a region, and adding factors to reflect desired economic growth and competitive posture.

Determining future port facilities needs is further complicated by the debate over port facility redundancy. Some studies show that ports have overbuilt in the past, resulting in excess U.S. port capacity (Frankel, 1973; U.S. Dept. of Transportation, 1977; Borland and Oliver, 1972). A national

In contrast to bygone days, modern ports must provide facilities to service the larger ships today. Requirements for deeper water, longer berths, larger warehouses, and more land area for container storage have made many former port locations obsolete. This recent photo shows a portion of the Garden City Terminals, Georgia Ports Authority, Savannah, Georgia. (Photo courtesy of Georgia Ports Authority)

Academy Panel (National Research Council, 1976), on the other hand, concludes that this is not the case. In fact, it suggests that excess capacity is desirable so that ports can remain competitive and can handle normally recurring peak loads. The panel also argues that judgments about efficiency should not be based on apparently underutilized facilities.

Regardless of the outcome of this debate, where there is much competition between ports and other users, coastal managers need to understand trade forecasting and facility requirements in order to balance port needs with other uses and to develop an appropriate allocation scheme. This will invariably involve close cooperation between port authorities and coastal management program officials. This cooperation should result in better knowledge and appreciation of the goals and methods of both port development and coastal management program development, which is the objective of this study.

STUDY METHODS AND DEFINITIONS

This study sought to characterize port authority and coastal management program relationships at a national scale, so a method that would permit national-level generalizations and provide useful information was needed.

To determine which ports and coastal states might best represent the country as a whole, certain criteria were developed that reflect the primary concerns of port authorities and coastal management programs, along with geographic, distribution, and program development factors. Table 1.1 describes eight criteria categories and the range of factors considered within each category, which are reflected in the six case study ports and states selected.

Ports from which the case studies would be selected were identified from 35 coastal and Great Lakes port cities of varied populations and with varying gross cargo tonnages in 1974 (Table 1.2). Two each were selected from large ports, medium ports, and small ports (Naval Oceanographic Office classifications in *World Port Index*, 1971). This sample did not include hundreds of very small port authorities because of the difficulty in conducting the research and because coastal management programs primarily concerned larger ports and port development issues.

The following six case study port areas were finally chosen (Figure 1.1):

1. Port of Milwaukee—Wisconsin coastal management program
2. Port of Philadelphia/South Jersey Port (Camden)—Pennsylvania/New Jersey coastal management programs
3. Georgia Port Authority at Savannah—Georgia coastal management program
4. Brownsville Navigation District—Texas coastal management program

5. Port of Los Angeles—California coastal management
   program
6. Port of Grays Harbor—Washington coastal management
   program

The ports represent variety in size, type of cargo handled, organizational level of the port authority in state government, and recent growth trends and problems. They also represent the coastal and Great Lakes regions of the country. Each state's approach to coastal management was considerably different and program efforts ranged from early stages of development (Pennsylvania) to a fully implemented program (Washington). (The case studies are presented in Chapter 7.)

Three key definitions were decided upon early in the study:

Public port authorities were chosen as the focus of study because they often represent a broad range of users concerned with trade and economic development in the coastal zone. (Limiting the study to public port authorities, however, excludes the many private ports, lessees of port facilities, and shipping firms that are all involved in aspects of port development.) Public port authorities would be the agency most often dealing with coastal management program officials.

Port development was limited to land- and water-use issues that arise out of proposals for new or expanded port and port related facilities, such as landfills for new terminals, channel dredging, and land acquisition for major expansions. Since physical facility development problems are of primary concern to

Table 1.1 Criteria for case study ports

1. Locational factor:
   (Mandatory: one port/area)
   A. North Atlantic
   B. South Atlantic
   C. Gulf coast
   D. Lakes
   E. North Pacific
   F. South Pacific

2. Port size:
   A. Large
   B. Medium
   C. Small

3. Port expansion factor
   A. Extensive development plans
   B. Moderate development plans

4. The role of the port
   A. Intermodal exchange
   B. Industrial development/promotions
   C. Landlord

5. Port administrative factor
   A. State
   B. Municipal
   C. Multiple-port organization

6. Human environment factor
   A. High density urban area
   B. Medium density area
   C. Low density area

7. State of coastal management factor
   A. Approved coastal management program
   B. Advanced state program
   C. Beginning state program

8. Priority of port problem determined through responses to Office of Coastal Zone Management questionnaire
   A. Primary concern
   B. Secondary concern

coastal management programs, problems of internal port management—financing, labor relations, trade promotion—were not
addressed except when they had a direct bearing on a physical facility project.

Table I.2. Size characteristics of selected U.S. ports

Port	Size of port[1]	1974 tonnage (millions of short tons)	City population
Great Lakes			
1. Duluth	M	40.3	100,578
2.* Milwaukee	M	4.2	717,099
3. Chicago	L	45.9	3,366,957
4. Detroit	L	27.5	1,511,482
5. Cleveland	L	21.9	750,903
Atlantic Coast			
6. Portland	M	27.6	65,116
7. Portsmouth	S	2.3	25,717
8. Boston	L	25.7	641,071
9. Newport	S	8.8	34,567
10. New Haven	S	12.0	137,707
11. New York, Elizabeth and Newark	(L)	195.6	7,894,862
12.* Philadelphia	L	59.9	1,948,609
13. Wilmington, DE	M	3.9	80,386
14. Baltimore	L	59.6	905,759
15. Hampton Roads	(L)	72.9	678,047
16. Wilmington, NC	M	8.7	46,169
17. Charleston	S	9.0	66,945
18.* Savannah	M	9.9	118,349
19. Jacksonville	M	14.8	518,131
Gulf of Mexico			
20. Tampa	M	40.9	277,767
21. Mobile	L	33.1	190,026
22. Pascagoula	S	13.1	27,264
23. New Orleans	L	144.2	591,502
24. Galveston	L	7.2	61,809
25. Houston	L	89.1	1,231,394
26.* Brownsville	S	2.8	52,522
Pacific Coast			
27. San Diego	M	2.1	693,931
28. Long Beach	M	26.9	358,633
29.* Los Angeles	L	25.9	2,816,061
30. Richmond	S	14.7	79,043
31. San Francisco	L	3.9	715,674
32. Oakland	L	6.8	361,561
33. Portland	L	20.7	382,619
34.* Grays Harbor	(S)	3.2	30,554
35. Seattle	L	14.3	530,831

*Case study port
[1]U.S. Naval Oceanographic Office, 1971. *World Port Index*, 4th Ed. (Washington,
D.C.: Government Printing Office). Numbers 11, 15, and 34 are disaggregated in
the *Index*.

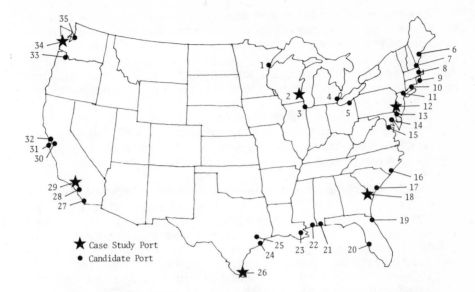

Figure 1.1 Thirty-five candidate ports including six case study ports. The numbers correspond to the port cities in Table 1.2.

Coastal management programs were defined as those governmental programs being developed and implemented pursuant to the federal Coastal Zone Management Act of 1972. This definition excludes many public and private activities—such as management practices of private owners, regulation by federal agencies, traditional city zoning along shorelines, or management by state land agencies—unless these activities are a formal part of a program developed under the Coastal Zone Management Act.

RELATED STUDIES

A number of studies conducted during the past decade have examined port development problems and issues, provided useful information about factors that influence port growth, and suggested public policy approaches to that growth. In some cases, public programs affecting ports have been initiated as a result of these studies.

In 1969, the Stratton Commission, a major federal study concerned with the nation's ocean-related efforts, recommended establishment of a national coastal and marine resources program (Comm. Mar. Sci., 1969). It recommended state-developed coastal management programs and a nationwide study to determine how and where ports should develop in light of rapid technological changes and increasing environmental constraints. Similar studies had been recommended earlier by the U.S. Marine Council, a federal interagency body coordinating marine affairs at the national level, and by the U.S. Corps of Engineers. The recommended national port facility needs study was not undertaken, however.

The public port industry was initially opposed to direct federal involvement in port development (other than traditional Corps of Engineers functions to maintain and improve navigable waterways). However, in the early 1970s port authorities began to recognize that limited federal technical and financial assistance could assist the industry. Subsequently, some larger public port authorities used federal funds to do regional trade forecasts to determine future facility needs and to counteract claims of overdevelopment (Wash. Public Ports Assoc. (WPPA), 1975 and N. Calif. Ports and Term. Bur., 1976). Currently, the port industry is lobbying for a federal law that would provide ports with funds to offset costs for federally mandated environmental protection, cargo security, and worker safety programs.

One project of the American Association of Port Authorities (AAPA) is worth special mention. In 1976, AAPA conducted a short study of port development and coastal management program development that described the port industry for the benefit of coastal management planners. It concluded that coastal management programs could be beneficial to port authorities if they provided adequate space for future port expansion.

University studies funded by Sea Grant and other agencies have also addressed port development (Schenker, Mayer, and Brockel, 1976; Frankel, 1973; Mayer, 1975; Borland and Oliver, 1972). In 1973, a national conference was held to discuss port planning and coastal environment interests (Schenker and Brockel, 1974). Subsequently, a National Academy of Science (NAS) study recommended a program of federal aid to ports (National Research Council, 1976). Another NAS study, now underway, is addressing the impact of maritime services on local populations and ways to avoid adverse impacts.

The subject of port development and coastal management programs is receiving increasing attention. The federal Coastal Zone Management Advisory Committee issued a resolution in 1977, calling on states to give ports priority consideration and to "designate port authorities as having responsibility within their jurisdiction for the development and implementation of aspects of coastal zone programs affecting their operations." The 1977 National Sea Grant Association Conference also dealt with port development: papers were presented by port officials, coastal management program officials, and academic investigators. A 1978 workshop held by the New England River Basin Commission addressed the relationship of New England's port authorities and emerging coastal management programs. Finally, a Department of Commerce task force is developing a comprehensive ocean policy study that addresses ports and coastal management programs, and is considering new policies and programs to enhance coordination between them.

Because the coastal zone is such an important region, and its resources are essential to many diverse groups and individuals, minimizing conflict between different users is long overdue. This study attempts to provide useful information to those people who face the conflicts between port development and environmental protection each day.

2 PORT DEVELOPMENT

A port is a dynamic and changing business whose growth or decline depends upon its ability to maintain and improve its competitive position. It must be able to respond to the pressures of an expanding local economy, the demands of shippers and transportation carriers for more storage space or better facilities, or its own need to improve its facilities to meet rapidly changing shipping and cargo-handling technologies. To meet these pressures a port may need new facilities, more land, or perhaps deeper channels to accommodate larger ships.

The port authority* is the central figure in such development (Figure 2.1). If the port commissioners decide that demands for the port's services warrant expansion of facilities, they ask the port director and his staff to develop detailed plans. These plans, once approved by the port, are submitted to local, state and federal environmental agencies to be reviewed for compliance with land- and water-use regulations. If the project involves channel deepening or other public water body improvements, the local sponsors may submit a civil works project request to the congressional delegation for study and possible implementation by the Corps of Engineers.

These four key elements of port development—the functions and organization of the port authority, the forces that create demand for port services, federal assistance programs for port development, and the land- and water-use regulations and agencies which must approve development projects—are discussed in this chapter.

PORT AUTHORITIES

Organization of Port Authorities

Since the turn of the century, public port authorities have become an important part of the American port industry. Most public port authorities derive their authority and obligations directly or indirectly from state law. In some states, port authorities operate directly under state statute as state-level departments or special districts. Others are controlled indirectly by states, with powers statutorily passed from the state to municipalities or counties which, in turn, create port authorities.

The types of port authorities vary among the states. Most ports operate within a legislatively or statutorily defined local region. California ports, with few exceptions, are departments of city government. In Washington and Oregon, port authorities are created under state enabling statutes, but operate at the local level. The ports of Texas derive their authority from the state, but operate as county navigation districts. Many East

---

*As discussed in Chapter 1, this study uses public port authorities as the representative of port development interests. Although the private sector has a major role to play in port development, the public authorities tend to interact more directly and regularly with coastal management program officials.

10

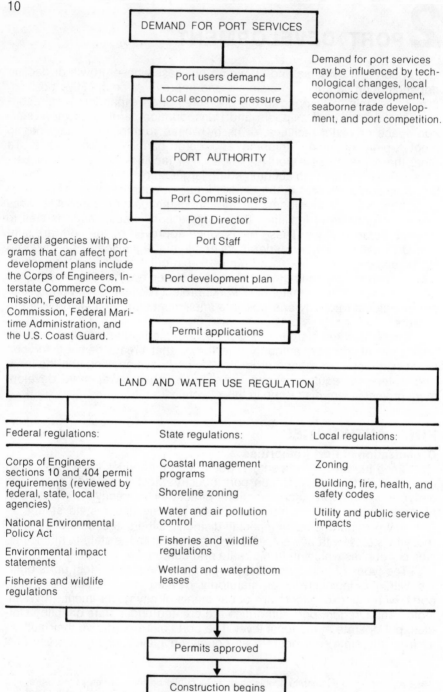

Figure 2.1   Port development process.

Coast states have a single, statewide port authority. Great Lakes port authorities represent a variety of all types that appear elsewhere. Despite the differences in organizational structure, there are several features common to enabling legislation in the various states:

1. The legislation creates a public role and responsibility to improve and develop waterborne commerce.

2. Port commissions are established to exercise that responsibility.

3. Port authorities are authorized to develop, build, finance, and promote facilities and services necessary to the public port enterprise and its objectives.

Functions of a Port Authority

The first function of a port is to handle the transfer of cargo among ships, barges, and inland carriers. Modern ports do more than transfer cargo, however. They store cargo, promote industrial development, and sometimes operate airports, bridges, transit systems, and recreational boating facilities.

Cargo transfer. Cargo transfer operations have changed rapidly in recent years. The new specialized ships—such as dry bulk carriers, container ships, automobile carriers, chemical tankers, etc.—require more specialized handling and storage facilities. Specialized cargo-handling equipment has in many areas displaced human labor because it can do the job much faster. Less than 20 years ago, it might have taken a week or more to load a 10,000-ton general cargo shipment. Today, with high-speed equipment, a 10,000-ton container cargo can be loaded in less than a day.

While improved cargo-handling methods have lowered per-unit shipping costs, they also represent a large capital investment for the port authority. Money must be available to install the new equipment as quickly as possible and to keep it operating in order to realize a positive return. Further, adequate space is needed for the new cargo-handling equipment.

Cargo storage. If the chain of transport between land and water modes is interrupted at the port, cargo must be stored. Storage facilities and the amount of land required vary from one type of cargo to another and are affected by the physical form of the cargo, the level of specialization of storage technology, and operations preferences of transportation carriers. For instance, storing 30,000 tons of logs requires about ten acres of land, but storing 30,000 tons of logs in the form of wood chips requires less than six acres (WPPA, 1975).

The number of containers stored per acre can be doubled or tripled, depending on the method of container stacking used. Some steamship lines prefer to store containers exclusively on-chassis (the set of highway trailer wheels), while others prefer to stack them off-chassis. The on-chassis approach permits faster access to containers but requires a larger storage area.

The cost and availability of land that is suitable for port functions also affects cargo storage. If land is scarce or high-priced, more intensive use of storage facilities and use of more sophisticated storage technology become economically attractive.

Industrial development. The fabric of port areas often includes other industries which choose to locate nearby for a number of reasons. Ship-building and marine repair and supply firms must be located adjacent to shipping traffic. Firms that depend on large quantities of imported raw materials (such as oil refineries) or export large quantities of finished goods often locate near a port.

Most port authorities promote industrial development to some extent, although the extent to which it is permitted by enabling legislation varies widely. Some ports are limited to promoting industry that directly requires port services. The Port of Grays Harbor, for example, has a broad county-wide industrial development mandate. It was instrumental in persuading a new chemical plant to locate in the county, which contributes to the county's economy, but is not physically near the port, is not on port-owned land, and does not ship or receive any materials through the port.

A port authority's financial resources and land holdings may reflect its involvement in industrial development. The Port of Brownsville, for example, owns 42,000 acres of land adjacent to the 17-mile-long Browns-ville ship channel. It actively promotes industrial development by perform-ing a number of services for its lessees; it acquires and prepares land, provides utilities and other infrastructure investments, and acts as agent in securing environmental permits.

Public Port Authorities and Private Ports

Ownership and operation of port facilities may be divided between public port authorities and private industry. Port facilities that are owned and operated by private companies in most cases consist of specialized, single-purpose piers or terminals for handling specific cargos, such as grain, logs, petroleum, iron ore, or coal.

A public port authority may own and operate piers, warehouses, ter-minals, and storage facilities. The Georgia Ports Authority at Savannah, for instance, owns and operates general cargo, container, and bulk cargo terminals on the Savannah River. There are also numerous privately owned and operated terminals along the same stretch of the river.

Sometimes, a public port authority owns the facilities, but leases the operation to private enterprise. The Port of Los Angeles, for example, owns many facilities, but leases them to private steamship lines and stevedoring firms. Leases vary widely. The operator/lessee might provide his own container cranes and improve the land, or the equipment and buildings may be provided by the port within the terms of the lease.

Port Financing

Because modern cargo-handling facilities require heavy capital investments, financing has become a major issue. From 1966-1972, United States ports invested over one billion dollars to expand and modernize facilities (Figure 2.2). Funds for capital improvements may come from reinvestment of port earnings, revenue bonds and general obligation bonds,

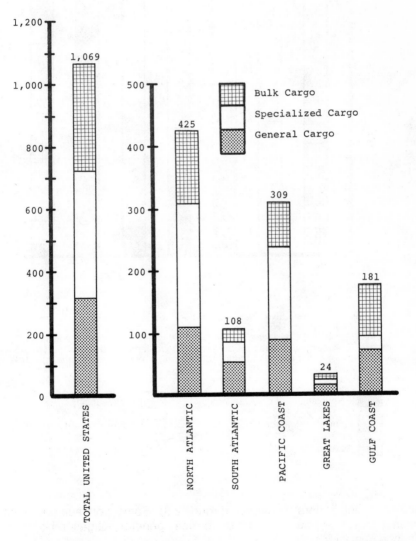

Figure 2.2 Port development expenditures, 1966–1972, for the United States and selected regions. Amounts are in millions of dollars. Source: U.S. Department of Commerce, Maritime Administration, *Public port financing in the United States,* June 1974, p. 10.

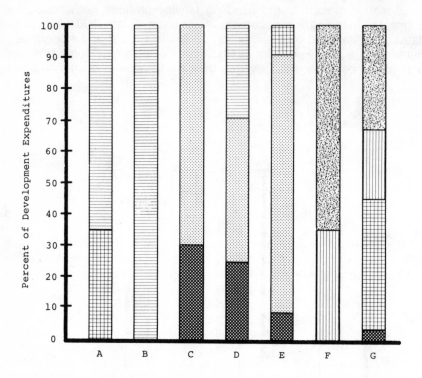

Figure 2.3   Representative financing methods for selected U.S. ports, development expenditures for 1966–1972. Ports: (A) Newport News, Virginia; (B) Portsmouth, Virginia; (C) Charleston, South Carolina; (D) New Orleans, Louisiana; (E) Houston, Texas; (F) San Diego, California; (G) Oakland, California. Source: U.S. Department of Commerce, Maritime Administration, *Public port financing in the United States,* June 1974, p. 39.

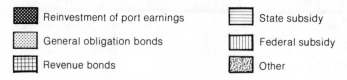

Reinvestment of port earnings   State subsidy

General obligation bonds   Federal subsidy

Revenue bonds   Other

and state and federal subsidies (Figure 2.3). Some port authorities have been granted the power of taxation to repay general obligation bonds or to finance operations.

Ports generate income from charges levied on shippers who use their facilities or services, but usually little of this income is available for capital improvement projects. Although many port authorities retain earnings to finance operations and capital improvements, others must return earnings to a governing body—for example, a city—which provides an annual operating budget.

The major source of capital improvement funds is public financing. Some ports have tax-levying authority, while others are authorized to issue general obligation bonds or revenue bonds. In the last two or three decades, there has been a general decrease in investment by private enterprise and a growing predominance of public agency investment in port facilities (AAPA, 1976). (Figure 2.3) Direct federal funding for development is not common, partly because of fear that federal aid could lead to federal control, but public subsidy at the federal, state, or local level is very common. The Corps of Engineers in effect subsidizes development by providing dredging and channel maintenance services, and the Economic Development Administration provides public works assistance funds in certain cases.

Port Planning

Every port performs some planning function, although few of them have large permanent planning departments. Some ports hire planning consultants from time to time, however the larger ones, like the New York/ New Jersey Port Authority and the Port of Seattle, maintain complete departments that are responsible for planning facility needs and evaluating trends in the industry. Even some smaller ports, like Grays Harbor, have a planning section within the management office.

There is a high degree of uncertainty involved in port planning, particularly long-term planning. Planners must consider rapid changes in shipping technology, trying to develop plans based on the future needs and requirements of ships the port will serve without knowing for certain the size and draft of the next generation of ships and future methods of cargo handling.

Port planners are also uncertain about future customers. A shipping company whose vessels are costly to operate must be flexible in its operation; it can change routes and ports of call fairly quickly. It is difficult for a port to plan new facilities, and even more difficult to obtain financing if it cannot prove well in advance that the facilities will be used. At the same time, ports must risk developing new facilities and services in order to have them ready when shippers and carriers need them.

Time scales of port plans are geared to immediate response planning, mid-range (up to five years) planning, and long-range (5-15 years) planning. Immediate response planning deals with day-to-day problems, such as pier maintenance and improvement. Mid-range planning is often concerned with major port capital improvement projects, such as the construction of a new container terminal. Long-range planning is a general master plan, which considers major future expansion, channel improvement, new cargo types, property acquisition, and other considerations.

On a spatial scale, port plans may involve only construction of a single pier or minor infrastructure changes, or they may propose expansion

16

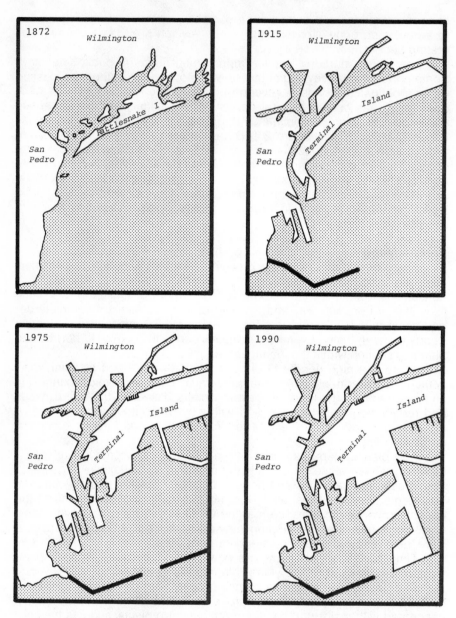

Figure 2.4 Historical and proposed expansion of the Port of Los Angeles by landfill, 1872–1990. Source: Port of Los Angeles, Comprehensive master plan 1990.

of an existing terminal or major dredging and filling projects. Figure 2.4, an example of major changes, shows the growth of the Port of Los Angeles since 1872 and the major landfill expansion proposed in the Los Angeles Port Master Plan of 1976.

In the last few years, port planners have been involved in regional planning. Some recent regional port studies were conducted as a result of state legislative pressures, and growing claims of overbuilt facilities. The Washington Public Ports Association (WPPA), which includes the Port of Portland, Oregon, conducted a data systems study and issued technical reports that describe the current system, give commodity forecasts, and develop a model to determine facility use efficiency. WPPA's members also formed a voluntary cooperative development committee to issue "certificates of need" to member ports on any new facility.

Another regional study, NORCAL (sponsored by Northern California Ports and Terminals Bureau), concerns ports in the San Francisco Bay area. Its principal purpose is to develop a method for determining port capacity and the need for future expansion. Similar studies are also being conducted in Florida, Texas, St. Louis, Mid-America (a 17-state region), and the Great Lakes.

DEMAND FOR PORT SERVICES

Seaborne Trade Development and Technological Change

The United States is a focal point of world trade. It is a major consumer of oil and raw materials and the largest distributor of manufactured goods and agricultural products. Since World War II, an overall growth in demand for port services has resulted in a corresponding increase in port development. Despite fluctuations, trade continues to grow (Table 2.1).

Table 2.1   Total world seaborne commerce, 1965–73

Year	Crude oil	Oil products	Iron ore	Coal	Grain	Other cargo	Total trade	% increase
			in 1,000 million ton-miles					
1965	2,480	640	527	216	386	1,600	5,849	
1966	2,629	700	575	226	408	1,700	6,238	7%
1967	3,400	730	651	269	380	1,800	7,230	16%
1968	4,197	750	775	310	340	2,000	8,372	16%
1969	4,853	760	919	385	307	2,150	9,374	12%
1970	5,597	890	1,093	481	393	2,200	10,654	14%
1971	6,554	900	1,185	434	406	2,250	11,729	10%
1972	7,719	930	1,156	442	454	2,400	13,101	12%
1973	9,171	1,010	1,398	467	622	2,700	15,368	17%

Source: United Nations Conference of Trade and Development *Review of Marine Transport*, 1974, p. 7.

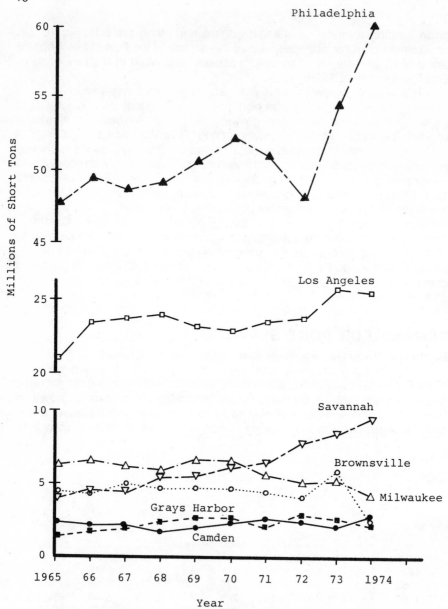

Figure 2.5 Net total cargo tonnages handled for six case study ports, 1965–1974. Tonnages shown are net tonnages for all cargoes moved through all terminals, public and private. Grays Harbor tonnages include vessel traffic, but exclude rafted logs. Source: U.S. Army Corps of Engineers, *Waterborne commerce of the United States,* 1974.

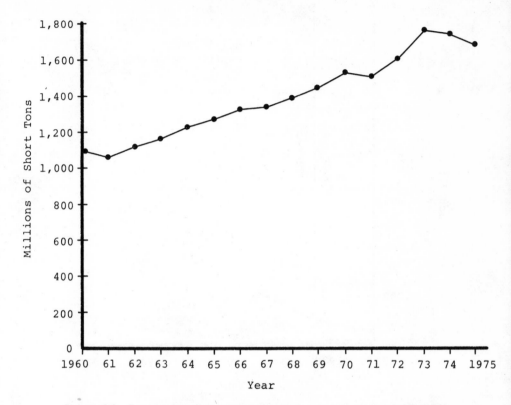

Figure 2.6 Total waterborne commerce of the United States, 1960–1975.
Source: U.S. Army Corps of Engineers, *Waterborne commerce of the United States*, 1975.

The average annual growth rate of U.S. seaborne trade was 9.7 percent in the early 50's, 11 percent in the late 60's, and 7 percent by the 1970's. During the early 70's, the rate of growth varied from 4 percent in 1971, to 6 percent in 1972, and to 11 percent in 1973, a year of strong economic activities and trade prosperity despite the continuing monetary instability. (Figure 2.5 shows tonnages for the six case study ports for these years. Total U.S. waterborne commerce in recent years is given in Figure 2.6; world and U.S. waterborne commerce projections are given in Figure 2.7.)

The merchant fleet increased in response to growing volumes of cargo. Larger vessels were built and there were rapid technological changes in ship operation and cargo-handling methods.

Until about 1950, ports saw only minor changes in cargo-handling methods. However, since then they have had to adapt to accelerated and profound technological changes. The general cargo ship of 25 years ago

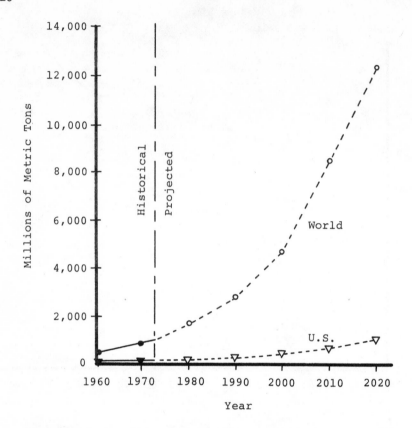

Figure 2.7   Historical and projected world and U.S. dry cargo trade. Source: NORCAL, *Trade outlook of the Northern California ports.* 1975. p. 57.

has been overshadowed by such new advances in shipping technology as container ships, ro-ro (cargo rolled on and rolled off via ramps in the side or stern of the ship), LASH (lighter aboard ship, small barges stored on a large mother ship), and very large crude carriers (VLCCs) of over 500,000 dead weight tons that draw over 90 feet of water. Ports that didn't modernize their cargo-handling facilities to service these larger and faster ships are now at a competitive disadvantage.

The new large, specialized ships are expensive to build and operate, so nonproductive time in port must be minimized. A decade ago, an estimated 60 percent of a conventional general cargo ship's year was spent in ports. Today's container ships, using the proper port facilities, reduce turnaround time by a remarkable 80 percent or more (Goss, 1968). Thus, shippers choose ports which provide the fastest, most efficient loading and unloading service. It is often the port authority which must bear the investment burden of providing the updated facilities that shippers and carriers demand.

Local Economic Impact of Ports

Ports are important contributors to the economic health of many coastal areas, both directly and indirectly. Jobs (hence incomes) and sales (hence revenues) immediately generated by port activity constitute the direct impact on local economies. The indirect impact comes from the use of these incomes and revenues to purchase goods and services within the local community. This "multiplier effect" creates more jobs, income, sales, and revenues, especially in retail and wholesale sectors of the local economy.

A number of port authorities have developed methods to determine the impact of their respective ports on the local economies. One of these methods (Hille and Suelflow, 1968) indicated that in 1968 a ton of general cargo passing through the Port of Baltimore generated more than $32 in the local economy and that a ton of bulk cargo moving through the port generated $7.69.

The ports of Seattle, Los Angeles, and Savannah, among others, have similar methods. There is no universally accepted procedure for calculating the multiplier effect or local economic impact of a port. Each port's method is likely to contain factors and assumptions unique to its individual economic environment. For this reason, it may not be possible to make direct comparisons between two economic impact methods.

Port Competition

Ports operate in a highly competitive environment. Traditionally, neighboring ports have vied with each other for cargo originating in or destined for a specific region or hinterland in which one port had attained a competitive edge. Hinterlands of adjacent ports often overlapped and shifted with time as transportation rate structures and inland transportation connections changed. An example of expanded overlapping hinterlands are the East and West Coast ports that compete with Great Lakes ports for much of the same cargoes bound for the Midwest.

Containerization has changed the patterns of economic hinterlands of ports. Large capital investments in specialized vessels and container-handling equipment have resulted in container traffic being concentrated in fewer, but larger ports, termed "load centers." Revised rate structures and the "minibridge" have greatly expanded many ports' hinterlands.

Minibridge is a unified land-sea rate structure which makes it competitive to ship a container, for example, from Rotterdam to Houston via a combined land-sea route, rather than an all-water route. A container might be shipped by water to the Port of New York/New Jersey and travel the rest of the distance by rail. Shippers save time and inventory costs by using the faster multimodal trip.

Critics of ports have occasionally charged that heavy competition among neighboring ports leads to overbuilding facilities and creating excess regional port capacity. One port may justify publicly the need for a new facility in terms of regional supply and demand, but be planning primarily on winning traffic from neighboring ports. If many neighboring ports follow this same strategy, more docks could be built than needed for the amount of cargo being transported.

FEDERAL PORT PROGRAMS

Although traditional port industry policy has been that ports should remain competitive and free to develop without federal control (Marcus et al., 1976), the U.S. government provides considerable direct subsidy and indirect financial assistance for port development and operations. The Corps of Engineers is a major source, funding civil works projects, such as channel widening and deepening, the construction of breakwaters and jetties, and channel maintenance. With the rising costs of these projects, ports are now being required to pay a larger share, which may include costs of dredged material disposal, purchase of disposal areas, and relocation of utilities and bridges.

Other port activities are aided or managed by federal agencies. The Coast Guard enforces regulations and standards pertaining to the safety of the port and vessel operations. In its regulatory capacity, the Coast Guard inspects vessels and waterfront facilities for compliance with applicable safety regulations, and installs and maintains navigation aids such as buoys, lighthouses, and beacons. A relatively new activity of the Coast Guard is the operation of vessel traffic control systems in congested harbors and inland waters. The vessel movement-monitoring role was expanded significantly in 1972 when Congress passed the Port and Waterway Safety Act.

The Maritime Administration (MARAD) is charged with promoting and developing federal policies and goals for U.S. ocean ports. Under section 8 of the Merchant Marine Act of 1920, MARAD is authorized to conduct developmental activities with respect to ports and port facilities, to maintain domestic and foreign port data, and to provide technical advice on port matters. Since 1965, MARAD has placed increased emphasis on its port development responsibilities, which include regional port planning and integrated transportation systems and deepwater ports research.

The two principal regulatory commissions involved in ports affairs are the Interstate Commerce Commission (ICC) and the Federal Maritime Commission (FMC). The ICC was created by the Interstate Commerce Act of February 4, 1887, to regulate transport in the United States and carriers engaged in interstate and foreign commerce. Under the Deepwater Port Act of 1974, the ICC is the authorized common carrier regulator of offshore ports and requisite storage facilities.

The Federal Maritime Commission was established in 1961 as an independent agency with jurisdiction over waterborne movements between the United States and foreign countries, and among noncontiguous ports of the United States. It administers certain provisions of the Clean Water Act of 1977, approves or denies proposed agreements between carriers, regulates common carrier practices, accepts or rejects rates and tariffs, and licenses ocean carriers. As new concepts in land-sea intermodal transportation have evolved, the complex jurisdictional authorities of the FMC and ICC have become increasingly overlapped because it is difficult to distinguish when waterborne commerce ends and general interstate commerce begins.

LAND AND WATER REGULATION

Several regulatory agencies at federal, state, and local levels are directly concerned with the land- and water-use aspects of new port facilities. (Figure 2.1 shows these regulations as they relate to port development. The scope of regulation in cross-section of a state (Washington) coastal regulatory program is shown in Figure 2.8.) These agencies have established criteria to deal with site selection, environmental impacts, and other aspects of the uses of coastal lands and waters. Although port developments occur in all states and locales, there are considerable variations among local selective criteria. Coastal Zone Management Act activities (described in Chapter 3) are designed to enhance the coastal resources management functions now performed by most state and local governments and to provide a link with the many federal agencies responsible for regulating coastal uses.

Federal Regulations

The Constitution authorizes Congress to regulate commerce among the states, and over the past century the courts have interpreted this power expansively. Today, the uses of virtually all U.S. waters are subject to regulation by Congress which has enacted legislation on matters ranging from navigational improvements to the protection of water quality.

There are a number of federal programs and agencies that directly affect port facility development:

1. Review of activities affecting navigable waters, including dredge and fill activities, by the Corps of Engineers;

2. Assessment of environmental impact by federal agencies, under the National Environmental Policy Act;

3. Protection of water quality, by the Environmental Protection Agency;

4. Maintenance and enhancement of fish and wildlife resources, by the U.S. Fish and Wildlife Service and the National Marine Fisheries Service.

These federal programs relate closely to one another and often have counterpart activities at the state and local level. Usually, each one of these agencies is involved in port facility development. Other agencies— U.S. Coast Guard, Maritime Administration, ICC-FMC—affect port development but are not directly concerned with related land- and water-use issues.

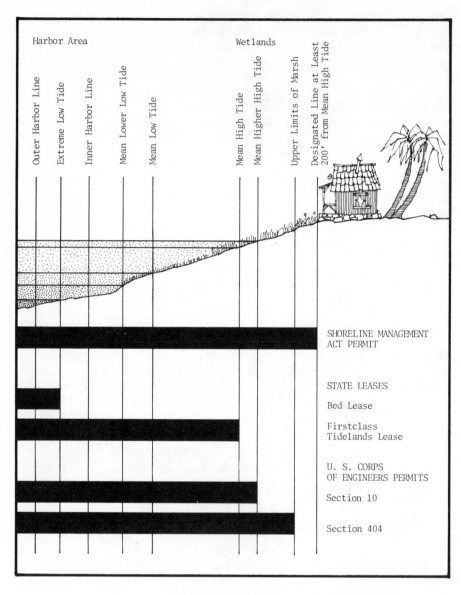

Figure 2.8   Types of shoreline alteration controls that might be applicable within city limits in the state of Washington. Source: Grays Harbor Estuary Management Program, Governmental jurisdictions technical memoranda, p. 128.

Corps of Engineers. Many agencies are involved in coastal management, and the Corps of Engineers is one of the most important. The Corps builds and maintains jetties, channels, and other public works. But in addition to these civil works functions, it also exercises two regulatory permit programs, one to review all activities affecting navigable waters (authorized under section 10 of the Rivers and Harbors Act of 1899, hereafter referred to as section 10) and another to regulate dredge and fill activities in navigable waters (authorized under section 404 of the Federal Water Pollution Control Act Amendments of 1972, hereafter referred to as section 404). Since most activities in navigable waters involve some type of dredging and filling, there is considerable overlap between the two permit programs. Constructing moorings for barges along a shoreline or emplacing pilings in navigable waters are examples that do not involve dredge and fill activities, but would still require a section 10 activity permit. Most port development activities, however, involve both permit pro-

The regulatory programs of the Corps are complex and cannot be dealt with in detail here; however, some important aspects of the programs should be mentioned. "Navigable waters" have been defined very broadly for dredge and fill purposes to include all tidal waters to the mean-high-tide line and wetlands that are wholly or partially covered at high tide, whether publicly or privately owned, and contiguous wetlands that are periodically inundated during storms or floods. A Corps decision to issue a permit is based on whether the overall public interest would be served, considering benefits and costs of the project, environmental and fish and wildlife concerns, flood protection, recreational needs, and other matters. These decisions are made only after consultation and review by other agencies of the federal government (Environmental Protection Agency and fish and wildlife agencies specifically, as discussed below), state and local agency review, and input from private parties.

As a matter of policy, the Corps does not issue a permit for a development activity if it is opposed by a state or local agency authorized by state law to review the project. Thus, the Corps acts as a clearinghouse for comment and review and normally will not act until issues raised by other agencies and parties are resolved with the applicant or with another agency. A very recent amendment to the section 404 program will allow a state to exercise 404 authority, rather than the Corps and Environmental Protection Agency, if the state regulatory program has sufficiently rigorous standards.

U.S. Fish and Wildlife Service/National Marine Fisheries Service. The Fish and Wildlife Coordination Act requires that the U.S. Fish and Wildlife Service and the National Marine Fisheries Service, plus the state fisheries and wildlife agencies, comment to the Corps of Engineers regarding the effect of any proposed development project on fish and wildlife resources. These agencies are concerned with the protection of fish and wildlife resources, their habitats, and the rights of the public to use the navigable waters of the United States. They have, over the past ten years, been the most vocal opponents of large developments in coastal areas, especially in regions were wetlands, marshes, mangroves, and other biologically productive environments are abundant. The Corps must consider their views in its decision making. An objection by a fisheries or wildlife agency that is not resolved at the local level must be resolved at the national level. In practice, very few appeals are heard; thus, the consent of the state fisheries agency is virtually mandatory before a development project can begin.

Because of the difficulties inherent in preventing losses to the environment and the pressures (often political) to approve project proposals, federal fisheries and wildlife agencies have required that developers provide mitigating features in their proposals to reduce overall damage to biological resources. For example, they might require that a three-acre wildlife preserve be purchased if three acres of productive wetlands are destroyed. This is a major point of controversy in coastal development permit applications.

Environmental Protection Agency. Although the Environmental Protection Agency's (EPA) primary responsibility is the control of air and water pollution, it also has authority to review the deposit of dredged material into the navigable waters of the United States. Dredged material can be polluted and depositing it in certain areas can degrade water quality and harm fish, wildlife, water supply, and recreational uses. Therefore, EPA reviews the quality of dredge spoils and the site into which they are to be placed. The legislation under which the EPA operates allows the agency to overrule a Corps dredge and fill permit on environmental grounds.

National Environmental Policy Act (NEPA). NEPA requires all federal agencies to pay careful attention to environmental objectives and to conform to strict procedural requirements when making decisions that significantly affect the quality of the environment. To ensure that the agencies implement this policy, NEPA requires each federal agency to prepare a detailed statement of environmental impact on every major federal action that might significantly affect the quality of the human environment.

Environmental impact statements have been prepared for most Corps of Engineers civil works projects designed to enhance port facilities and operations. The Corps often prepares an environmental impact statement before issuing a section 10 permit authorizing new port facilities requiring bulkheading and landfill. The statement must discuss any adverse environmental effects that cannot be avoided should the proposal be implemented, alternatives to the proposed action, the relationship between local short-term uses and the enhancement of long-term productivity, and any irreversible and irretrievable commitment of resources which would be involved in the proposed action. It is circulated for comment to other federal agencies, state and local governments, and the public.

State Regulations

Since their establishment, state governments have been concerned with the management and productive use of the resources owned by the state and held by the state in trust for its citizens (waterbottoms, water, fish, etc.). States have also been concerned with the enactment of laws and regulations under the police power to protect the health, safety and welfare of citizens. In earlier years these powers were often delegated to local governments since state government did not have the appropriate management apparatus and was removed from the problem. Today, state-level agencies are directly involved in managing resources. Also, many new programs in the areas of environmental protection and control of critical land areas are implemented, administered, or guided at the state level, with varying degrees of local government involvement and assistance. Thus, port facility development requires many state agency approvals, the more important of which are discussed below.

Waterbottom leasing. States own and manage the waterbottoms within their jurisdictions, covering three primary functions:

1. Minerals management—sand, gravel, oil, etc.;

2. Living resources management—shellfish, finfish;

3. Leasing for fill and other purposes.

A state assumes a proprietary role in waterbottom management, generally allowing waterbottom use or resource production so long as it receives a royalty or rental. In some states, submerged lands were sold to private interests in past years, but generally this practice is no longer allowed, although submerged lands and tidelands are leased by the states for resource utilization purposes. Most port facility development projects require a long-term waterbottom lease or outright ownership. All states accommodate port waterbottom needs by allocating priority uses to ports in harbor areas (as in Washington), or outright conveyance (as in Texas, until 1973). Usually, leases and conveyances limit the use of waterbottom to navigation and commercial use. Most are for at least 30 years, and some are for 99 years.

State fisheries and wildlife agencies. Almost all states have declared ownership of all animals free in nature; thus, all fish existing in the waters of the state can be regulated by the state. Because of the common property aspect of fisheries, states have developed management programs in order to protect living resources and to reduce conflicts among those who want to exploit them. State management programs and protection laws are usually organized around a particular species, such as shrimp, oysters, salmon, menhaden, and other species.

An additional responsibility of the state fish and wildlife agencies is to provide input to the Corps of Engineers about the effect of dredge and fill on fish, wildlife, and the aquatic environment. Federal law requires the Corps to consider the views of state fish and wildlife agencies in their decision making, so Corps projects in the coastal zone are reviewed by state fisheries agencies to determine measures that should be taken to prevent loss of fish and wildlife resources and recreational opportunities. For example, if a Corps permit is required for dredging waterbottoms for a port project, state recommendations from the fisheries agency will be important in the Corps' decision.

State environmental laws. Almost all states have passed comprehensive laws addressing pollution control. These laws deal with water pollution, air pollution, and solid waste control, but often they address other problems too, such as oil spills, noise, radiation, and pesticides. Most of these programs are administered at the state level and may affect aspects of port development.

A more pervasive environmental law, which addresses many forms of development within a state, has come to be known as state environmental policy acts, or SEPAs. Following the National Environmental Policy Act of 1969, discussed above, a number of states have passed laws requiring environmental impact statements for nonfederal projects. The adoption by states of these "little NEPAs" results in the application of the environmental impact statement procedure to a wide range of state and local actions. Three of the case study states (California, Washington, and Wisconsin) have passed such laws.

State coastal resource protection laws. Environmental laws that can directly affect port development have been adopted by many states over the past decade. These laws deal with wetland protection, beach and dune protection, dredge and fill controls, oil spill prevention and clean-up, energy facility siting, erosion prevention, beach access, and shoreland zoning. No state has adopted all these measures; however, quite a few have adopted three or four of them and almost all have at least one such law. These programs usually require permit review before a development project can begin. Each one deals with some aspect of coastal development and meets special critical problems in the coastal zone. The federal coastal management program is designed to build upon these coastal resource programs by providing coordination among state agencies, building in the interests of local government and federal agencies, and providing better technical information and analytical tools as a basis for coastal decisions.

Local Regulations

Four sets of controls that affect port development are usually found at the city or county level of government:

1. Land-use controls, such as zoning and subdivision controls;

2. Police power ordinances concerned with health, safety, and fire protection;

3. Provision of public services, such as roads, water, sewers, utilities, and others;

4. Local components of state coastal resource programs (discussed in the previous section).

Land-use controls. Zoning is a means of controlling land use where an area is divided into districts, in each of which preferred or allowed uses and density restrictions are listed. Land uses are segregated into general categories such as residential, commercial, and industrial, and are further divided into numerous subcategories. In most cases, ports and port-related land uses are classified as industrial uses.

Police power ordinances. Local governments provide for fire, police, health, and safety protection programs, which affect port development activities when building and construction codes must be satisfied. Most of these considerations have been integrated into the design and engineering of facilities and are no longer policy problems or constraints to development.

Public services. Public services—water supply, sewerage and waste disposal, streets and right-of-way, and police powers mentioned above—can directly affect port development.

The control of public services by cities can determine the location and timing of all development activities in a city or county. Before new facilities can be operational, port authorities must have the public services, such as access to streets and highways, and water and sewer services. Ports and local governments have a long tradition of interaction regarding provision of public services, and the issue has not raised major policy concerns in recent years.

Local implementation of coastal resource protection laws. A recent local-level control that does affect port development is the local implementation of coastal resource programs, such as local shoreland management, local wetlands control, local administration of set-back lines to protect beach resources, and others. These are often implemented by local ordinance, or incorporated into local comprehensive plans and zoning controls. In the case of some rural counties, these local shoreline or wetland programs have been the first experience of counties in planning and land-use control. Usually, these programs are developed pursuant to a state law authorizing or encouraging their development. Coastal management programs that develop under the federal Coastal Zone Management Act usually incorporate these local activities.

3 COASTAL ZONE MANAGEMENT PROGRAMS

During the past decade, the federal government and state governments have actively responded to coastal resource problems. Generally, these problems fell into two categories: resource problems arising from use conflicts, public access, and environmental degradation; and organizational problems, such as overlapping jurisdictions, lack of coordination among decision makers, and insufficient use of information in decision making (Englander et al., 1977). While individual states tried a variety of solutions, they tended to focus on a particular natural resource—such as wetlands—rather than attempting comprehensive solutions.

Concurrent with state efforts, the federal government was also studying coastal zone problems. The Stratton Commission, the Marine Council, the National Estuary Study, and the National Estuarine Pollution Study all drew attention to the national value of coastal resources, the effects of destruction and degradation of these resources by man, and conflicts among coastal users. They concluded that states should have primary responsibility for coastal management, but they also found that local and state organizations were inadequate to handle national resource problems and recommended their management roles and capabilities be enhanced (Senate Report 92–753).

Based on these findings and recommendations Congress passed the Coastal Zone Management Act of 1972. It gave the states primary responsibility for developing management programs which would "preserve, protect, develop and, where possible, restore or enhance" coastal resources. (CZMA section 303 [a]) States are directed to achieve wise use of the resources by "giving full consideration to ecological, cultural, historic, and aesthetic values as well as to needs for economic development." (CZMA section 303 [b]) Moreover, federal agencies are admonished to cooperate with states in this task, and all levels of government and the public are actively encouraged to participate (CZMA section 303 [c] [d]). By encouraging states to assume greater responsibility in coastal planning and decision making, the federal program supplemented state efforts that were already underway.

While states are not required to develop coastal management programs, the Coastal Zone Management Act included incentives to encourage them to assume this responsibility. Development and administration funds are provided to states, along with funds to accomplish specific program objectives—such as beach and estuarine acquisitions, education and training programs, and energy impact programs. Originally, two-thirds of the cost of development and administration was provided; however, 1976 amendments to the act increased the federal share to 80 percent. Another major incentive is that federal agencies are required to be consistent, to the maximum extent practicable, with state programs.

These incentives, along with public pressure for coastal resource protection and better government decision making, have convinced all eligible states and territories that they should participate in this program. To do so, they must conform to criteria established in the federal statute and in implementing regulations. These criteria are flexible, however; broad management categories are identified, but the specific content of each program is left to the states. This way, states have latitude to develop unique and innovative approaches which are applicable to their own political and environmental situations.

States developing coastal management programs must satisfy certain federal requirements before seeking approval (Figure 3.1 outlines the steps of program development and implementation).* First, they must identify the permissible land and water uses and establish priorities among them, and establish the coastal zone boundaries. (These first steps are interrelated tasks, since the boundary must extend inland to include all uses which have a direct and significant impact on coastal waters.) Areas of particular concern within the coastal zone must then be identified. These are areas that have critical management problems or contain unique environmental resources. Organizational arrangements must be established to insure cooperation among agencies with responsibilities in the coastal zone. Finally, the authority for implementing the coastal management program must be determined either by coordinating existing legislation or enacting new comprehensive legislation.

Once a state feels confident that its program meets federal standards, the program is submitted to the Secretary of Commerce for approval. There, the Office of Coastal Zone Management evaluates the proposal. Other federal agencies and interested parties can also review and comment on the state program and the environmental impact statement which must accompany it. Arrangements for state-federal interaction are determined, and questions of national interest are reviewed during this period.

If the program satisfies the requirements of the federal legislation and meets no substantial resistance from federal agencies, the Secretary of Commerce approves it and the state can then apply for grants to implement it. To date, all coastal and Great Lakes states and U.S. territories are developing coastal programs. Some programs have satisfied the federal requirements and been approved by the Department of Commerce (programs approved as of September 1978 are noted on page 2).

STATE COASTAL PROGRAM DEVELOPMENT

Permissible Land and Water Uses

Defining permissible land and water uses within a coastal management program involves several prescribed steps. First, states must inventory their coastal areas to identify the kind and distribution of resources— both natural and manmade—and the range of existing land and water

---

*The federal Office of Coastal Zone Management summarized program development guidelines and requirements in seven informal threshold papers (OCZM, 1976). Threshold papers were in use when the case study research was done, but early in 1978 new regulations were implemented to replace them.

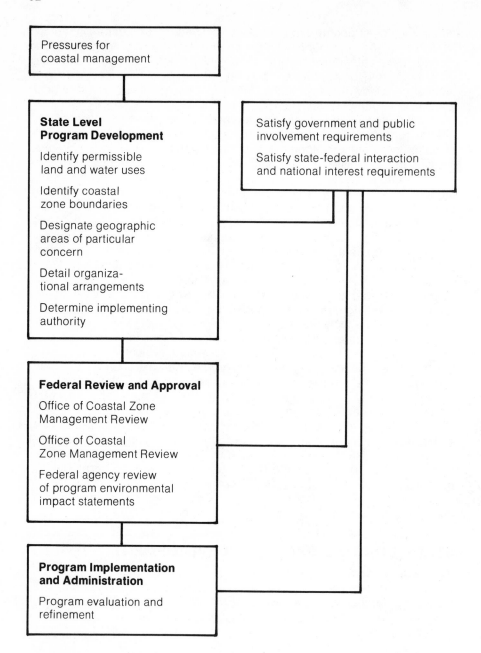

Figure 3.1   State-level coastal zone management program development under federal Coastal Zone Management Act of 1972.

uses. Second, coastal uses must be distinguished from inland uses. Only those uses which have both a "direct" and "significant" impact on coastal waters need to be considered in a coastal program. The third step is to develop a method for determining the capability and suitability of each segment of shore for supporting different uses. Fourth, these determinations then must be combined with an analysis of local, regional, state, and national needs in order to identify permissible coastal uses.

After the permissible uses have been identified, states must establish priorities among them according to three geographic scales:

1. Uses that are broadly defined and generally applicable to all coastal development;
2. Uses that are more specific, referring to certain coastal environments, such as wetlands or natural estuarine areas;
3. Uses that are site specific, referring only to a particular location.

Last, states must create a management process to plan for impacts of coastal energy facilities, including those involved in transportation of energy resources such as coal, oil, and liquefied natural gas. They must also address the questions of beach access and beach erosion. These last requirements received added attention with the 1976 amendments to the Coastal Zone Management Act.

Several approaches may be used to implement land- and water-use policies. One approach is highly structured: specific policies are related to particular uses occurring in certain types of coastal environments. A less site-specific approach is to develop policies only with respect to major categories of coastal uses, such as transportation and recreation, and activities such as dredging and filling of coastal waters. A third approach is to apply performance standards to control environmental impacts rather than to regulate particular uses. Some standards, such as air and water quality standards, must be included in all management programs regardless of the approach selected (OCZM, 1976, paper no. 2, p. 4).

Examples. Washington State relies primarily on the first method of managing coastal uses. Local governments are required to classify all shores according to the intensity of development. Generally, four environmental designations are used to depict the level of development: urban, rural, natural, or conservancy (Washington Department of Ecology, 1976, p. 123). Specific policies have been developed to identify permissible uses in each environment. Ports are a preferred use in urban environments but are excluded in natural or conservancy environments.

Texas, a strong home rule state, relies primarily on performance standards. Each project application is assessed for its environmental impacts in accordance with a systematic activity analysis involving three steps:

1. The activity and its location are identified.

2. The effects of environmental alterations on the pertinent ecological system are analyzed.

3. The likely economic and social consequences, environmental alterations, and possible mitigating or enhancing features for each are considered.

Since performance standards are stressed in the Texas program, coastal authority rests in reacting to proposed projects rather than allocating particular uses to certain environments in advance.

Relationship to ports. Because port functions are water dependent, ports have priority among coastal users in all case study states. However, coastal programs are beginning to differentiate among such port facilities as general cargo, commercial fishing, small-craft, hazardous materials, and energy-related facilities. For example, in California, the extent of autonomy given to ports varies according to the type of proposed development. Energy-related facilities require state review while a cargo-related facility can be approved by the port if it is consistent with the port's certified master plan.

Ports are not the only priority users in the coastal zone, however. They must compete for waterfront space with other water-dependent or public uses. This competition is evident in Washington where the state statute, the Shoreline Management Act of 1971, explicitly recognizes the water dependency of port activities and lists port development among the uses granted priority for altering the natural shoreline of the state. Yet, the statute places equal importance on other uses which are water-dependent or uses which increase the public's ability to enjoy the shoreline.

Determining Coastal Zone Boundaries

One of the primary requirements of a coastal zone management program is a determination of management boundaries. Seaward boundaries are legislatively defined as the outer limits of the territorial sea (usually three miles). Great Lakes boundaries are the state or the international boundaries. Inland boundaries are flexible but must extend inland "to the extent necessary to control . . . uses . . . which have a direct and significant impact on coastal waters" (CZMA section 304 [a]). Since the land- and water-use and boundary-determination elements of program development are defined with respect to direct and significant impact, they must be compatible.

There are many methods for determining the coastal boundaries of a state (Table 3.1). Biophysical characteristics (such as topographic features or vegetative cover), uniform distance from a tidal mark, political jurisdiction boundaries (such as county lines), manmade features (such as highways), or planning units (such as census tracts or regional agency jurisdictions) may be used singly or in combination to define coastal areas (OCZM 1976, paper no. 1, p. 7). Minimum inland boundaries to estuarine areas must include all waters with a measurable quantity of seawater but

Table 3.1 Approaches to defining inland coastal boundaries

Type of boundary	Case study examples
Fixed set-back line	Washington Shoreline Management Act (200 feet inland from MHW) California Coastal Act (1,000 yards) Wisconsin Shorelands Act 300 feet inland from rivers and streams 1,000 feet inland from lakes
City and county line	Georgia Coastal Area Planning and Development Commission (CAPDC) planning boundary
Census tract boundary	Pennsylvania coastal planning boundary
Rights-of-way of coastal highways, railroads, pipelines, etc.	New Jersey boundary of Coastal Area Facilities Review Act (CAFRA)
Elevation contour line	Louisiana (proposed)
Mountain ridge crest	California
Special resource areas (dunes, flood plains, estuaries, marshes)	California
Special adjustments to exclude areas in which development would have little or no effect on resources or public access	California (certain urbanized areas)
to avoid bisecting a parcel of land or to conform to an identifiable natural or manmade feature	California (up to 100 yards)

may be extended to include all areas of tidal influence.

Some states employ a "two-tiered" approach to determine coastal boundaries in which a distinction is drawn between a planning area and a coastal management area (OCZM 1976, paper no. 1, p. 7–8). The management area—the first tier—is narrower than the second, and all uses in this area usually are closely regulated. The planning area—the second tier—is more broadly defined and often encompasses the entire coastal county. Planning and development in this area are monitored for consistency with the management program in the first tier.

Examples. Washington's two-tiered program illustrates a variety of the possible management approaches. The first tier, the management area, is based on the boundaries defined in the Shoreline Management Act. A uniform distance of 200 feet inland from the ordinary high tide line forms the standard boundary. Natural features such as bogs, swamps, and flood plains are also included and may extend the 200-foot boundary further inland (Washington Department of Ecology, 1976). The second tier, the planning area, follows county lines, which in turn generally coincide with a natural boundary, the crest of the Cascade mountain range.

Many of the case study states have not yet adopted a coastal boundary. However, studies of coastal ecosystems which have been undertaken in Georgia and Texas are intended to provide the resource information for boundary determinations. Scientists have mapped biological and geological information to identify the inland extent of marine influence.

New Jersey will rely on its Coastal Area Facility Review Act (CAFRA) to define the boundary for that segment of the coast under CAFRA jurisdiction. CAFRA boundaries are defined on the basis of manmade features. Since the CAFRA segment specifically excludes the areas in which the Port of New York/New Jersey and the Delaware River ports are located, the New Jersey coastal boundary applicable to ports is still undetermined.

Relationship to ports. Since coastal boundaries should incorporate those lands where activities can have a direct and significant impact on coastal waters, the boundaries usually extend a considerable distance up coastal rivers. Although ports located along these rivers and navigation channels are considered seaports and have direct linkages with ocean-going vessels, some port officials argue that the coastal program boundaries extend too far inland. The officials maintain that their ports are outside the coastal zone. For example, officials at the Port of Philadelphia and the Port of Brownsville do not consider the marine influence in their vicinity sufficient to include their holdings in the coastal zone.

Another argument to exclude many onshore port developments from management programs is that urban boundaries in the coastal zone should be limited to the high-water mark on bulkheads. Under this argument, only fill operations or other changes in the bulkhead lines would be subject to the management programs, because only those changes affect coastal waters. (See Chapter 6, boundary definition recommendations, where these arguments are refuted.)

Since port development functions may extend far inland, an individual port may be in both tiers of the coastal zone or may straddle the inland boundary of the coastal zone. Where a portion of a port project lies within the management area, courts in both California and Washington have ruled that the whole project is subject to the regulations governing coastal development.

Geographic Areas of Particular Concern (GAPC)

The Coastal Zone Management Act requires states to designate geographic areas of particular concern (GAPCs) in the coastal zone. Federal regulations defined the scope of GAPCs to include "transitional or intensely developed areas where reclamation, restoration, public access, and other actions are especially needed; and those areas suited for intensive use or development. In addition, immediacy of need should be a major consideration . . ." (OCZM 1976, paper no. 3, p. 1). As a result, GAPCs are useful for achieving both economic and environmental goals.

States must consider the variety of purposes and environments to which a GAPC designation can be applied. These areas can represent a type of shore (such as wetlands) or a specific site. In either case, the rationale for selection, the exact location of boundaries, and the methods of control must be stated explicitly in state proposals.

Examples. Several methods for designating geographic areas of particular concern were used in case study states. Table 3.2 illustrates the variety of ways California uses GAPCs. They range from the entire coastal zone to small sensitive resource areas.

The Washington legislature, in the Shoreline Management Act, specified certain shores as "shorelines of statewide significance." These areas

Table 3.2 Types and functions of geographic areas of particular concern (GAPC) as defined in California

This list of geographical areas of particular concern defined in the California Coastal Act (1976) illustrates the many uses possible for GAPCs. Basically, any area of the coast may be designated a GAPC to receive special protection, funding, planning effort, or to preserve specific rights or administrative jurisdiction for the State Coastal Commission. The following seven types of GAPCs are outlined:

Entire coastal zone in general

18 specific estuarine, habitat, or recreational areas designated in the California Coastal Act

More specific areas of concern, a list of which serves as a standard for reviewing local coastal programs for compliance

    Sand transport systems
    Offshore islands
    Degraded wetlands
    Public trust lands
    Prime agricultural land
    Commercial timber lands
    Corridors for boating access
    Highly scenic areas
    Seismically hazardous areas
    Archeological resources areas
    Industrialized port areas
    Public works facilities
    State colleges and universities

Sensitive coastal resource areas that cannot be protected by local zoning ordinances alone

State Coastal Commission's reserved jurisdiction before certification of local coastal programs

State Coastal Commission's appeal jurisdiction after certification of local coastal programs

Areas purchased for public preservation and restoration

exhibit unique environmental characteristics and are regulated by more restrictive standards and greater state authority than other state shore-lines. Alterations to the natural shoreline are permitted only when specific criteria are met. The state coastal agency also identified administrative GAPCs, which may be temporary. They were selected for intensified coastal management on the basis of three criteria: (1) potential conflicts among user groups and regulatory agencies; (2) environmental features of greater than local concern; and (3) recognition by other state agencies, programs, and ownership characteristics as an area of particular concern (Washington Department of Ecology, 1976, p. 12).

Wisconsin proposes to use geographic areas of particular concern as a cornerstone in its coastal program. Those areas, along with a limited number of coastal uses, are the only ones identified as management areas within their broad planning boundary. Types of areas which may be desig-nated include areas of significant natural, recreational, scientific, or his-toric value which require either management or protection; areas espe-cially suited for water-related economic development—ports, hazard areas, and approved power plant sites; and areas marked for restoration.

Relationship to ports. Waterfront areas with obsolete port facilities or with development potential can be designated as geographic areas of particular concern. This helps port officials plan future facilities locations with certainty and provides both port officials and coastal management personnel with a specific reason to cooperate in implementing the coastal program. In Washington, the Grays Harbor estuary has been designated as a GAPC because of intense use conflicts. The Port of Grays Harbor ac-tively participates on the task force attempting to resolve the conflicts. Georgia's urban centers of Savannah, Brunswick, and St. Simons are pro-posed to be GAPCs for economic development. Port uses proposed by the Georgia Port Authority and economic uses promoted by the Savannah Port Authority are appropriate in these areas. Alternatively, port expansion into Georgia's coastal marshlands, which are proposed to be GAPCs for preservation, would likely be prohibited.

Use of geographic areas of particular concern with respect to port activities is explored in greater depth in Chapters 4 and 5.

Organizational Arrangements

A primary goal of the federal coastal legislation is effective coordina-tion among all federal, state, and local agencies with responsibilities in the coastal zone—natural resource management, land and water space allocation programs, and environmental protection. To meet this goal, states are required to establish methods for coordinating these agencies' activities. Four methods are normally used:

1. Coastal statutes may prescribe agencies' interrelationships.

2. Interagency committees or designated individuals within agen-cies may be used to facilitate coordination.

3. Ad hoc committees may be established to resolve specific coastal issues.

4. Executive reorganization may integrate resource protection and resource management functions in the same agency.

Examples. A special section in the California coastal legislation explicitly details the relationship between the coastal commission and other state agencies. The commission is authorized to submit recommendations to state agencies which detail how these agencies may implement their programs to conform with, and to help implement, the Coastal Act. If the agencies do not implement these recommendations, they must justify their decision to the Governor and legislature. No particular forum is recommended for coordination among all state agencies; however, specific types of coordination are required between the commission and individual departments, commissions, and boards (California Coastal Act, PRC, sections 30400–30418).

Washington's program relies on an existing, well-developed network of agency coordination. In addition, ten state agencies have designated "coastal zone management contacts" to coordinate coastal-related affairs, such as review of local master programs, permit applications, and environmental impact statements. Coastal zone management funds are used to hire the "contacts" within the state agencies. Coordination with local governments is achieved through implementation of the state shoreline management statute.

In New Jersey, the responsibility for environmental protection and resource management rests within the Department of Environmental Protection, thereby combining management of waterbottoms or fill activities and the environmental protection of coastal resources in the same agency. This arrangement provides a unique opportunity for close coordination of these activities. Funds for coastal management planning have been used to integrate four management activities: (1) administration of the wetlands program, (2) review of coastal facilities, (3) issuing of riparian leases and licenses, and (4) issuing of waterfront development permits.

The New Jersey coastal program also depends upon ad hoc coordination with the State Department of Labor and Industry, to provide input on the economic effects of coastal regulations and the economic needs in particular coastal regions. The department's economic researchers have prepared numerous issue papers and frequently participate in coastal planning meetings.

Relationship to ports. Because port development issues usually involve state waterbottoms, the coordination element of coastal management programs is especially important for ports. Expansion plans that involve critical estuarine areas may conflict with conservation statutes, such as the Georgia Coastal Marshlands Protection Act, Washington's Shoreline Management Act, and the federal Fish and Wildlife Coordination Act. Coastal management programs will not repeal these existing statutes, but if there is cooperation among affected users and agencies and consistency of federal activities, much of the uncertainty surrounding permitted land and water uses should be eliminated and beneficial uses can be expected to proceed without excessive permit delays.

Implementing Authority

Under the Coastal Zone Management Act (section 306 [d] [1]), state coastal management programs must have the authority to—

1. Administer land- and water-use regulations;

2. Control development to insure compliance with the coastal program;

3. Resolve conflicts among competing uses.

Before a mechanism is selected, states are required to inventory existing laws, regulations, judicial opinions, etc., to establish where authority lies.

There are three techniques for program implementation (section 306 [e] [1]) that may be used singly or in combination:

1. State establishment of criteria and standards for local implementation, subject to administrative review and enforcement of compliance;

2. Direct state land- and water-use planning and regulations;

3. State administrative review for consistency with the management program of all development plans, projects, or land- or water-use regulations, including exceptions of variances thereto.

Although any number of government agencies may have authority to implement the coastal management program, only one state-level office (identified by the Governor) can be responsible for receiving and administering coastal program funds.

Examples. Two approaches for implementing coastal programs emerged from the case studies: (1) "networking" existing authorities, and (2) enacting new comprehensive legislation.

Networking involves coordinating existing governmental powers to achieve coastal management goals. Some states, such as Massachusetts and Wisconsin, propose networking the existing local and state powers and state-implemented federal programs. Management tools may include zoning, air and water quality standards, resource management agency standards (such as forest practices), submerged-land lease criteria, state health standards affecting sewage and shellfish management, energy facility siting criteria, fisheries management, and wildlife agency regulations.

Texas is using a network of existing state authorities to implement its coastal program. The Interagency Council on Natural Resources and the

Environment, an executive branch council, was reorganized, renamed the Natural Resources Council, and given responsibility for regulating coastal land and water uses based on a standard analysis procedure. Only matters of state and national interest are regulated; local matters are reserved for local decision makers.

Other states have legislated new management systems and special permit procedures to implement their coastal programs. Washington requires permits for all substantial development in the first tier of the coastal zone. While certain uses—such as single-family residences, docks and bulkheads for single-family residences, and certain agricultural uses—are exempt from permit requirements, all other substantial developments, including port development, are included (Shoreline Management Act, RCW 90.58.030 [3] [e] [i to vii]).

California also has comprehensive coastal legislation. Impetus for this legislation was a public initiative, Proposition 20 (California Coastal Zone Conservation Act of 1972); however, it created only an interim coastal management program. Permanent legislation enacted in 1976, the California Coastal Act, now requires permits for all major developments within the 1,000-yard coastal zone. Local governments are responsible for developing detailed programs for implementing state policies. Until they are developed and certified, however, the State Coastal Commission, assisted by regional commissions, will issue permits as they did under Proposition 20.

Both California and Washington have quasi-judicial appeal boards to hear disputes over coastal permits, the Shorelines Hearings Board in Washington and the California State Coastal Commission.

A principal distinction between these two programs is the special treatment California gives to the ports of Hueneme, Long Beach, Los Angeles, and the San Diego Unified Port District. (San Francisco Bay ports are not included since they lie within a different coastal management jurisdiction.) These four ports will develop "port master plans" in their jurisdictions. Once the plans are certified by the coastal commission, the ports must insure that all new developments comply with the plan. Developments that appear to violate the certified port master plans may be appealed to the coastal commission (California Coastal Act, PRC, Division 20, Chapter 8).

Relationship to ports. Using the network approach entails administrative cooperation and coordination, using traditional formal and informal connections among the ports and government agencies.

Comprehensive legislation, as in Washington and California, often adds new administrative or regulatory mechanisms to state and local agencies. Although they may create initial uncertainty for ports and be a source of annoyance, they may also provide more concrete rules for decision making. California's comprehensive legislation, for example, gives four ports the authority to plan and regulate activities within their jurisdiction.

Public and Governmental Involvement

The Coastal Zone Management Act mandates that programs be developed "with the opportunity of full participation by relevant federal agencies, state agencies, local governments, regional organizations, port authorities, and other interested parties, public and private . . ." (section 306 [c] [1]). To do so, states must—

1. Distribute information about their programs so that participants can easily understand program elements;

2. Provide ample opportunity for interested and affected persons and groups to comment and offer suggestions;

3. Demonstrate that this input is seriously considered (OCZM 1976, paper no. 4, pp. 1–5).

States have considerable latitude in determining the mechanisms to insure full participation; public hearings are the only technique specifically required (section 306 [c] [3]).

Examples. States use various methods to assure participation. Newsletters are published and widely distributed in Texas, Pennsylvania, Washington, and Wisconsin. Frequently, advisory committees are appointed to provide technical advice and public and governmental viewpoints.

Wisconsin has provided multiple opportunities for advisory committee participation. Its Coastal Zone Coordinating and Advisory Council is composed of representatives from state agencies, regional planning commissions, local government, and university and public interest groups. Its efforts are coordinated with the Wisconsin planning office before policy recommendations are made to the Governor. The council, in turn, receives advice from a Citizens' Advisory Committee, composed of citizens and public interest groups. Additionally, each of Wisconsin's three regional planning commissions, with jurisdictions on Lake Michigan and Lake Superior, have citizen and technical advisory committees which review and comment on coastal management policies. A Coastal Council and Citizens' Advisory Committee has also been recommended to implement the coastal management program. Film clips, talks with local interest groups, and media coverage supplement these formal mechanisms.

Relationship to ports. Ports are permitted full opportunity to participate in coastal management program development and to express their needs and interests.

State-Federal Interaction and National Interests

After a program is approved, federal agency actions must be consistent with it to the maximum extent practicable (CZMA section 307 [c] [1] [2] [3]). Disagreements between these agencies and state programs which cannot be resolved informally can be settled through a mediation procedure established in the federal statute (section 307 [h]).

All coastal states must consider the national interest in "siting of facilities necessary to meet requirements which are other than local in nature" (section 306 [c] [8]). Energy facility needs must be given special attention under the 1976 amendments. In addition, states that are

Table 3.3 Requirements which are other than local in nature
and in the siting of which there may be a clear national interest
(with associated facilities and cognizant federal agencies)

Requirements	Associated Facilities	Cognizant Federal Agencies
1. Energy production and transmission.	Oil and gas wells; storage and distribution facilities; refineries; nuclear, conventional, and hydroelectri powerplants; deepwater ports.	Federal Energy Administration, Federal Power Commission, Bureau of Land Management, Atomic Energy Commission, Maritime Administration, Geological Survey, Department of Transportation, Corps of Engineers.
2. Recreation (of an interstate nature).	National seashores, parks, forests; large and outstanding beaches and recreational waterfronts; wildlife reserves.	National Park Service, Forest Service, Bureau of Outdoor Recreation.
3. Interstate transportation.	Interstate highways, airports, aids to navigation; ports and harbors, railroads.	Federal Highway Administration, Federal Aviation Administration, Coast Guard, Corps of Engineers, Maritime Administration, Interstate Commerce Commission.
4. Production of food and fiber.	Prime agricultural land and facilities; forests; mariculture facilities; fisheries.	Soil Conservation Service, Forest Service, Fish and Wildlife Service, National Marine Fisheries Service.
5. Preservation of life and property.	Flood and storm protection facilities; disaster warning facilities.	Corps of Engineers, Federal Insurance Administration, NOAA, Soil Conservation Service.
6. National defense and aerospace.	Military installations; defense manufacturing facilities; aerospace launching and tracking facilities.	Department of Defense, NASA
7. Historic, cultural, aesthetic, and conservation values.	Historic sites, natural areas; areas of unique cultural significance; wildlife refuges; areas of species and habitat preservation.	National Register of Historic Places, National Park Service, Fish and Wildlife Service, National Marine Fisheries Service.
8. Mineral resources.	Mineral extraction facilities needed to directly support activity.	Bureau of Mines, Geological Survey.

developing coastal management programs must coordinate program development with federal agencies; prior to approval, the federal Office of Coastal Zone Management must give these agencies an opportunity to comment on the proposed program (section 307 [a] [b]).

National interests. Defining "national interests" has been extremely difficult. Federal agencies don't have to define them; instead, federal regulations guide states in identifying activities and associated facilities which may have a clear national interest and are other than local in nature (Table 3.3). These guidelines note the potential national interest of ports and harbors.

States can fulfill the national interest requirement by allowing federal agencies to (1) assess energy facility sites, (2) coordinate and exchange viewpoints, and (3) continue to interact with the state through an established process (OCZM, 1976, paper no. 5, p. 13).

Federal agency coordination. All relevant federal agencies which must be formally contacted for coordination have been identified by the Office of Coastal Zone Management. Measures that can be used to satisfy the state-federal coordination criterion on a continuing basis include technical or advisory assistance (through informal but documented contacts or through advisory committees), bilateral discussion, invitations to meetings and hearings, federal coordination bodies (regional councils or river basin commissions), and review of draft documents (OCZM, 1976, paper no. 5, p. 7–9).

Federal consistency. The federal consistency clause requires federal agencies to conduct their activities and development projects in a manner that is consistent with approved state programs "to the maximum extent practicable" (Table 3.4). (CZMA section 307 [c] [1] [2] [3] and [d]) State coastal programs can veto issuance of permits, leases, licenses, and grants from federal agencies, but these vetoes may be appealed to the Secretary of Commerce.

Examples. The Washington coastal program provided the first opportunity to assess standards for fulfilling the obligation of federal involvement. The Shoreline Management Act, the core of the Washington program, both predates federal legislation and places primary responsibility at the local level. Federal agencies were invited by the state to attend planning meetings and to participate on master program review committees. The significance of federal participation, however, was not appeciated by either the state or federal agencies until Washington submitted its coastal management program for approval in 1975. The round of negotiations which followed Washington's application was the first serious, concerted attention federal agencies gave to coastal management program development.

Washington's approved program builds on an existing federal review

Table 3.4 Federal consistency matrix diagram.

CZMA Section	307(c)(1) & (2) (Subpart C)	307(c)(3)(A) (Subpart D)	307(c)(3)(B) (Subpart E)	307(d) (Subpart F)
Federal action	Direct federal activities including development projects	Federally licensed and permitted activities	Federally licensed and permitted activities described in detail in OCS plans	Federal assistance to state and local governments
Coastal zone impact	"Directly affecting the coastal zone"	"Affecting land or water uses in the coastal zone"[1]	"Affecting any land use or water use in the coastal zone"[1]	"Affecting the coastal zone"[1]
Responsibility to notify state agency	Federal agency proposing the action	Applicant for federal license or permit	Person submitting OCS Plan	A-95 Clearinghouse receiving state or local government application for federal assistance
Notification procedure	Alternatives chosen by federal agency (subject to NOAA regulations)	Consistency certification or equivalent procedure set forth in CZM Program	Consistency certification	OMB Circular A-95 notification procedure
Consistency requirement	Consistent to the maximum extent practicable with CZM Program	Consistent with the CZM Program	Consistent with the CZM Program	Consistent with the CZM Program
Consistency determination	Made by federal agency (review by state agency)	Made by state agency	Made by state agency	Made by state agency
Federal agency responsibility following a disagreement	Federal agency not required to disapprove action following state disagreement (unless judicially impelled to do so)	Federal agency may not approve license or permit following state agency objection	Federal agency may not approve federal licenses or permits described in detail in the OCS Plan following state agency objection	Federal agency may not grant assistance following state objection
Administrative conflict resolution	Voluntary mediation by the Secretary (Subpart G)	Appeal to the Secretary by applicant or independent Secretarial review[2] (Subpart H)	Appeal to the Secretary by person or independent Secretarial review[2] (Subpart H)	Appeal to the Secretary by applicant or independent Secretary review[2] (Subpart H)
Associate Administrator reporting of inconsistent federal actions	(Subpart I)	(Subpart I)	(Subpart I)	(Subpart I)

Source: *Federal Register,* Volume 42, No. 167, pages 43588-89, August 29, 1977

[1]These terms all have the same meaning.
[2]Voluntary mediation by the Secretary is also available in certain cases.

process, A–95, to identify questions needing state-federal coordination. A–95 review is a coordinating procedure which enables state and local agencies to review federal grants to states to insure their compatibility with existing state and local planning programs. The state has also created a state-federal coordinator position in the state coastal management office.

Most other states will also incorporate the A–95 review process into their federal coordination process. During early phases of program development when states are identifying national interests and developing policies, this review process may be supplemented by other procedures. For example, Louisiana and Texas conducted a survey of all federal agencies having a coastal management interest to get their view of national interest.

Since Washington's program was the first one approved, it provides the only examples of federal consistency in operation. The consistency issue arose in connection with the Navy's construction of a large pier for the Trident Nuclear Submarine Base on Hood Canal and also in connection with a lawsuit challenging Washington's Tanker Safety Act, which imposes state standards for moving oil by tanker on Puget Sound. In the first case, the state believed the Navy pier, designed for refitting large submarines, would be inconsistent with the state's coastal management program. Even though the Coastal Zone Management Act excludes federal lands from the coastal zone, the pier would impact upon the state's waterbottoms and fishery resources. Since the Secretary of Commerce could overrule the state's determination based on national security reasons, the state agreed to allow the construction because of the clear national security aspects of the submarine base.

In the second case, the state argued that the Tanker Safety Act was part of its coastal management program and therefore the Coast Guard's regulation of oil tanker safety and movement should conform to state law. This argument was rejected by the lower court which heard the case. The court believed that Congress did not intend that the Coastal Zone Management Act should result in the negation of other federal statutes and programs. The U.S. Supreme Court found part of Washington's tanker law unconstitutional, but in deciding the case made only passing reference to the Coastal Zone Management Act.

In another case, federal approval was denied a project which had received state approval. The Port of Tacoma obtained a state permit to develop a marina, but because of federal Fish and Wildlife Service objections, a Corps of Engineers permit has been held up. In this instance, federal consistency requirements do not compel the Corps to issue a federal permit even though the state has approved the project. It is safe to conclude that Congress intended that the Corps be consistent as often as possible, but did not mandate consistency in each and every instance.

Relationship to ports. Federal regulations identify port development as an activity with national interest implications. Because port projects frequently involve a federal navigation improvement project or require federal and state permits for filling or dredging, state-federal coordination is an important issue when port developments are proposed. As the Navy Trident pier and Tacoma marina examples show, questions of federal consistency have already arisen and are likely to continue to do so in the future.

FEDERAL REVIEW AND APPROVAL

State programs are continually reviewed by the federal Office of Coastal Zone Management. During the development of a program, section 305 grants may be terminated if a state does not demonstrate that it is making progress toward developing an approvable coastal management program. After a program is approved, the federal office conducts ongoing reviews of state performance to insure adherence to the approved coastal program.

An intensive federal review of the coastal management program occurs when the state submits the program for approval. Federal review involves the Office of Coastal Zone Management (OCZM) and federal agencies with an interest in the coastal zone. OCZM reviews state programs for consistency with the federal statute and program approval regulations, and for compliance with the National Environmental Policy Act.

On the basis of an environmental impact assessment submitted with the state program, OCZM prepares a formal environmental impact statement (EIS) for programs submitted for final approval. When an EIS is issued, it is circulated for review along with the state program. Public hearings are then held to review the EIS prepared by the federal office and the program approval application prepared by the state.

Since federal agencies must comply with state coastal management programs to the maximum extent practicable, they have a great interest in carefully reviewing each program submitted for approval. Copies of the proposed program and draft EIS are circulated to national and regional offices of federal agencies. Although the agencies are not formally involved in preliminary approvals, they are encouraged to review each program proposal carefully. If a state decides to apply for preliminary approval while its program is being reviewed, issues raised by federal agencies must be considered before the program is reaccepted for final approval.

PROGRAM IMPLEMENTATION AND ADMINISTRATION

Federally approved programs are eligible for continuous funding under section 306 of the Coastal Zone Management Act. Typically, a portion of the funding will be used for implementing a special permit system or the networking of existing regulatory programs. Additional uses of administrative funds may include upgrading portions of a coastal program, or completing detailed local plans to implement state policies. Both Washington and the San Francisco Bay Conservation and Development Commission (BCDC) have used considerable portions of section 306 grants for refining their coastal programs. In both cases, funds are being directed toward more specific planning for shoreline use and protection. Washington's program has also allocated implementation funds to study natural resource systems in Puget Sound, the Strait of Juan de Fuca, and along the Pacific coast, and to develop a coastal atlas for state and local planners.

Continued development of state programs requires increased attention to program evaluations. Since techniques for evaluating coastal management programs are still in the development stage, implementation funds may be geared to both developing evaluation techniques and conducting evaluations (Englander et al., 1977).

The Office of Coastal Zone Management has interpreted section 306 liberally. As is illustrated above, many aspects of program implementation may be funded under this provision, and imaginative use of these funds provides a state with many options for improving management programs. Only capital investments or long-term scientific investigations are not allowed.

ASPECTS OF COASTAL MANAGEMENT PROGRAMS ADDED BY 1976 AMENDMENTS

Interstate Coordination (Section 309)

To facilitate interstate coordination of shared coastal areas, a special section was added to the Coastal Zone Management Act in 1976. No funds have been appropriated to implement this as yet, although regulations have been promulgated. Presently, there are numerous interstate activities in existence which would benefit from the assistance. For example, the Great Lakes Basin Commission has appointed a standing committee on coastal zone management. The committee provides a forum for addressing such matters as costal zone boundaries at state lines and national interest. And in the Northeast, a Coastal Zone Task Force, organized through the New England River Basins Commission, includes representatives from the five New England coastal states and New York.

In other cases, interstate studies that are currently funded by state coastal management funds might be more appropriately funded under section 309. For example, Washington and Oregon appointed a joint estuary study team for the Columbia River (CREST) to deal with land- and water-use allocation problems in the estuary. CREST is funded by program development funds in Oregon (section 305) and implementation funds in Washington (section 306). Duluth, Minnesota and Superior, Wisconsin are conducting joint research on their port facilities, which is presently funded by the federal Office of Coastal Zone management and the Department of Housing and Urban Development.

Research Training and Technical Assistance (Section 310)

A special program to encourage research, studies, and training in support of coastal management was established by the 1976 amendments. The purpose is to sponsor research, management training programs, and technical assistance at the national and state levels to aid in the development and implementation of the program. The section has not been funded as yet, but many research and study efforts have been supported under the more general provisions of sections 305 and 306. Special studies on selected topics, such as ports, erosion, outer continental shelf impacts, and coastal ecology, have already been produced, and others probably will follow. In addition, funding would permit continuing education programs and internships, which would enhance the ability of present and future coastal agency personnel to manage coastal resources effectively.

Coastal Energy Impact Program (Section 308)

A major addition to the federal coastal management program in 1976 was the creation of a coastal energy impact program. The purpose of this program is to assist local and state governments, through grants or loans, to meet the immediate costs associated with growth resulting from offshore energy development and to pay for unavoidable environmental damages. The eligibility for assistance, allocation of funds, and determination of amount of assistance are highly technical issues, which are just now being resolved. Under this program, port authorities are eligible to receive loans or grants if they are the governmental unit needing assistance to meet outer continental shelf facility requirements. New amendments to this program will probably take effect in 1978.

Estuarine Sanctuary and Marine Sanctuary Grants (Section 315 and Title III, Marine Protection, Research, and Sanctuaries Act of 1972)

The 1976 amendments require planning for the protection of, and access to, public beaches and other public areas along the coast. Grants can be made to states to cover 50 percent of the cost of access rights to beaches or other coastal areas.

Grants are also appropriate if a state wishes to acquire, develop, and operate estuarine sanctuaries in order to create natural field laboratories where natural and human processes in estuaries can be studied. The federal office has identified a number of types of estuaries existing around the country from which selected sanctuaries will be established. A limited number of sanctuaries have been designated to date.

Marine sanctuaries are authorized under the "Ocean Dumping Act" (Keifer, 1975). The marine sanctuary program is administered by the Office of Coastal Zone Management. Sanctuaries as far seaward as the continental shelf or in the Great Lakes may be nominated by any individual, organization, or government body to achieve any of five purposes:

1. Preservation, protection, and management of a particular ecosystem (e.g., coral reef);

2. Protection of selected species;

3. Protection of the recreational and aesthetic character of a seascape;

4. Protection of an area in order to conduct long-term research;

5. Protection of special geologic, oceanographic, historic or living resource features.

SUMMARY

Federal coastal zone management guidelines provide a framework that gives states considerable freedom to develop coastal programs which meet their unique needs. This federal framework is currently being re-fined. Continued refinement can be expected as states and the federal government gain experience in managing the coastal resources. Future evaluations of the effectiveness of various management techniques will enhance these efforts.

4 LAND- AND WATER-USE PROBLEMS AND EMERGING POLICIES

Certain land- and water-use issues emerge when ports consider new development projects and if coastal management programs are to be successful they must be able to resolve these problems effectively and quickly. Ten problem areas common to most development activities emerged from the six case studies and are discussed in this chapter. The first three arise from the environmental impacts associated with construction projects, maintenance activities, and day-to-day port operations. They are (1) management of landfill, (2) management of dredging and dredged material disposal, and (3) air and water quality degradation.

Measures to ameliorate such impacts present two more issues: (4) mitigation and compensation for environmental damage, and (5) public access and aesthetics. Mitigation measures may take several forms: restoration of biologically degraded areas, dedication of similar areas for public purposes, collection of in-lieu payment, or public access to waterfront to offset loss of public tideland areas.

In addition to environmental issues, certain marine facilities raise two special problems that coastal management programs are addressing; (6) siting of hazardous facilities and (7) small-craft harbor facilities. Facilities for storing or transferring hazardous cargoes—such as liquid natural gas (LNG)—have raised safety hazard questions requiring special siting regulations. Small-craft harbors are in critical short supply and often compete with larger marine trade facilities for scarce waterfront and harbor space.

For ports to proceed with development plans they must know how much suitable waterfront land is available to them and they must be certain that construction can proceed on schedule. These problems are covered in the next two issues discussed: (8) allocation of waterfront land and (9) streamlining of permit procedures. Environmental and siting reviews by public agencies can be lengthy and project approval uncertain. This makes planning difficult and even speculative since ports must consider both short-term (shippers) needs and long-term economic development. If a port can't plan future capital expansion with some degree of certainty, its competitive posture and economic growth goals are jeopardized. Some coastal management programs are addressing these problems by providing adequate waterfront space for immediate and foreseeable port growth and adding procedures designed to streamline the permit review process.

Finally, there is the problem of future use of obsolete waterfront facilities (10). As port technology changes, older facilities become obsolete and there is emerging public pressure to redevelop these facilities for commercial and public uses.

Coastal management policies which address these issues are found in existing state laws and regulations, court and hearing board decisions, or in newly developed coastal management documents. In many cases the policies are very general, but as coastal management programs mature they will become more specific and will address particular aspects of land

and water uses. California, the San Franciso Bay area, and Washington are now formulating more specific policies. In Wisconsin, Pennsylvania, New Jersey, Georgia, and Texas, general policies are still being debated.

1. MANAGEMENT OF LANDFILL

Ports need waterfront land to accommodate the new shipping technologies (such as containerized cargo), which require large land areas adjacent to lengthy bulkheads. Industrial users need it because they want to be near transportation facilities. The primary means for satisfying increasing demands for waterfront land is often landfill. Ports that do not have large reserves of undeveloped land create it by filling between existing, outmoded finger piers, or by filling nearby wetlands and shallow bottomlands to an elevation above high water.

Landfill issues generate conflicts between port authorities and competing coastal users which center around adverse environmental impacts, the purpose and justification for the project, and regional landfill management. Before examining the issues in detail, however, it is important to delineate some of the engineering and economic constraints in using landfill to create new facilities.

Water depth. Landfill becomes impractical and prohibitively expensive in water depths over 50 feet.

Site availability. Existing finger piers or other structures on the site must be cleared and the cost of acquiring and filling the site must compare favorably with the cost of alternative sites.

Availability of fill material. Landfill projects may require extensive amounts of fill. Often, a major landfill project is planned to coincide with major dredging activity, to make use of available dredged material. Because it is expensive to transport dredged material more than a few miles, the landfill site must be close to the dredging site and be prepared to receive the material when dredging begins.

Suitability of fill material. Sand and gravel generally make excellent fill material because they dewater (drain) quickly and develop soil bearing capacities needed to support heavy structures. Fine-grain silts are less desirable—they may take months or years to dewater and may be limited in soil bearing capacity. Polluted dredged material in a landfill may require special treatment or isolation to make the landfill safe for development.

Cost of fill material. The cost of dredging, placing, containing, and shaping a landfill may dictate a project's financial feasibility.

Environmental impact. Strict environmental controls which are designed to maintain water quality or protect fisheries resources during the project may significantly raise the cost. In many cases, these costs do not include final site preparation needed to make the land useable.

Environmental Impacts of Landfill

There are adverse environmental impacts of landfill projects that coastal management programs have to deal with. The configuration of a landfill may modify water circulation and change patterns of sediment erosion or deposition. Dredging and placement of the fill material may release suspended sediment in the water column, degrading water quality and possibly smothering communities of benthic organisms with a blanket of silt. Increase in pollutants and decrease in dissolved oxygen may accompany stirring of the sediments, making the area hazardous for aquatic life. Landfill may also harm spawning, breeding, or feeding areas for fish, birds, and terrestrial animals.

Most of the coastal management programs studied have formulated general policies to deal with at least some of the adverse environmental impacts of landfill. For example, Georgia's Coastal Marshlands Protection Act requires landfill permits from the state's Department of Natural Resources, which shall "consider the public interest" by analyzing possible alterations in stream flow, potential increases in erosion or siltation, and the effects on finfish and shellfish, wildlife, water quality and other marine resources. The California Coastal Act of 1976 (section 30706) requires that port landfills be the minimum size necessary for the project, be constructed in accordance with "sound safety standards," and "minimize harmful effects to coastal resources, such as water quality, fish and wildlife resources, recreational resources, or sand transport systems, and . . . . minimize reductions of the volume, surface areas, or circulation of water."

Washington State Department of Ecology (1972) guidelines note that "significant damage to existing ecological values or natural resources" should not occur and that "such factors as total water surface reduction, navigation restriction, impediment to water flow and circulation, reduction of water quality, and destruction of habitats should be considered." Similar policies are incorporated into each city and county shoreline master program. In addition, state resource agencies may review and impose standards on landfill in the interest of protecting a natural resource, such as Department of Fisheries standards for landfill location and construction.

Federal resource management agencies have paramount rights to review environmental impacts of landfill projects in navigable waters, so coastal management programs must consider their policies during program development and implementation. By statute and interagency agreement, the Environmental Protection Agency (EPA), the U.S. Fish and Wildlife Service (FWS), and the National Marine Fisheries Service (NMFS) review and comment to the Corps of Engineers on sections 10 and 404 permit applications for construction or discharge of material in navigable waters of the United States. The review criteria includes strict standards to protect fish and wildlife resources, wetlands, and water quality. If one or more of the agencies objects to granting a permit, it may be denied or the case may be appealed to a higher authority in the Corps of Engineers and the resource agency.

The Port of Grays Harbor landfill projects illustrate the interaction of agencies and indicate that current coastal management landfill policies are too general to resolve controversy and effectively incorporate all federal agency interests. In the absence of suitable upland sites, the port depends on landfill to make low-lying waterfront marshland useful for port purposes. Several projects have been delayed because of disagreements over the effects of fill on important fish and wildlife habitats. The issue is complicated by the fact that the wetlands are not pristine, but have been used as dumps for a sawmill waste for many years.

In the case of a proposed landfill to accommodate a steel corporation's plans for an offshore oil drilling rig assembly yard (Figure 4.1), the U.S. Fish and Wildlife Service recommended denial of the Corps of Engineers permit because of potential adverse impacts to an important feeding ground for juvenile salmon. But political pressure was exerted based on the assertion that national offshore energy development policy superceded fisheries habitat protection, and the FWS withdrew its objection, the permit was approved, and construction began. Grays Harbor County's Shoreline Master Program landfill guidelines did not resolve the steel plant landfill problem, however, because they were too general and they did not reflect federal resource agencies' policies as they related to specific sites in the estuary.

Purpose and Justification for Landfill

It is common for coastal management programs to outline permissible purposes for landfill in general terms. The California Coastal Act of 1976 states (section 30705) that water areas may be filled for ". . . facilities as are required for the safety and the accommodation of commerce and vessels to be served by port facilities, . . . new or expanded facilities or waterfront land for port related facilities, . . . commercial fishing,. . . recreational boating," and other minor activities.

Washington's guidelines are less specific, stating only that "priority should be given to landfills for water-dependent uses and for public uses." Seattle's master program is equally nonspecific, permitting landfill for "water-dependent uses when no feasible alternative exists and the applicant can demonstrate a clear public benefit." In a recent case in Seattle, demonstrating a "clear public benefit" proved difficult—the need for the facility and alternative uses for the presently underutilized site were debated at length by planners, economists, and port officials before the port was finally permitted to proceed with the project.

Managing Landfill Within a Region

To avoid dealing with landfill on a project-by-project basis, attempts have been made to focus on landfill within a region, such as an estuary or

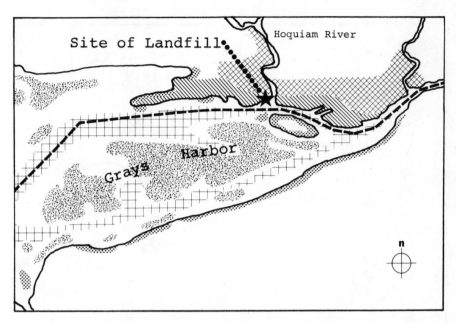

Figure 4.1 Conflict over industrial development of the fill site at the mouth of the Hoquiam River centered on the potential adverse environmental impacts to wetland areas, fish-rearing areas, and commercial salmon and sturgeon fishing grounds directly adjacent to the site. Source: Grays Harbor Estuary Management Program. Maps of vegetation and wildlife and natural resource use.

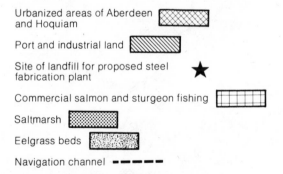

Urbanized areas of Aberdeen and Hoquiam

Port and industrial land

Site of landfill for proposed steel fabrication plant

Commercial salmon and sturgeon fishing

Saltmarsh

Eelgrass beds

Navigation channel

bay. A dramatic example is in the San Francisco Bay area. A Corps of Engineers study (1959) noted that the Bay had shrunk from 680 to 437 square miles, primarily due to extensive filling which had continued unregulated since about 1850 (Figure 4.2). Some conservationists expressed concern that soon there would be only a few narrow channels left of the once extensive Bay. This concern led to passage of the McAteer-Petris Act in 1965 and the establishment of the Bay Conservation and Development Commission (BCDC). One of its first tasks was to slow the rapid filling of the Bay. Through an interim permit system, filling decreased from

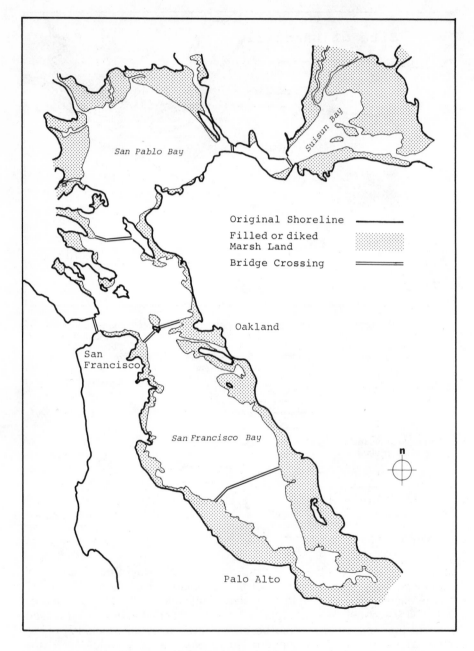

Figure 4.2   The San Francisco Bay system has been reduced in size by diking and filling from 787 square miles in 1850 to 548 square miles in 1968, a loss of 239 square miles. Source: San Francisco Bay Conservation and Development Commission.

an average annual rate of 1700 acres per year before 1965 to 61 acres per year after 1965 (Swanson, 1975).

In areas outside of San Francisco Bay, California's program allows landfill in those regions where port development has already occurred. The California Coastal Act states: "Existing ports shall be encouraged to modernize and construct necessary facilities within their boundaries in order to minimize or eliminate the necessity for future dredging and filling to create new ports in new areas of the state."

Most coastal management programs have not identified specific areas where landfill is allowed or encouraged. Yet, the pressure for development and expansion of port facilities continues to grow, resulting in landfill decisions that are made on an ad hoc, case-by-case basis. The need for more explicit landfill planning within coastal management programs is illustrated by the Port of Seattle, which is short of land for long-term future development. The port's development plans for the next five to ten years in Elliott Bay include landfill between a number of old finger piers to create new quay-type berths for container and general cargo terminal expansion. When these plans are completed, the port will have nearly exhausted all possible future sites for new landfill within its jurisdiction. Further major expansion will require wholly new facilities in remote areas, since water depths up to 600 feet in Elliott Bay preclude large landfill areas. The Seattle Shoreline Master Program will have to address this problem in the future.

A final issue often raised by resource agencies is how to manage the cumulative effects of many small landfill projects within a region. One landfill project by itself may have only minor impacts on fish and wildlife habitats or on reducing the total water surface area of a bay, but hundreds of such projects spread over several decades can have far-reaching impacts.

Although none of the case study programs yet provides specific approaches to this problem, coastal management personnel want to be able to predict the cumulative effect of each additional project and determine the ultimate limits of landfill development within a region. In Grays Harbor, for example, state and federal resource agencies refused to agree to new landfill activities until cumulative effects or ultimate development limits are known. In a Los Angeles case, before a small landfill project was approved, the applicant was required to show whether his project could be accommodated in a 1034-acre landfill proposed in the Port of Los Angeles master plan.

2. MANAGEMENT OF DREDGING AND DREDGED MATERIALS DISPOSAL

For a port to be competitive, it must maintain channels to handle longer, wider, and deeper-draft ships. Shipping industry trends are toward larger ships with increased drafts: most of the supercarriers already in service require water depths of at least 65 feet. The typical average depth of a U.S. port ranges from 30 to 40 feet, thus, a large percentage of the world fleet cannot enter many existing ports unless deeper and wider channels are dredged. Further, many natural and manmade ports require maintenance dredging to keep the channel free from silt and other obstructions. Ports with deep natural harbors and ports that succeed in getting federal navigation improvement funds will have a competitive advantage in the future.

Dredging and dredged materials management is primarily the concern of the Corps of Engineers, in cooperation with a local government agency, often a port authority. Federal funds for construction and maintenance dredging are appropriated by Congress to cover the dredging phase, but the "local cooperator" is required to pay for the disposal site and right-of-way acquisition, utility relocation, and other costs incurred in dredged materials disposal.

Dredging and dredge disposal problems seen in the case studies include disposal site selection, review of dredging needs, and interstate coordination of dredging and disposal between two or more adjoining states. Each of these is discussed below.

Disposal Site Selection

Selecting suitable dredged material disposal sites requires balancing dredging and disposal costs with environmental protection requirements. The cost per cubic yard of dredging is influenced by a number of factors— the type of material dredged (hard or soft), type of dredge used, water depth, distance from the dredging site to the disposal site, cost of dikes for confined disposal, and special environmental protection measures.

Disposal areas may be limited to upland sites (above the high-water mark), contained or uncontained wetland sites (diked or uncontained areas subject to tidal influence), and open-water sites. Construction dredging projects generate large amounts of material over a short time, requiring disposal areas suited to that purpose. The material generated by maintenance dredging requires disposal sites continuously available over a longer period of time. Dredged material that is polluted with heavy metals or toxic organic compounds poses special technical and cost problems and must be disposed of in contained upland sites. The material must be stabilized to prevent erosion or leaching of pollutants into neighboring water bodies.

Traditionally, the Corps of Engineers, the local sponsor, and concerned state and federal agencies are primarily responsible for choosing disposal sites. But a trend noted in Washington and California—fostered by coastal management programs and federal environmental protection legislation—has been to encourage more public, and local, state, and federal agency participation in decision making. Federal resource protection agencies—notably the U.S. Fish and Wildlife Service, the Environmental Protection Agency, and the National Marine Fisheries Service— are the most visible and active advocates for the protection of living resources in connection with dredging activities. Federal statutes and interagency memoranda of understanding permit these agencies to review and comment on proposed federal dredging projects.

Regulations and guidelines governing dredging differ considerably among coastal management programs. The Coastal Marshland Protection Act in Georgia requires developers to consider the effects of the proposed dredging on stream flow, erosion or siltation patterns, fish and wildlife, water quality, and other marine resources. The act specifically exempts federal dredging projects from permit requirements, however. While Georgia does not include provisions for long-range planning of dredged material disposal, Washington State Department of Ecology guidelines (1972, p. 15) state that "local governments should control dredging to minimize damage to existing ecological values and natural resources of both the area to be dredged and the area for deposit of dredged materials." Local master programs are required to develop long-range plans for the disposal or use of dredged material.

The Shoreline Master Program for Grays Harbor County (1975) illustrates how the state guidelines have been applied at the local level:

1. Dredging should minimize damage to existing ecological values, natural resources, and the river system of both the area to be dredged and the deposit area, and shall also minimize water quality degradation.

2. Spoil deposit sites in water areas should be identified in cooperation with the State Departments of Natural Resources, Game, and Fisheries. Depositing dredged materials in water areas should be allowed only for habitat improvements, to correct problems of material distribution affecting adversely fish and shellfish resources, or where the alternative of depositing it on land is more detrimental to shoreline resources than depositing it in water areas.

3. Dredging of bottom materials solely to obtain fill material should be discouraged.

4. Ship channels and turning and moorage basins should be identified and no new areas prepared or used without sufficient evidence that existing channels and basins are inadequate.

5. The use of dredge spoils for purposes other than landfill is encouraged.

Grays Harbor requires constant maintenance, and an extensive channel improvement project is being studied. The proposed project is generally accepted as necessary to preserve the port's competitive position, given the ever increasing size of ships. In the past, dredged material has been deposited in both deep water and uncontained disposal areas in wetlands. Much of the new land created by dredged disposal is now prized as productive wildlife habitat. Wetlands that haven't yet been filled are now considered unacceptable for dredged materials disposal, which

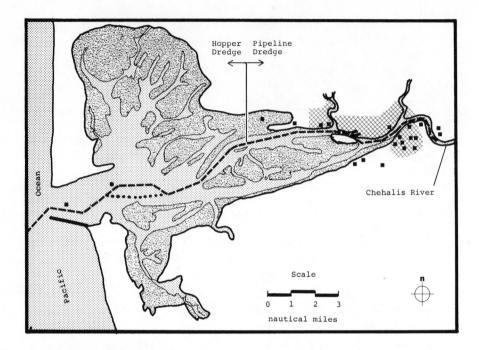

Figure 4.3 Eighteen alternative dredge spoil disposal sites have been chosen by the Corps of Engineers in the Grays Harbor Estuary. Final site selection has not been completed, but past selection has been by site-by-site review of economic, political, and environmental factors conducted by local government, the port, and state and federal environmental resource agencies. Local government and resource agency involvement is concentrated in the final selection of sites from among alternatives initially preselected by the Corps. Source: Corps of Engineers, May 1976. *Grays Harbor widening and deepening draft environmental impact statement.*

has resulted in a conflict between the port and the Corps of Engineers, on one side, and the U.S. Fish and Wildlife Service, the State Department of Fisheries, and conservationists on the other.

A number of disposal sites have been identified for Grays Harbor's proposed channel improvement project, but no final selection has been made. The Grays Harbor Estuary Task Force may examine the issue and could refine the existing criteria for choosing disposal sites as part of the management program now being developed (see Figure 4.3).

Review of Dredging Needs

Coastal management programs normally have not questioned the need for major federal dredging projects, since most were authorized long before coastal programs were initiated. States vary widely, however, in the degree to which they review the purpose, justification and need for smaller, non-federal projects. The Washington State guidelines do not limit the purpose of dredging (beyond prohibiting dredging solely for fill material) and do not require justification of need for a project. The California Coastal Act (1976, section 30705 [a]) requires dredging in port areas to be consistent with a certified port master plan, and limits the permissible purposes of dredging to construction, modification and maintenance of shipping channels, port facilities, commercial fishing and recreational boating facilities, and a handful of minor, incidental purposes.

Interstate Coordination of Dredged Material Disposal

The Philadelphia region has the dual problem of where to dispose of maintenance dredged material in an urban area that has few disposal sites, and how to build interstate cooperation between Pennsylvania, New Jersey, and Delaware—the states that share access to the Delaware River. Presently, the City of Philadelphia is considering withdrawing the major regional disposal site from use so it may be developed.

The Pennsylvania coastal management program, in its draft policies on the Delaware River, identifies the need to establish suitable sites and develop criteria for assessing environmental impact but does not specifically mention interstate solutions to the problem. The key New Jersey coastal management legislation (the Coastal Area Facilities Review Act) does not currently include in its jurisdiction the section of the Delaware River where Camden's port facilities are located. There has been no serious attempt by either state to resolve the dredge disposal problem at a bistate level.

More advanced planning is occurring in Washington and Oregon, where the Columbia River Estuary (CREST) study is developing an interstate strategy to select sites for dredged material disposal. Disposal sites on the Columbia River are selected by defining the maximum possible dumping distance for dredged material and then excluding water areas, prime agricultural land, refuge lands, and wetlands. Lands not otherwise constrained are examined in further detail, and the final selection is made by local elected officials. Local governments, state and federal environmental resource agencies, and the Corps of Engineers are involved in the selection process from the beginning.

3. AIR AND WATER QUALITY DEGRADATION

An additional problem often associated with port development projects is air and water quality degradation. Since air and water pollution control predates coastal management programs, federal and state statutes already provide for specific pollution abatement procedures, such as point-source permits, treatment plant construction, planning programs and others.

When the Coastal Zone Management Act was passed in 1972, Congress recognized the possibility that states might create duplicate air and water quality programs for coastal areas. Therefore, the act requires that the provisions of the federal Water Pollution Control Act and the Clean Air Act, together with state and local programs developed pursuant to those acts, be incorporated into state coastal management programs and "shall be the water pollution control and air pollution control requirements applicable to such program(s)" (CZMA section 307 [f]).

Except in limited instances, coastal management programs have not modified or created new programs to address air and water quality in the coastal zone. Coastal management programs deal primarily with land- and water-use planning and allocation, leaving specific resource management responsibilities, such as water pollution control, in the hands of single-purpose resource agencies.

There are exceptions, however. By passing specific coastal legislation that amends or strengthens existing water and air quality statutes, some states have changed pre-existing practices. In California, the Coastal Act generally avoids duplicating existing state agency missions. Two exceptions are noted in the water resources area. First, the State Coastal Commission retains jurisdiction over coastal wastewater treatment plant siting, size, and phasing of services, and delineation of service areas (section 30412). Since the availability of wastewater treatment in developing areas directly affects the pace and density of growth, it is an issue important to the commission. Second, the Coastal Act contains an explicit policy for maintaining or restoring water quality in biologically sensitive coastal areas, such as estuaries and coastal wetlands (section 30231). Techniques to implement this policy include controlling both point and nonpoint discharges, avoiding depletion of ground waters and, encouraging wastewater reclamation. Section 15 of the Coastal Act amends the California Water Code to be consistent with the coastal policies. Thus, the Coastal Act alerts the California Resources Agency, the Water Resources Control Board and the federal Environmental Protection Agency to the high priority placed on maintaining and enhancing coastal water quality.

A similar observation could be made concerning Seattle's Shoreline Master Program (1976, p. 36) requirements dealing with air and water quality at cargo-handling facilities. These policies call for cargo-handling equipment that is designed to avoid accidental discharges of particulates into the air and water and require measures that are adequate to treat or clean up spilled materials. It is very difficult for federal and state pollution control agencies to require certain equipment and to monitor the clean-up of accidental spills. In this case, the Seattle master program complements the efforts of broader environmental protection programs.

Finally, in Texas, the Brownsville Navigation District has assisted an industrial lessee on port-owned land to comply with waste discharge requirements of the Texas Water Quality Board. Two wastewater aeration lagoons were constructed using a $4,600,000 pollution control bond sponsored by the port. The port, in this instance, facilitated the achievement of water quality standards. Actions of this type could be encouraged by the policies of coastal management programs.

4. MITIGATION AND COMPENSATION FOR ENVIRONMENTAL DAMAGE

In many areas, port development projects which require dredging, filling or channel modification of existing water bodies or wetlands are essential to the continued economic viability of the port. Although some of the harmful effects of dredging and filling may be minimized by permit conditions on dredging operations, disposal methods, and better engineering design, other environmental effects are more difficult to ameliorate. These are the degradation or permanent loss of fish and wildlife habitats in bottomlands, tidelands, marshes, and other wetlands. These habitats are valuable natural resources that have a variety of functions:

- They provide spawning, nursery, and feeding grounds for finfish.

- They contain commercial or sport shellfish beds.

- They are shelter, nesting, feeding, and breeding areas for migratory birds.

- They provide nutrients and planktonic forms for many levels of the food chain.

Dredging and filling projects may alter or destroy fish and wildlife habitats: they change circulation patterns, introduce heavy suspended sediment loads into the water which eventually smother aquatic plants and shellfish beds, cover the habitats completely by filling above the water line or dredging the area to a deeper depth, or release toxic substances into the water as dredging churns up polluted bottom sediments (Clark, 1974).

The permanent alteration of habitat types may have beneficial as well as undesirable results. In many areas along the east coast, material was disposed of by creating small islands of fill next to the navigation channel. Over the years, new vegetation has covered these dredge islands, which have become valuable habitats for waterfowl and small animals. New intertidal and shallow-water communities have developed where dredged material has filled previously deep water up to a shallower depth. In both cases, the existing communities were either destroyed or severely altered, but new communities—also valued as natural resources—have established themselves gradually over time.

Requirements for Mitigation

The present thrust of resource management agencies has been to require mitigation and compensation measures where fish and wildlife habitats will be significantly altered or destroyed by dredging or filling. Such measures may be required by state fisheries or game departments, state or local coastal zone management programs, and the U.S. Army Corps of Engineers acting together with the Environmental Protection Agency, the National Marine Fisheries Service, and the Fish and Wildlife Service.

The terms mitigation and compensation are defined differently by different people. According to *Webster's* the word mitigate means "to make less severe, less rigorous, less painful; to moderate," and the word compensation means "anything given as an equivalent, or to make amends for a loss, (or) damage." In practice, the Corps of Engineers uses numerous terms. For example, the Seattle District Corps of Engineers office uses the following definitions:

Mitigation reduces the harmful environmental effects of a project.

Compensation provides equal replacement of biological resources.

Enhancement restores more productivity than was taken away.

State coastal management programs, by and large, do not contain detailed definitions of mitigation and compensation or what measures are appropriate for certain development activities. Two exceptions to this are Oregon and California. The Oregon Land Conservation and Development Commission's guidelines permit only restoration of wetland areas in the vicinity of the landfill and specifically exclude transfer of ownership, compensatory recreational facilities and land acquisition by public agencies. The California Coastal Act (section 30607.1) specifies "either acquisition of equivalent areas of equal or greater biological productivity or opening up equivalent areas to tidal action; provided, however, that if no appropriate restoration site is available, an in-lieu fee sufficient to provide an area of equivalent productive value or surface area shall be dedicated to an appropriate public agency, ..." These provisions apply to all wetlands outside established port areas, and the act contains no specific mitigation requirements within the existing ports of Port Hueneme, Los Angeles, Long Beach, and San Diego. This represents a significant departure from the Coastal Plan developed under Proposition 20 which required that new habitats be created on an acre-for-acre basis to compensate for environmental damage in all areas, including ports.

The Texas coastal management program has not yet defined appropriate mitigation and compensation measures, and the program's hearing draft contains no detailed discussion of the problem. A bill addressing fish and wildlife mitigation passed the 1977 Texas legislature but was vetoed by the Governor.

Washington Department of Ecology guidelines (1972) do not directly define mitigation or require specific measures, but they do permit the use of dredged material for habitat improvement. In states such as Washington, which has an approved coastal management program, the practice of mitigation may exist even though it is not specifically treated in the legislation and guidelines. For example, the Shorelines Hearings Board has required mitigation measures as conditions for approval of appealed permits. The Georgia Coastal Marshland Protection Act does not define mitigation nor does it require specific mitigation measures. Similarly, the Pennsylvania and Wisconsin coastal management programs have not yet defined mitigation and specified measures. But states such as Wisconsin and Pennsylvania, whose coastal management programs are still being developed, may follow in the footsteps of federal resource agencies and specify requirements as their programs mature.

The most visible forces behind mitigation requirements for projects that alter or destroy fish and wildlife habitats have been the U.S. Fish and Wildlife Service, the Environmental Protection Agency (EPA) and the National Marine Fisheries Service (NMFS). By statute and interagency agreement, all three of these agencies provide important input into Corps of Engineers sections 10 and 404 permit review (see Chapter 2). The Fish and Wildlife Service, in its published regulations, may require "compensational measures" (Department of Interior, 1975) to protect resources. NMFS and EPA are developing similar mitigation policies at the district and regional levels but no national agency policies have been formally published.

Two examples of mitigation requirements were observed in this study. In Seattle, filling between finger piers in the southwest harbor area meant the loss of fish habitats among the pilings of the old piers. Compensation measures requested by the State Department of Fisheries called for the development of a public fishing pier elsewhere in Elliott Bay. The Department of Fisheries plans to build the pier on land contributed by the port. The new pier does not restore biological productivity or provide replacement habitat area, but it does provide compensation to the general public in the form of better access to sport fishing. A submerged artificial reef at the end of the pier will attract fish to the location.

Under the California Coastal Zone Conservation Act (1972) and the Coastal Plan (now superceded by the California Coastal Act of 1976), landfill projects had to include an acre-for-acre replacement of productive areas as compensation. The Port of Los Angeles calculated that providing the replacement land stipulated by the Coastal Plan's mitigation requirements would cost $53 million compared to the $12.5 million cost of the development project (Weir, 1976, p. 119). As a result of the mitigation requirements and other policies in the Coastal Plan, the port fought for special individualized treatment under the new Coastal Act. In the new California Coastal Act, port districts are specially exempt from the mitigation requirements.

Mitigation Cost and Financing

Private interests or local or state government must pay for mitigation requirements imposed on non-federal dredging and filling projects. Mitigation has been attacked by port interest groups as being prohibitively expensive and they argue that the costs involved can reverse the financial feasibility of a project.

Three promising concepts for funding mitigation—two in use, the other under study—may help resolve the problem of costs:

1. On federal Corps of Engineers projects in navigable waters, section 150 of the Water Resource Development Act (1976)

authorizes the Corps to spend up to $400,000 per project to develop wetlands as part of water resources development projects.

2. In Florida, the Tampa Port Authority has implemented a temporary "Environmental Protection Service Charge" of 2¢ per net ton on all export bulk cargo, which will be dropped when revenues have reached the $5 million mark. These revenues are earmarked for mitigation projects in conjunction with the Corps of Engineers Tampa Harbor Deepening Project.

3. In the Columbia River Estuary, the Columbia River Estuary Study Task Force (CREST) is discussing the concept of a "mitigation bank" of potential sites for replacing biological productivity lost by dredged material disposal. State and local governments bordering the estuary would contribute funds to acquire sites, which would be selected according to the type and level of biological productivity possible. Users of disposal sites whose biological productivity is reduced would purchase a given number of "replacement units of biological productivity" from the "mitigation bank." This revenue would be used to acquire additional mitigation sites. The concept is in preliminary phases of discussion and has not been fully developed or approved.

5. PUBLIC ACCESS AND AESTHETICS

Limited and diminished public access to the nation's shores and beaches was a major concern leading to passage of state coastal management statutes and the federal Coastal Zone Management Act (Englander, 1977). The act calls for participating states to "[develop] a planning process for the protection of, and *access* to, public beaches and other public coastal areas . . ." (emphasis added). It also calls for protection of aesthetic values (section 305 [b] [7]). Because of the subjective nature of aesthetic values, they have not been dealt with as rigorously as public access requirements in coastal management programs.

Federal and state regulations give attention to both physical *and* visual access to the shoreline. Ports that propose new or expanded developments in urban waterfronts are encouraged or required to provide public access in their site planning. But such requirements, unless carefully carried out, could conflict with both the security and safety of port operations. Occupational safety laws and regulations preclude public access to working port areas and the security of general cargo might be compromised by unrestricted access to docks, wharves, and sheds. There are, two kinds of public access that can be realized:

1. Physical access via secure sections of the waterfront on port-owned land, through easements or dedication;

2. Visual access to the water, achieved through careful siting and landscape design of the facility, or from special structures such as observation towers located to command views of port operations.

Washington, California, and Massachusetts provide the best examples of public access and aesthetic requirements in state coastal management efforts. Specific policies are included in these programs and agency decisions affecting port development require public access features in the development project.

At the state level, in 1976 California established the California Coastal Conservancy which authorizes the acquisition of public access-ways and reservation of significant coastal resource areas for public use and enjoyment. A bond issue of $280 million passed by the voters partly finances this acquisition program.

Washington's shorelines management regulations require local governments to include a public access element in their master programs. On "shorelines of statewide significance" this requirement is given higher priority and local jurisdictions are admonished to "(i) increase public access to *publicly owned* areas of the shorelines" (emphasis added, Department of Ecology, 1972, 173-16-040 [5] [e]). Ports are singled out for special attention in this regard: "port facilities should be designed to permit viewing of harbor areas . . . which would not interfere with port operations or endanger public health and safety." (173-16-060 [10] [b]).

At first glance, Seattle appears to apply these guidelines vigorously. Clear standards for public access in both public and private shorelines have been developed. Table 4.1 lays out the physical and visual access requirements of Seattle's master program. The Port of Seattle, however, effectively resisted a provision to require public access in port areas devoted to water-dependent uses and, as a result, received an exemption (see Table 4.1, item 4).

The issue is far from settled, however. During review of a major renovation and expansion project for a new container terminal, the city pressed the Port of Seattle to provide onsite public access. In spite of the master program provisions, the port refused and instead agreed to build a public observation tower on a port-owned pier adjacent to the project site. Serious consideration is being given to amending the public access provision of the master program and removing the exemption granted the port.

Often, coastal management programs will allow less desirable development if public access is provided. For example, non-water dependent uses of shorelines in Seattle require public access. Consequently, public access is still required if the Port of Seattle leases a portion of the harbor for industrial or commercial uses that do not require access to the water. Whether, in fact, this will deter non-water dependent uses of the shorelines remains to be seen. Another example is the California Coastal Act which allows ports to justify minor fills if they improve shoreline appearance or facilitate public access. A trade-off is made between policies that

68

Table 4.1 Public access requirements
of the Seattle Shoreline Master Program

Type of Property	Regulated Public Access
1. public property—public use(s)	required
2. public property leased or rented for private, non-water dependent use(s)	required
3. central waterfront—public and private property	15% of total water area covered by structure(s), or 5,000 square feet, whichever is greater
4. public property leased or rented for private, 100% water-dependent use(s)	not required
5. public or private property, 100% water-dependent use(s)	not required
6. private property, non-water dependent use	required, if four or more residential units and 100 or more of water-frontage, shoreline PUD, or commercial or industrial use, unless exclusively residential development on saltwater shoreline and public access to shoreline from street is available within 600'
7. private multiple residential development on saltwater	required if not within 600' of public access to water

Source: Seattle Shoreline Master Program, Seattle Department of Community Development, 1976

discourage fill and the goal of protecting "scenic and visual qualities of coastal areas."

Aesthetic considerations are more troublesome aspects of coastal management programs. While the Coastal Zone Management Act calls for protection of aesthetic values (section 305 [b] [7]), it is difficult to implement because aesthetic tastes vary widely. Restrictions on development which are labeled "aesthetic" deal mostly with height, bulk, and site coverage restrictions to insure visual access.

Port facilities usually are large scale, prominent industrial landmarks, composed of massive, skeletal cargo-handling structures, and large vessels at dock or in transit. Views are blocked and then revealed as containers and ships are moved about the harbor and terminal area. To some individuals observing the hustle and bustle of a port is exciting. To others it is visually abhorent.

Two management concepts—water-dependency criteria and urban waterfront redevelopment—have a bearing on both public access and the visual amenities of port areas. Locating non-water dependent industrial developments on upland sites conserves waterfront areas for uses requiring water access. In Seattle, for example, the space between the port's grain elevator and the loading dock provides bike and pedestrian pathways along the shore, which the grain conveyer system passes over. Similarly, separating oil terminal facilities from tank farms that are located inland, can provide the public with access along the shore. The Union Oil products terminal in Seattle is arranged in such a manner and this principle could be applied to other liquid and dry bulk terminal facilities where space permits.

Redeveloping obsolete finger piers for retail shops, promenades, and public waterfront parks can conserve the scale and texture of old port structures, provide physical access, and in some cases produce commanding views of active port areas on adjacent or nearby sites. In New Orleans, through a joint port-city effort, a small section of riverfront terminal facilities was razed to visually link the historic French Quarter and the Mississippi River. Standing on the levee, an observer can view both the operations of the port and the activities in Jackson Square in the French Quarter, thereby gaining a sense of New Orleans' riverport origins and her historical port dependency.

The Massachusetts coastal program anticipates that successful revitalization of the urban waterfront will depend upon integrating harbor

Myrtle Edwards Park, sponsored jointly by the Port of Seattle and the City of Seattle, follows the waterfront along Elliott Bay for some 4000 feet past the port's Pier 86 grain elevator. (Photo courtesy of the Port of Seattle)

views with development. Proposed development guidelines recommend that marine terminal development should conform as much as possible to existing shoreline configurations, height should be limited, and "seafairing" qualities should be maintained or enhanced.

Where massive industrial structures dominate an urban shoreline, other techniques can be used to mitigate their visual impact. The Boston-gas LNG tanks were decorated with super-graphics by a commissioned artist. What was just another huge structure is now an attractive visual landmark visible from the Southeast Expressway. Had the same facility been constructed on a rural shoreline, the tanks could have been painted in earthy, muted colors to blend with the natural landscape (Mann Associates, 1975, p. 129).

These examples illustrate ways that ports and their industrial lessees can mitigate the visual impact of shoreline facilities. Coastal management programs generally have addressed coastal aesthetics through broad policy statements only; project-by-project review must deal with site-specific visual impacts during the design phase of project development. Seattle's master program is explicit here: any *public* development may be reviewed for visual design quality by an ad hoc panel of design experts prior to a formal application for a shoreline substantial development permit. Such a review applies to port-owned developments but not to those of its lessees (Seattle Department of Community Development, 1976, section 21A.39).

6. SITING HAZARDOUS FACILITIES

Hazardous facilities are those facilities which manufacture, store, or utilize commodities having a high risk of fire, explosion, or leakage of toxic or dangerous substances. Nuclear, petrochemical, and other facilities are hazardous if accidents or improper operations should occur. Liquefied natural gas (LNG) is one type of hazardous facility receiving attention in coastal management programs. It is discussed here as an example of how coastal programs deal with siting hazardous facilities.

Declining domestic production and increased industrial use have resulted in significant increases in imported natural gas. Special tankers are equipped to transport natural gas, which is liquefied at extremely low temperatures, to $-259°F$, and reduced to one six hundredth of its former volume. The tankers unload the liquefied natural gas into cryogenic storage tanks at coastal locations. Current technology requires that the tanks be located at the point of unloading to avoid the risks involved in pumping LNG through pipelines over long distances (Massachusetts Office of Environmental Affairs, 1977, p. 227).

The 600-fold reduction in volume achieved by cryogenic liquefaction results in substantial economies in shipping natural gas, but there are problems associated with transporting and storing this volatile material. The risk of fire during vessel movement in port, offloading, and storage imposes constraints in siting LNG facilities. Furthermore, LNG tanks are large, obtrusive elements in the landscape and decisions to site LNG facilities in sparsely populated rural areas carry with them a visual amenity cost. Finally, LNG tankers have drafts of approximately 40 feet and therefore require deep-draft channels—either existing channels or new dredged channels (likely to be necessary in a remote area).

Given these risks and tradeoffs, how have coastal management programs addressed the LNG facilities siting question? California has recently established a separate siting procedure for LNG facilities. Washington and Massachusetts have created, by legislative action, special energy facility siting councils, with explicit responsibility to recommend sites for power plants, refineries, and LNG and other energy-related facilities.

California's LNG Terminal Act of 1977 gives licensing authority to the Public Utilities Commission (PUC), but requires the State Coastal Commission to study potential sites and make recommendations to the PUC. The PUC has exclusive authority to issue a single permit for one LNG facility, preempting any other local or state license or permit previously required. The PUC is required to select the site given the highest ranking by the coastal commission unless it can either show deficiencies in the evaluation process, or determine that the site selected imposes unreasonable construction delays that will adversely affect adequate gas supply. Among the conditions imposed on the facility by the act are its size, origin of gas shipments, timing of construction (related to demand and existing supply factors), and maximum population densities at various distances from the site. This last provision is explicit: within a one-mile radius of the site, population density may not exceed ten persons per square mile; within four miles of the site permitted density is sixty persons per square mile. Power of eminent domain given to the successful permit applicant may be exercised to restrict or reasonably reduce population densities to meet this requirement (LNG Act, section 5590 [b] and [c]).

The Energy Facilities Siting Council (EFSC) in Massachusetts and the Energy Facilities Site Evaluation Council (EFSEC) in Washington State have similar, but less extensive mandates than those given the PUC in California. Each can override local government zoning and land-use decisions and preempt other state permit and license requirements. Further, each has sole responsibility for preparation of an environmental impact statement. However, the councils are not restricted to single-site limitation, as in California, nor is the coastal management agency in either state mandated to conduct independent siting studies—this is the role of the councils. Further, the councils' jurisdictions extend beyond LNG facilities to include power plants and refineries. (The California LNG Terminal Act also calls for the State Coastal Commission to study potential sites for monobuoy, offshore oil terminals).

Under Washington's EFSEC certification procedure the substantive requirements of other state regulatory programs must be respected. Whether such requirements include the policies of local shoreline master programs is in doubt, however. A 1977 legislative battle raged over the provision in the Energy Facilities Siting Act allowing EFSEC to override local zoning.

A memorandum of understanding between EFSC and the lead coastal management agency in Massachusetts provides for assessment of environmental and safety risks, evaluation of the size of buffer zones around facilities, and an assessment of the impacts on *"existing or future port operations"* (Policy No. 30, emphasis added). In addition, a four-part procedure for assuring consistency with coastal management program policies is created:

1. Restricted areas such as coastal wetlands and ocean sancturaries will be avoided.

2. In evaluating energy needs and site suitability, the policies of the state's coastal management program are incorporated into the decision process.

3. During review of the project, adverse impacts will be mitigated in conformance with resource management provisions of the coastal management program's lead agency, and local governments will have an opportunity to review the project for conformance with local zoning.

4. If conflicts arise between the applicant and local or state government over conditions or delays imposed on the project, the EFSC can override other state or local agencies' objections (Massachusetts CMP, p. 259).

Could the California, Massachusetts, and Washington energy facility siting programs allow an LNG terminal in an existing port area? In California it appears that LNG facilities will not be sited in existing public ports. In fact, the favored site, and one against which others will be assessed, is at Point Conception, northwest of Santa Barbara.

In Massachusetts and Washington, the siting councils could approve a site within an existing harbor area. Three LNG facilities are located on the waterfront within the Boston metropolitan area—one at Dorchester (Bostongas), and two at Everett (Bostongas and Distrigas). A major expansion plan at the Everett location is awaiting permit approval from the Energy Facilities Siting Council. New federal regulations, however, may limit all future LNG facilities to remote sites.

Beyond state authority to regulate LNG facilities siting, any proposals for a new or expanded LNG project are subject to the licensing requirements of the Federal Energy Regulatory Commission (FERC). An executive interagency task force on liquefied natural gas imports is currently assessing, among other factors, safety and siting questions of LNG facilities. Given the national interest and federal consistency requirements of the Coastal Zone Management Act, the findings of this task force will have important implications for state coastal management programs and for public port authorities within whose harbor areas LNG facilities may be sited.

7. SMALL-CRAFT HARBOR FACILITIES

The demand for small-craft moorage is exceedingly high throughout the country, but supply, in some areas, is very low. Coastal management programs are beginning to address aspects of this problem. First, they are trying to find ways to meet part of the demand while protecting coastal environments from excessive development activity. Second, because commercial fishing boats cannot compete financially with recreational boaters for limited dock facilities, special protection for commercial fishing vessels is being considered. Finally, to avoid navigational hazards when small craft and ocean-going ships use the same harbor, provisions for separating the moorage facilities of the two classes of vessels are being considered.

Growth in water-based recreation activities is accelerating rapidly and there is a critical shortage of adequate moorage facilities to accommodate small craft. Slips and docks for larger, nontrailerable sailboats and powerboats, charter fishing vessels and, in some cases, commercial fishing boats are needed. With the creation of the 200-mile offshore fishing zone and the likely expansion of the U.S. fishing fleet, some coastal states will need additional or expanded harbor facilities to accommodate more and larger fishing vessels.

Both public and private small-craft harbors serve this accelerating demand. Private marinas often operate in protected bays, coves, lagoons, and estuaries where extensive navigation improvements are not needed for harbor development. Such sites, however, contain sensitive environmental resources and public pressure is against development in those locations. The trend, then, is toward large, public harbors, developed in less sensitive environments, where private lessees manage moorage and boat service yards (e.g., Marina Del Rey, California), or where facilities are managed entirely by public agencies, often public port authorities (e.g., Shilshole Marina, Port of Seattle).

Coastal management programs tend to support small-craft harbor development because the use is water dependent and it provides access to the water for recreational use. Further, the facilities provide essential services to the important commercial fishing industry. However, because small-craft harbors require dredging, filling, and bulkheading, severe restrictions are sometimes placed on their development in order to achieve environmental protection goals. Even when coastal programs lean in the direction of allowing marina development, resource protection agencies, such as the U.S. Fish and Wildlife Service and state fish and game agencies will often insist on high environmental protection standards.

Massachusetts, Washington, and California provide examples of differing approaches to the small-craft harbor problem taken by coastal management programs. In Massachusetts' proposed coastal management program, the pace and types of new harbor development is controlled. Recreational small-craft harbor planning is tied to state capital budgeting. Highest priority for state recreational funds is given to public boat ramps.

Expenditures for dredging new moorage facilities are restricted except where a regionwide boating public is to be served, or where there is no other way to resolve conflicts between recreational boating and commercial fishing.

Washington's program deals with marinas by analyzing the impact of new proposed facilities. State guidelines for local master programs address marina siting and design questions (Department of Ecology, 1972, 173-16-060 [5]). Through the Shorelines Management Act and the State Environmental Policy Act, the Department of Ecology (DOE) and other agencies review specific marina proposals for consistency with local master programs and identify significant adverse effects on the environment. Planning and siting of marinas still remain the prerogative of local government, for the most part, and significant variations in the treatment of marinas is evident (Goodwin 1976, 1977, and Department of Ecology, 1976, Vol. 2, pp. A9-A45). Nevertheless, the state can influence the location and size of marinas in ways other than the shorelines management program. For example, the Department of Natural Resources submerged lands leasing policies, leasing rates, and lease terms affect the location and profitability of new or expanded marina facilities. Further, the Inter-Agency Committee on Outdoor Recreation (IAC), which dispenses Federal Bureau of Outdoor Recreation (BOR) funds, and local governments using unclaimed state marine gas tax rebates for public recreational facility construction and land acquisition, can influence public sector investment decisions. Finally, state resource agencies can object to particular projects and require significant modifications or offsite mitigation. These requirements are often reinforced by federal reviewing agencies during sections 10 and 404 permit reviews by the Corps of Engineers (Goodwin 1977).

In a populous state like California, the virtually unlimited demand for recreational boating is recognized and technological alternatives to the proliferation of "wet" moorage are encouraged. Of these, dry storage, upland facilities, dredged back shore marinas, and public boat launch ramps have received prominent attention in coastal management programs. In a move to deflate demand, California's Coastal Plan also included a policy to encourage the cooperative ownership of recreational boats; it was deleted in the Coastal Act, however.

An additional problem facing coastal management programs is the accommodation of commercial fishing docks, vessel and gear repair yards, and processing plants. Normal economic pressures would result in the conversion of fishing harbors and yards to recreational boating areas, because of the high price yachters are willing to pay for moorage. Further, fishing fleets are often out of the harbor for extended periods and there is a high turnover in occupancy. Thus, the recreational boater is the higher paying, more stable tenant, and the only tenant the private marina operator can afford.

The public marinas, and small public port authorities, tend to provide the space and services for the commercial fishing vessels. Public ports will often set aside special facilities for fishing vessel permanent moorage, which minimizes conflicts between fishermen and recreational boaters. Dock space is provided for storing and repairing fishing gear, loading supplies, and unloading the fish catch. Shoreside space is made available for marine fishing supply houses, boatyards, marine electronic businesses, and other ancillary services. Restaurants capitalizing on the general public's fascination with the colorful fishing vessel harbor activities are also frequently located in these harbors. Revenues derived from these dockside businesses often are used to subsidize deflated moorage rates for fishing vessels.

California's Coastal Act mandates that California ports protect commercial fishing harbor space, unless adequate facilities are provided elsewhere or there is no longer a need for such facilities. Further, recreational marina facilities must not interfere with commercial fishing operations.

Finally, there are potential navigation and safety hazards when large ships and small craft move about in the same harbor. The proposed master plan for the Port of Los Angeles, which if approved would become a part of the California coastal management program, requires the separation of marina and fishing fleet facilities from industrial port uses in order to minimize potential navigational conflicts.

8. ALLOCATION OF WATERFRONT LAND

An issue common to coastal management programs, and one of direct importance to ports, is the allocation of waterfront land among competing industrial, commercial, residential, natural habitat, and public recreational uses. The principal objective of established and developing policies is the conservation of waterfront land for uses dependent upon a waterfront location. As programs mature and are refined the water-dependency concept is being debated rigorously. New interpretations of dependency include the recognition that various uses derive different kinds of benefits from their waterfront location. These benefits can be assessed and can guide coastal management decisions affecting the allocation of scarce waterfront land.

Beyond knowing the degree of water dependency that characterizes various uses, coastal management officials need to know the likely demand for waterfront land for those uses. Ports, which are recognized as principal waterfront users in most coastal management programs, develop in response to changes in maritime trade—patterns which often are difficult to forecast. Given the paucity of adequate deep water sites for expansion, ports, nonetheless, must plan for probable future expansion in order that their needs be accommodated in coastal management programs. Regional port facility planning studies can be useful in augmenting ad hoc trade projections made by individual ports.

Once water-dependent uses are identified and likely future demands on waterfront land known, coastal management programs have several available mechanisms to implement specific allocation schemes. These

Table 4.2. Three alternatives for determining water dependency of industries or suitability of waterfront land for water-related industries

Alternative 1: Washington State

Classifications of the Washington Department of Natural Resources specify maximum lease terms for leasing state lands in harbor areas.

Priority	Use examples	Maximum lease term

I	Water-dependent commerce
	   public or private port terminals
	      handling general commerce
	   ferry and passenger terminals
	   marine construction and repair
	      facilities
	   marinas and moorage areas
	   tug and barge companies
		30 years with unrestricted renewal

II	Water-oriented commerce
	   single-user terminals, usually
	      handling raw materials
	   pulp, paper, lumber and
	      plywood mills
	   seafood processing plants
	   sand and gravel companies
	   petroleum handling and
	      processing plants
		30 years with limited renewal provisions

III	Other water-dependent and water-
	   oriented uses
	   uses making limited contributions
	      to navigation and commerce
	   ecological and scientific reserves
	   waterfront parks and beaches
	   public resorts, aquariums,
	      restaurants
		20 years with no renewal

	Other uses
	   apartment buildings
	   hotels, taverns
	   private residences
	   warehouses not directly associated
	      with waterborne commerce
	   retail sales outlets
		No new lease issued.
		Existing leases for 10 years, limited renewal provisions

include "districting" (similar to zoning) and the planned use of public infrastructure investments for guiding private sector investments.

The discussion which follows examines policies, criteria, and implementing mechanisms that coastal management programs are using to guide the allocation of waterfront land, specifically as they address the problems of port development.

Water-dependency Criteria

Water dependency is an innovative decision-making criterion being used more and more frequently in coastal management programs. The

Table 4.2. *(continued)*

Alternative 2: San Francisco Bay Area (*Present*)

The preservation of adequate waterfront sites for future water-dependent industry is a major concern in the San Francisco Bay area. The San Francisco Bay Plan (1969) presents a rating scale for comparing the physical infrastructure characteristics of different parcels of waterfront land in different locations. The higher the total score, the more desirable the land for siting water-dependent industry. (Bay Plan, p. 18)

Characteristic	Maximum Points
Channel or pipeline access	20
Rail access	10
Freeway access	10
Major highway access	5
Size of land area	15
Grade of site	10
Foundation suitability	15
Size of ownership units	5
Present use	10

Alternative 3: San Francisco Bay Area (*Proposed*)

A study of waterfront industry, done by a private consultant, recommends that the Bay Conservation and Development Commission revise its definition of water-related uses to identify industrial uses which "gain real economic benefit by being located on the water." The report suggests the following definition:

> "To be water-related, an activity or firm must gain cost savings or revenue-differentiating advantages, neither of which is associated with land rents or costs, from being located on the bay shore that it could not obtain at an inland location." (p. S-1)

principle behind the criterion is that only those uses dependent upon a waterfront location should be permitted to locate there. A shoe factory, for example, should not be permitted on the waterfront even if the manufacturer is willing to pay more for the land than the shipyard owner or the marina developer. Implicit in this approach is the desire to conserve scarce waterfront land for those uses that must be located there.

Although the principle is appealing, water dependency is not an easy concept to apply. Table 4.2 shows three contrasting types of water-dependency criteria. The first approach, used in Washington State, lists three categories of uses by priority: water-dependent commerce, water-oriented commerce, and other water-dependent and water-oriented uses. These priority listings help the Washington State Department of Natural Resources give preference to water-dependent uses over non-water dependent uses in leasing public lands. Those higher on the priority list of water dependency get longer leases and better lease terms.

The second approach, used by the San Francisco Bay Conservation and Development Commission, applies a point rating scale to various parcels of land to determine those most suited for water-dependent industry. The rating scale recognizes that priority of use should be based on factors other than the need for channel access. Industry requiring good rail access may tend to locate in the coastal zone because rail facilities are heavily concentrated there. Similarly, industries requiring large, level sites may locate in the coastal zone because much of the region's flatland may be there.

The third approach applies an "economic benefit" test to determine if an activity or proposed use is water related. If real cost savings or revenue advantages can be attributed to a waterfront location (unrelated to land rents or costs), the use is considered water related. This approach is being studied for possible application by the San Francisco Bay Conservation and Development Commission.

Water-dependency criteria are used explicity or implicitly in coastal management programs. The Washington coastal management program has explicit water-dependency definitions, which differ from those used by the state's Department of Natural Resources (shown in Table 4.2). Three categories of uses are established (Washington DOE, 1976):

1. Water-dependent uses, those which cannot exist in any other location but on the water;

2. Water-oriented uses, those which may be helped by location on the water, but which could function away from the water;

3. Non-water oriented uses, those which can locate equally well away from water.

These definitions are imprecise, however, and conflicting interpretation has led to delays in approving permits for a new sawmill in Grays Harbor. The sawmill receives logs by truck and exports metric standard lumber by ship to the Far East. Proponents of the mill claim that it is water dependent or water oriented because it exports lumber by ship from the nearby pier; opponents claim it need not locate in the coastal zone because it could truck its product to the waterfront. This problem is being negotiated as part of the Grays Harbor Estuary Study Task Force, and refined use classifications and definitions may be included in the management plan now being developed.

The Massachusetts coastal management program has developed a "preferred industries" concept within the classification of water-dependent uses. Specific industries are designated to receive highest priority for coastal locations, as are those industries which will be discouraged. This concept is applied to specific locations within Boston Harbor. For instance, because of their importance to the local economy, commercial fishing and fish processing receive high priority in the vicinity of Boston's Fish Pier and in several of the state's smaller ports, including Gloucester and New Bedford.

Oil transfer facilities are deemed vital to the Massachusetts economy, but they consume much scarce waterfront land in Boston Harbor. Massachusetts proposes a policy to encourage siting new tank farms inland, connecting them to waterfront transfer terminals via pipelines, and to phase out existing waterfront tank farms (Policy 30). This policy would be implemented by the Energy Facility Siting Council, using its permit and review process.

Even if explicit water-dependency criteria are not developed, state coastal managers tend to apply them implicitly when commenting on proposed development projects. For example, in Massachusetts, a conflict arose over a plan to locate a new community college at a site on Town Bay that is adjacent to a 35-foot navigation channel and is now zoned industrial. Coastal managers considered this poor planning and a violation of the principle of water dependency.

In Philadelphia, the Navy has built single-family housing at the Philadelphia Navy Yard on one of the few remaining tracts of undeveloped waterfront land in the city. City officials attempted, without success, to influence the Navy to relocate this non-water dependent use to an inland location, which the city would provide, and make the waterfront property available for port-related uses. State and city officials were powerless to stop the project, because it is within a federal enclave, exempt by federal law from state and local control. If Pennsylvania had had an approved coastal management program, the Navy would have been required to determine the consistency of its housing project with the program.

The use of water-dependency criteria is not limited to state and local government programs that affect coastal areas. The U.S. Fish and Wildlife Service is authorized to consider whether a project is water dependent or non-water dependent. Where biologically productive wetlands are involved and where other upland sites are available, the Fish and Wildlife Service usually recommends denial of a (Corps) permit unless the public interest requires further consideration (Department of Interior, 1975). In the previously mentioned example of a sawmill in Grays Harbor, the Fish and Wildlife Service objected to issuing the permit on the grounds that the sawmill was not water dependent.

Conserving the Future Supply of Waterfront Land

In ports where developable land is in short supply, coastal management agencies and port authorities are beginning to take steps to use existing land more intensively.

The Port of Seattle, facing a growing shortage of waterfront land for new container facilities, has adopted a strategy of "building up" by stacking containers more densely, decreasing on-chassis storage, and storing empty containers at inland locations. Such measures increase the intensity of use for port operations and enhance the conservation of land for other water-dependent uses.

The Port of Grays Harbor recently raised its tariff on log storage at port-owned terminals, which was followed by an unexpectedly sharp

Stacking containers four high means more can be stored, thereby reducing the demand for waterfront land. Containers are accessible using four mobile overhead "transtainer" cranes visible in upper right. (Photo courtesy of Port of Seattle)

decline in the number of logs stored. Log storage was shown to be very price sensitive, and logging companies chose to store logs at their own inland yards or to leave the timber standing. Reducing the number of logs stored was not the purpose of the tariff boost, but the example illustrates the possibility of using rate structures to encourage more intensive use of existing facilities.

Some coastal management programs are addressing the problem of development overflowing into undeveloped rural areas. The Massachusetts coastal management program, for example, viewed Boston Harbor as the preferred location for a new container terminal and it is their policy to discourage such major new facilities being located in undeveloped areas elsewhere along the coast.

The new California Coastal Act (1976) contains a strong statement limiting new port development to existing port districts:

". . . Coastal planning requires no change in the number or location of the established commercial port districts. Existing ports shall be encouraged to modernize and construct necessary facilities within their boundaries in order to minimize or eliminate the necessity for future dredging and filling to create new ports in new areas of the state." (section 30701 [b])

This policy is implemented in part by the provisions allowing Southern California ports to prepare their own master plans.

Regional Port Facility Planning

Individual port authorities decide when and where new facilities should be developed based on their own analysis of future trade needs and their ability to finance new land acquisition and facility construction. In intensely developed urban areas, where other uses compete for scarce waterfront land, ports will increasingly be called upon to justify the need for new facilities and provide the public with better documentation of siting decisions. Proponents of regional port facility planning cite examples of redundant facilities in neighboring ports and stress economic efficiency and conservation of land as reasons why regional facility planning is desirable. But the port industry is largely opposed to regional planning efforts, alleging that it stifles healthy competition among ports and that market forces best determine the composition and location of new facilities.

Two West Coast examples show attempts to coordinate port expansion on a regional scale. One is a voluntary certification-of-need program operating in Washington State; the other is a regional planning activity underway in the San Francisco Bay area. The Washington Public Ports Association's (WPPA) Ports Systems Study (1975) forecasts the demand for waterborne commerce and changes in shipping technology through the year 2000. Existing port capacities were compared with projected demand, and a voluntary industry-based committee was established to review proposed new port facilities. In planning for new facilities, a member port applies to WPPA's Cooperative Development Committee (CDC), for a "certificate of need" stating that the facility is in harmony with regional port development needs. The certification mechanism has been used by member ports only once. The procedure—established in response to proposals for a Puget Sound regional port authority being discussed in the Washington State legislature—is, admittedly, a self-policing practice of the industry association and has no legal sanction.

Regional coordination of port facilities in the San Francisco Bay area has been a controversial issue for more than 10 years. The San Francisco Bay Conservation and Development Commission's 1969 Bay Plan noted that a more definitive regional ports plan was needed. The Metropolitan Transportation Commission (MTC) began to study ports under its regional transportation mandate. But Bay area ports, in an effort to avoid MTC regulation, commissioned their own regional facility plan under the auspices of the Northern California Ports and Terminals Bureau (NORCAL, 1976). The Corps of Engineers began a third study of port facilities and demand for waterborne commerce. These studies resulted in a range of forecasts for new facilities: MTC's forecast was low, NORCAL's was high, and the Corps' was in between.

The 1969 Supplement to the Bay Plan notes that lack of coordination of facilities planning has resulted in duplication of facilities, conversion of scarce land which could have served purposes other than port use, and extensive unnecessary filling of the bay. Each port's cargo demand projections have tended to be of existing trends, without consideration of regional development objectives. The Supplement (p. 210, 211) recommends that a regional authority coordinate port facility planning for the Bay area, although it need not be an operating authority. The Bay Plan recommended a number of potentially desirable sites for new and continued port expansion.

Presently in the Bay area, MTC has made preliminary identification of 63 sites for new and continued port expansion. A continuing study will refine projections of demand and determine which of these sites are best suited to port development. The concept of a regional port authority has not been implemented, but continues to be a controversial topic.

Priority of Use through Environmental Area Designations

A mechanism for allocating waterfront land through coastal management programs is to establish environmental area designations in particular coastal areas and prescribe what uses may take place in them—a procedure similar to zoning but involving broader considerations. For example, the Washington State guidelines establish four broad categories of land and water use (Department of Ecology, 1972, p. 32-34):

1. Natural, land to remain relatively free from human influence;

2. Conservancy, land where resource management and public recreation will be permitted;

3. Rural, intended to protect agricultural land from urbanization;

4. Urban, development permitted provided other criteria are met.

Environmental areas are designated in local shoreline master programs, which, because they become incorporated into the state administrative code upon approval by the Department of Ecology, supercede local zoning regulations. Local governments must then either modify their zoning regulations to comply with master programs, or create special shoreline districts to replace zoning regulations. Seattle chose the latter method. The city's master program, issued in ordinance form, creates a series of special districts with detailed regulations and conditions imposed on permitted uses. It is more common, however, for local governments to use zoning regulations to complement their master programs' environmental area designations, to give shape to their community development goals, and to provide a consistent pattern of regulations between shoreline and upland use regulation.

Environmental area designations extend zoning-like regulation in an additional important way by dealing with water uses to the limits of local jurisdiction. Marinas, aquaculture activities, and even deepwater sites for dredged material disposal lie within the purview of local shoreline master programs.

Experience in Washington suggests that environmental area designations alone will not be the primary means of controlling shoreland allocation. Other criteria—such as environmental impact, water dependency, and public access—are applied to uses and often determine, utlimately, which uses are permitted. Prescribing uses within a district initially screens out only those which are least desirable. Further, giving a district a broad heading, such as "urban," does not resolve competing use problems since many competing uses may be authorized within the same district. This problem arose in Grays Harbor, where local government rezoned an area in the port district to allow a hotel-convention center complex. This controversial rezone occurred within an "urban" classification of the shoreline master program.

Influencing Facility Location through Public Infrastructure Decisions

Public investment in roads, water supply, sewers, and other infrastructure improvements has a direct bearing on where port facilities are located and when they are built. An example of how purposefully using public investment can guide the development of a new container facility is evolving in Boston. The Massachusetts coastal management program acknowledges the need for a new container facility, and would like to see it located in Boston Harbor, rather than in an undeveloped area. It has encouraged the Massachusetts Port Authority (Massport) to build a new truck access route to a promising South Boston site, which is plagued by poor highway access, in an effort to improve its suitability for development and reduce noise and congestion on city streets.

Public infrastructure investment decisions influencing water access to port facilities are even more crucial to site development. The location and extent of dredging for channel maintenance or construction in many ports often determines which sites are suitable for development. Ports request funds for engineering studies and capital construction projects by working through their congressional delegation. Congress then directs the Corps of Engineers' District Office to conduct studies and develop the project using federal funds and local cooperating agencies. State and local coastal management programs have not, for the most part, stepped into this federal political arena to influence facility location. However, because of the federal consistency provisions of the Coastal Zone Management Act, local programs will have a greater role to play in planning future federal dredge and fill projects.

9. STREAMLINING ENVIRONMENTAL PERMIT PROCEDURES

Since 1970, a spate of environmental legislation at both federal and state levels has required additional planning for new or expanded facilities in marine and shoreland environments. These statutes might require development permits in wetlands, environmental assessments or impact statements for significant developments, compliance with land- and water-use plans, and maintenance or enhancement of air and water quality.

This incremental, piecemeal approach to environmental management has lead to duplicative, uncoordinated, multiagency review of projects proposed in the coastal zone. Excessive delays in processing permit applications cause project costs to escalate beyond original estimates. In some cases, detailed engineering designs necessary to support permit applications must be amended or discarded as a result of an agency's review. Capital tied up in anticipation of project approval incurs interest costs, which—in the case of public ports projects—are partially borne by the local taxpayers. Port planning can become speculative—the uncertainty of agency approval may spur many project proposals with the hope that some will pass the agency review process. A port's competitive advantage may be eroded if shippers' needs for waterfront facilities are not met in a timely fashion. Port development opponents can and have delayed construction through lawsuits that rest on narrow procedural questions rather than substantive issues of siting, design, or environmental impact.

In a nutshell, port capital improvement projects face a high degree of uncertainty which results in additional costs to society. Coastal management programs are directed by statute to develop mechanisms to ameliorate this uncertainty. Specifically, they must—in cooperation with the policies of federal, state, and local agencies—determine permissable uses, designate geographic areas of particular concern, and establish use priorities. Ideally, coastal programs are designed to be able to tell ports and other users, in advance, how and where development may proceed. However, site-specific allocation of uses has occurred only in limited instances. Coastal agencies are still developing better methods for prescribing site-specific use designations. In the interim, coastal management programs are requiring coordinated multiagency review of proposed coastal developments. To facilitate this coordination, programs are addressing the following permit-related issues:

- Identification of required permits
- Consolidation of permit information requirements
- Sequence of permit applications
- Timeliness of review
- Preliminary informal review of proposed projects
- Simplified procedures for minor projects

Identification of Required Permits

While most port planning staff are familiar with permits required by state and federal resource and environmental protection agencies, their lessees may not be. Procedures have been developed to require some government agencies to identify required permits.

In Washington State, the Environmental Coordination Procedures Act (ECPA) provides that, where more than one state agency permit is required for a development, the applicant may submit one "master" application to the Department of Ecology (DOE), which circulates copies to all other state agencies. Each agency receiving a copy of the master application must respond within 15 days of receipt, or forfeit the right at a later date to require a permit for that development. Each agency requiring a permit notifies the DOE, which mails to the applicant all required permit forms. The applicant returns the completed forms to the DOE, together with a certification from local government of compliance with local ordinances. The DOE then forwards the applications to the appropriate state agencies, collates agency responses in one document, and returns this to the applicant.

Local governments may opt to use the same procedures to process rezones, variances, and conditional uses. To implement the Environmental Coordination Procedures Act, the DOE disburses funds to local governments to defray administrative costs. The act provides for voluntary compliance by local government, but does not require it. Some critics argue that this is a major weakness in the procedure.

In other states, the permitting divisions of resource agencies may fall under one "super-agency." A central permit clearinghouse coordinates permit applications required of each of its divisions. In Georgia, the Department of Natural Resources houses fisheries, wildlife, parks, air and water quality, coastal erosion, and coastal marshlands protection functions. Similarly, in New Jersey, the Department of Environmental Protection has integrated its resource management functions. An Environmental Coordination Section in the Division of Marine Services identifies all marine-related state permits required in coastal wetlands, waters, and water bottoms under state jurisdiction.

Consolidation of Permit Information Requirements

Permits required by different agencies in various levels of government may require similar information concerning the proposed development and its environmental impacts. In some cases, master applications have been developed to standardize the information asked of developers.

In Georgia, the Department of Natural Resources and the Corps of Engineers have agreed upon a standard form to be submitted for both state and federal coastal development permits. Because of the Department of Natural Resources' broad resource management authority and the standardized permit application form, Georgia's coastal management program has the potential for realizing a one-stop, state-federal permit procedure for coastal development projects. Local permit requirements will remain in force, however.

The California Coastal Act instructs local governments to "endeavor to consolidate the coastal permit application and hearing with other required procedures. . . ." A parallel requirement at the state level mandates the State Coastal Commission to "establish a joint development permit application system with (other) permit issuing agencies, where feasible."

Under Washington's State Environmental Policy Act (SEPA) a standard "environmental checklist" has been developed to determine whether or not the applicant must prepare an environmental impact statement. Together with architectural or engineering plans for the project, the checklist is circulated among state and local agencies for review and comment. Any agency can determine that a full environmental impact statement needs to be developed using this "threshold determination." Further, any application for a development project falling within the jurisdiction of the Shoreline Management Act (SMA) is submitted on a standard form, regardless of the local government involved. This is important since SMA permits are issued by local governments—of which there are 226 abutting Washington's marine and freshwater shoreline.

Sequence of Permit Applications

The order in which permit applications must be submitted, and in some cases approved, can delay final approval of port projects. Attempts to allow concurrent permit applications are evident among the case study states. Under Washington's Environmental Coordination Procedures Act, applicants for state and local permits may, at the discretion of local government, submit concurrent applications for state and local permits. Final action by state agencies, however, is contingent upon compliance with local ordinances. Similarly, while Corps of Engineers permits may be processed concurrently with state and local permits, final action must await approval by state and local agencies.

Legislation to allow delegation of Corps of Engineers section 404 permit authority to the states was enacted by the Congress late in 1977. It had been anticipated by several states. In Texas, the Dredged Materials Act (1977) states:

> "Effective and efficient regulation of such (dredged material discharge) activities can best be accomplished at the state level, and it is the proper role of state government to take responsibility for such regulation" (section 2 [c])

Texas' detailed scheme for rationalizing the review of state permits through the restructured Natural Resources Council (formerly the Interagency Council on Natural Resources and the Environment) would be strengthened were section 404 delegation to occur. State agencies would not be required to review the same proposal twice, and would be unable, therefore, to alter their decision, as has sometimes been the case when time elapses between state permit reviews and the section 404 federal permit review.

Timeliness of Review

Statutory minimum and maximum times to respond to, process, and act on permit applications have been incorporated into state environmental policy laws modelled after the National Environmental Policy Act (sometimes known as "little NEPAs"). In Washington, the State Environmental Policy Act (SEPA) requires the preparation of an environmental impact statement for projects having a significant impact on the environment. Statutory minimum and maximum times are provided to complete consulting agencies' reviews of draft and final environmental impact statements, to establish the need for public hearings, and—as with the Environmental Coordination Procedures Act—to identify agency jurisdiction or expertise affected by the proposed action or project. An agency that fails to respond to the lead agency cannot allege a defect in the environmental impact statement at a later date. A final environmental impact statement must be completed within 75 days of the draft review date, subject to extension for large or complex projects.

All agencies, including local governments implementing Washington's State Environmental Policy Act, are required to establish guidelines for determining completion times for environmental impact statements. Seattle's Department of Community Development (1976) has prepared a 14-page public information document on the act which contains a simple flow chart outlining the process and timing of environmental reviews conducted pursuant to it.

The Wisconsin Environmental Policy Act and its guidelines establish similar statutory minimum and maximum times for permit processing. It should be noted, however, that statutory times refer only to the process of review and comment, public hearings, and agency actions, and do not include the time needed to prepare draft environmental impact statements. For projects having a significant impact on the marine environment, data gathering, sometimes involving field measurements, can be particularly time consuming.

Concern for timely permit review prompted a spokesman for the Brownsville Navigation District to comment in support of the proposed Texas coastal management program:

"We think that the improvement in this permitting authority, at least as far as navigation districts are concerned, would come with a better coordination among the state agencies. We find that many of our permits are held up for one reason and another, because it is set on somebody's desk in a state agency and does not get back to the Corps. I think that is one of the vital functions of the Interagency Council on Natural Resources and the Environment. If they could have a uniform policy under which these permits are reviewed, better applications can be made and certainly it would speed up the way of doing it." (Lantz, in Brownsville Hearing)

In the Natural Resources Council Act, (1977, section 3 [c]) the legislature declared that it is the "policy of the state that . . . state permitting processes be refined. . . ." and that "systematic, fair and prompt review of such (state and federal) permit applications is essential to protect public and private interests on the Texas Coast." (section 2 [e]). The act passed into law the intent of the proposed Texas coastal management program, described in the *Hearings Draft* (General Land Office, 1976). The need for streamlined permit procedures, proposed as part of the "activity assessment routine," appears prominently in these documents.

The Wisconsin coastal management program lead agency is studying the potential for county or regional level "One-stop shopping centers" for information, technical assistance and review of potential coastal management activities. Presumably, permit information would be one of the functions provided.

Preliminary Informal Review of Proposed Projects

Delays and unnecessary engineering and design work revision caused by agency objections to development projects could sometimes be avoided if the applicant and agency reviewers were able to conduct formal, but not necessarily binding, early negotiations to identify serious conflicts or problems. Coastal zone legislation, in some cases, includes provisions for such consultation.

In Texas, the Coastal Coordination Act (1977), section 5 [d]) provides that

"(a) prospective applicant . . . may obtain a preliminary analysis of the proposed activity for which the permit is sought, or a reasonable number of alternative proposals for performances of the activity, from any state (permitting) agency . . . *such preliminary analysis shall be held confidential* . . . (and) shall not be a final decision, and neither the agency . . . nor the applicant shall be bound by the results. . . . No state agency . . . shall on the basis of such analysis express such an opinion of the likelihood that a permit . . . will be granted or denied." (emphasis added)

The assurance of confidentiality is important for ports and other coastal users operating within the vagaries of the marketplace. The competitive advantage gained by a port's initiative to capture trade through expansion or change of technology could be lost if competitors learned of those plans at the preliminary inquiry stage.

The preapplication conference has been used successfully in New Jersey's coastal area. Under the Coastal Area Facilities Review Act (CAFRA), all major coastal projects must acquire a permit from the Department of Environmental Protection (DEP). The proponent is required to develop an environmental impact statement which, if the project permit is denied, imposes nonrecoverable costs. Prior to formulating specific land use designations in the coastal area, the DEP produced interim development guidelines against which projects would be assessed. To assist the developers in insuring that their projects will be compatible, a preapplication conference is held between DEP staff and the developer.

". . . the developer can test how project proposal fits with the guidelines. He can negotiate with the state staff to relax some requirements in exchange for ultimate approaches or mitigating measures. . . . They will match the proposal against the guidelines to indicate the projects likelihood of being disapproved, approved, or approved with conditions—along with the kinds of conditions likely to be imposed. The developer can respond by making modifications or counter proposals and can maintain contact with the staff as final designs are being prepared for permit application.

No commitments are made by the state or the developer in these sessions: a permit application is required under law before any final decisions. But the procedure establishes a clear picture of likely outcomes." (Rivkin, 1976)

Washington's State Environmental Policy Act Guidelines provide for a "pre-draft consultation" between the developer and consulted agencies prior to preparation of a draft environmental impact statement. Such a consultation can be initiated by a request to the lead agency from the applicant. Washington's experience is noteworthy in two other instances:

1. At local government levels, there is usually an informal, pre-submittal consultation between planning staff and applicants seeking shorelines "substantial development permits."

2. Where local government decisions are appealed to the Shorelines Hearing Board, informal, prehearing conferences provide a setting in which "out of court settlements" may be negotiated between the applicant and agency representatives.

At an informal monthly meeting of state and federal agency permit review officials in Washington State—known as the "Musk-Oxen Club"—prospective project applications are reviewed in advance of formal submittal to determine the major concerns of the agencies. This arrangement provides an opportunity for conflicting agency opinions to be resolved prior to formal review. Naturally, no binding commitments can be made, but since the personnel who review permits are present at the informal meetings, it is unlikely that serious reversals of opinion will occur later. It should be noted that attendance is voluntary on the part of agency personnel.

Simplified Procedures for Minor Projects

Where small projects that will have only insignificant environmental effects are proposed, simplified or streamlined procedures have been developed to accelerate agencies' actions. In California, the state and regional coastal commissions place groups of small projects on a "consent calendar," obviating the need for full hearings on each individual project, unless such a hearing is specifically requested (Coastal Act, section 13100-103). In addition, port projects that conform with the ports' state-certified local coastal programs are exempted from appeal to the State

Coastal Commission except for certain energy-related facilities, non-port related activities, and roads not principally intended for internal port use. (Coastal Act, sections 30715 [a] thru [f]).

At the federal agency level, the Corps of Engineers issues "nation-wide permits" for certain small, replicative activities involving discharge of dredge and fill material under section 404 jurisdiction. (Corps of Engineers, 1977, 303.4-2 through 4-4). The District Engineer can override such provisions and require individual or "general" permits at his discretion: the "general" permits may be issued for other minor, replicative projects within his jurisdiction. The intent of both "nationwide" and "general" permits is to minimize paperwork for minor projects. For important port expansion projects, however, the Corps of Engineers will continue to require sections 10 and 404 permits. In a recent amendment, states can be given authority under section 404 if their programs meet certain minimum standards.

10. FUTURE USE OF OBSOLETE WATERFRONT FACILITIES

Traditionally, ports were located adjacent to a city's central business district because most of the cargo was destined for local markets and the labor force was nearby. Modern shipping and cargo-handling methods have altered historical trade patterns and created demands for new types of port facilities. Space requirements for port operations have expanded and outgrown the capabilities of city-center sites, where the large parcels of land and expanded backup space that is often needed is not available. When a port moves to a new location or discontinues certain trade, obsolete or unused port facilities remain and their future use becomes an important coastal issue.

Many urban areas are taking an active interest in revitalizing their waterfront area. Growing interest in commercial, recreational, educational, and residential uses is providing ports and cities with viable alternatives for unused waterfront property. Coastal management programs are addressing these urban waterfront redevelopment needs.

In Georgia, efforts have been made to transform obsolete port facilities to non-shipping uses. The colonial quay in Savannah has been renovated as a promenade with public-oriented commercial enterprises. The Port of Los Angeles allocated old shipping property to a "Ports of Call," which contains shops and a restaurant. The Port of Seattle has worked with the City of Seattle and private concerns to convert unused piers to non-port uses amenable to public access: new uses include parks, shops, restaurants, and an aquarium.

A major renovation project along a half mile of the Delaware River in the center of Philadelphia's historical district is the Penn's Landing redevelopment project, a joint effort between public agencies and private enterprise. City-state funding created the landfill site, bulkheading, and public improvements (e.g., utilities, paving, landscaping, etc.). The

Philadelphia Port Corporation provided technical support for the landfill and bulkheading operation but private developers will complete the project with shops, restaurants, entertainment facilities, and an apartment-office-hotel complex. Less massive efforts have also been undertaken along Philadelphia's waterfront to reuse obsolete port facilities. Upstream from Penn's Landing, moorage is provided for two yachts which have been converted into restaurants; downstream is a warehouse which has been converted into tennis courts.

Studies conducted under Pennsylvania's coastal program explicitly address the issue of revitalizing the urban waterfront, with specific reference to obsolete finger piers. Pennsylvania's draft objective does not discuss the major effort occurring at Penn's Landing, but supports the principle by promoting new uses for abandoned or vacated waterfront.

The Massachusetts coastal management program has incorporated policies for urban waterfront renovation which directly support ongoing efforts of the City of Boston. On its downtown waterfront, Boston has adapted old wharves and a market building for new uses. This redevelopment emphasizes such goals as encouraging a mixture of land use,

The two old finger piers shown here were no longer usable for port cargo-handling purposes, so they have been redeveloped to provide recreation, education, and public access opportunities. the pier on the right contains a restaurant, shop space, and a public fishing area. Pier 59, to the left, and the modern concrete structure to the left of it, house the new Seattle Aquarium. Between these piers is the new Waterfront Park. (Photo courtesy of the Port of Seattle)

promoting marine or marine-oriented activities to stimulate tourism and symbolize Boston's historic connection to the sea, and providing public parks which enhance pedestrian access to the harbor (Tobin, 1977).

The preliminary Massachusetts coastal plan sets forth policies pertaining to ports and harbors which encourage water-dependent economic development activities. However, on shores no longer suitable for shipping, the program encourages "urban waterfront redevelopment and renewal in developed harbors in order to link residential neighborhoods and commercial downtown areas with physical and visual access to the waterfront." (Policy 20) This policy is harmonious with current restoration activities along Boston's waterfront, and the program proposes to actively promote it using existing state and federal programs. The program will—

1. "Champion" applications to the U.S. Department of Housing and Urban Development (HUD) through the Housing and Community Development Act of 1974 and Community Development Block Grant Program;

2. Disburse Coastal Zone Management Act implementation funds (section 306) to support the preparation of harborfront plans aimed at improving public access;

3. Advocate proposals for U.S. Bureau of Outdoor Recreation funding under its land and water conservation fund;

4. Encourage the Urban Mass Transportation Administration to provide grants and loans for the Department of Public Works to provide transit projects for the area, develop bikeways and walkways, and insure that new or improved roads and bridges provide visual and physical access;

5. Insure that the Massachusetts Waterways Program actively supports bulkhead, public pier, wharf, jetty, and shore protection projects which aid redevelopment;

6. Utilize the information channels of Massachusetts Environmental Policy Act, National Environmental Policy Act, and A-95 reviews to encourage waterfront redevelopment. (Massachusetts Office of Environmental Affairs, 1977, pp. 2-E 23-25)

5 PORT PARTICIPATION IN COASTAL MANAGEMENT PROGRAMS

Policies are needed to resolve land and water issues that both port officials and coastal managers can agree upon. Arriving at mutually agreeable policies will require interaction between these two groups. The case studies provide examples of three areas of interaction: (1) information exchange and forums for port involvement during coastal program development; (2) possible roles for port authorities in coastal program implementation; and (3) organizational arrangements to help resolve port-related coastal management problems which cross jurisdictional lines. Those interactions and the attendant organizational arrangements are described and, where possible, those that have been successful are identified in this chapter.

PARTICIPATION AND INFORMATION EXCHANGE DURING PROGRAM DEVELOPMENT
Requirements and Problems of Port-Coastal Relations

The Coastal Zone Management Act mandates that the development and implementation of coastal management programs include all interested parties (it specifically mentions ports) and governmental units. Beyond this mandate, however, there is a history of communication between port authorities and land and water regulatory agencies that predates the Act by many years. Because these regulatory agencies are often the same ones charged with developing coastal management programs, port authorities often will be dealing with familiar agency personnel and well-established lines of communication. Moreover, contact between coastal management and port personnel is unavoidable because the two activities have mutual areas of interest: comprehensive coastal management programs must consider marine transportation needs since transportation is an important coastal use; port developers must consider coastal management policies since future port facilities normally require coastal locations. The key question is how interaction can be most effective.

Ideally, contact between port authorities and coastal managers should be frequent, timely, and ongoing—occurring at different administrative levels within the respective organizations and addressing many different issues. But there are practical limitations. Although ports must deal with many environmental and land-use programs, only the larger port authorities have sufficient staff to follow the developments in all these programs. Similarly coastal management programs must deal with all coastal land and water users. Since the Coastal Zone Management Act only allows four years for program development, with a one-year transition period, not every user group can be given in-depth attention. However, once programs are approved and implemented, particular users can be given closer attention and programs can be refined. Thus, continued development and improvement of aspects of coastal programs affecting ports can be achieved after program development ends and program administration begins.

Another limitation to effective interaction between ports and coastal management programs has been that port authorities have hesitated to assist actively in the early stages of policy development. Because these programs are recent, with only broadly stated goals and objectives, their impact on port planning and operations have become apparent only as state programs begin to establish boundaries and to air policy alternatives regarding permissable uses and their priorities.

Involvement in early formulations of policy has frequently been affected by a port authority's governmental level relative to the level at which a coastal management program operates. Public port authorities are organized at various governmental levels: city, special district (usually county or multicounty), or state. Coastal management programs, though many are still being developed, tend to fall into one of three categories:

1. Programs which rely heavily upon the coordination of existing state authorities to regulate coastal uses;

2. Programs which delegate most authority for program development to local levels of government, but where the state retains a strong oversight and intervenor role;

3. Programs in which existing local regulation of land and water use remains the principal authority.

Where the port authority and coastal management program level are closely aligned (as in Georgia, where the focus of both efforts is at the state level), communication has been facilitated early in program development. In Georgia, the state port authority director sits as an equal with other state agency heads on the Governor's advisory council, a policy-advising group directly overseeing coastal program development. Similarly, in Washington, coastal programs and ports both are focused at county and regional levels—a situation which has facilitated early and ongoing interaction.

Where the governmental levels of ports and coastal management programs are different, special arrangements must be made to encourage interaction. In some cases, these arrangements have not been effective. In Texas, where ports are local-level districts and the coastal management program operates at the state level, the port representative on the coastal management advisory committee speaks for port interests in general terms but does not represent the views of all ten coastal port authorities. In California, after attempts to interact effectively with the State Coastal Commission failed, the California Association of Port Authorities created a special committee to lobby for port interests during the development of coastal legislation. An accord was hammered out at the very last minute. In both of these cases, port personnel monitored the progress of coastal management program development; but while the port authorities urged that ports be explicitly recognized, they did not formulate specific policy recommendations prior to receiving draft policies from coastal management programs. When draft policies were circulated, ports reacted vigorously, however, providing valuable feedback to coastal management officials at public hearings and in less formal settings. Thus interaction began in earnest late in the development process and only when ports recognized potential impact on port development. Had interaction occurred at earlier stages, some friction might have been avoided and policies developed that were acceptable to both parties.

In Wisconsin, where ports are city departments, the state coastal management agency commissioned an independent assessment of Great Lakes ports and provided for the appointment of one port director to the Citizens' Advisory Committee. Though the coastal program and ports are at different levels of government, the result has been a highly visible and positive program to encourage the revitalization of Great Lakes ports.

Despite these institutional barriers to interaction, however, once involved in a dialogue with coastal management program personnel, port directors and their staff have sought to insure recognition of port values as a part of coastal management programs.

Methods for Information Exchange

In all case study states, some information about port-related problems in the coastal zone has been shared between coastal management personnel and port officials. The form of this exchange has varied considerably, but because of the variability among ports and coastal management programs, it is difficult to state with certainty that one form worked better than another.

All coastal management programs have public participation programs. Most ports participate directly on advisory committees or councils where policy preferences and information can be exchanged in a face-to-face setting. Public information documents—such as newsletters, surveys, tabloid brochures, and draft policy papers—have been used extensively in some cases and virtually ignored in others. Public hearings, too, have ranged from perfunctory to extremely effective. Finally, special studies and reports have sometimes been commissioned by port associations and coastal management agencies.

Table 5.1 provides a summary of the kinds of interaction occurring between port and coastal management program personnel in the case studies. Communication forums or techniques which appear to be most effective are asterisked. The discussion that follows emphasizes communication techniques employed in the case study states. While there are no findings that can be applied nationally, there are examples that individual port authorities or coastal management programs might find useful.

Advisory committees and councils. State-level advisory committees and councils are the primary contacts between ports and coastal management programs in Wisconsin and Georgia. The director of the Port of Milwaukee, a municipal port authority, serves on the Governor's Citizens'

Table 5.1. Mechanisms for information exchange

Port	Advisory committees or councils	Public information documents or surveys
Milwaukee, Wisconsin	*Port Director is a member of Citizens' Advisory Committee to the Governor's State Advisory Council, and the Technical Advisory Committee to the S.E. Wisconsin Regional Planning Commission.	Public opinion questionnaire run in the newspaper included ports among the CZM issues. Citizens' Committee developed an information worksheet on ports for public information. State CZMP and DOT funded a background and future alternatives study for Wisconsin's Great Lakes Ports.
Ameriport Philadelphia Port Corp.	Delaware River Port Authority is a member of the CZM Steering Committee	Port Corporation receives public information documents from CMP agency
South Jersey Port Authority		Port Corporation receives public information documents from CMP agency
Port of Georgia at Savannah	*Port Director is a member of State CZM Advisory Council, Chairman of the Subcommittee on Ports and Waterborne Commerce, and serves on the Industrial Development Subcommittee	**
Brownsville Navigation District	Port Director is Chairman of Transportation Subcommittee of the Brownsville City Planning Commission. Counsel for Port of Corpus Christi is a member of CZM Advisory Committee, and represents port interests on Texas coast.	*"Hearings Draft" CZMP document and appendices mailed to coastal user and interest groups prior to ten regional public hearings with CZM Agency Director and consultants present. Texas Coastal and Marine Council publications on ports and related issues are widely distributed and receive legislative attention.

*Mechanisms which appeared to be unusually effective.

**These states have public participation programs, but no particular significance to ports was noted during case studies interviews, due to early state of program development.

Public hearings	Legislative involvement	Informal contacts
* *		
* *		*Key staff person in city planning is an unofficial information liaison between the port and CZM. DRPA initiates contacts with New Jersey coastal program.
. * *		Special assistant to the mayor is an unofficial information liaison between the port and CZM.
* *		Through close association with the Savannah Port Authority, GPA stays in touch with local planning agencies

Port Engineering Director represented Port at CZMP Hearing in Brownsville.

98

Table 5.1. (*cont.*) Mechanisms for information exchange

Port	Advisory Committees or councils	Public information documents or surveys
Los Angeles, California		*Draft coastal plan elements containing restrictive port development policies were circulated statewide.
Grays Harbor, Washington	During master program development an official port representative served on the Citizens' Advisory Committee. *Port is an active charter member of the Regional Planning Commission. Port participated with RPC in early CZM study. Port serves on Grays Harbor Estuary Task Force.	

*See legend on previous page

**See legend on previous page

Advisory Committee. This body provides public input to the Coastal Coordinating and Advisory Council, which is composed of state agency representatives and locally elected officials, including a representative from the City of Milwaukee. The director of the Georgia Ports Authority (GPA), a state agency, participates with other state agency directors on the Georgia coastal zone management advisory council. Because GPA's director has equal status, he has a stronger position with respect to policy formulation than his Milwaukee counterpart and is potentially more effective.

The Port of Brownsville is not represented on the coastal zone management advisory committee in Texas. In fact, during program development the only port representative on the council was the lawyer for the Port of Corpus Christi. Indirectly, however, major coastal industrial corporations who lease port landholdings represented marine commerce and industry interests on the council. When the governor appointed the advisory board to the Natural Resources Council, no maritime, coastal, or environmental interests were selected. Strenuous lobby efforts on the part of port, fishing, marine recreation, and environmental interests are expected and may cause this advisory committee to be reconstituted.

Public hearings	Legislative involvement	Informal contacts
Legislative aide and planning department staff attended hearings throughout the state, during development of California's Coastal Plan.	*Port Director played a primary role in making CAPA the spokesman for California ports during CZM negotiations. CAPA's first lobbyist was an excellent mediator. Port's legislative aide performs a formal liaison function with city government.	The port/environmental division head has informal contacts with commission staff.
Public hearings were held to review local master program before formal adoption.	Port assisted in drafting the Shoreline Management Act in response to an environmentally more restrictive initiative measure. Ports resisted legislative proposals to create a state port authority.	*Past director or regional planning commission is present port planner. Present director of RPC maintains informal liaison with port.

In Washington State, there was active public participation during the preparation of local shoreline master programs. A port employee served on the Grays Harbor citizens' advisory committee, but there is no conclusive evidence that his presence enhanced the port's position during the development of the local master program.

Three regional planning commissions whose constituent jurisdictions abut Wisconsin's Lake Michigan and Lake Superior shorelines have citizens' or technical advisory councils. These councils review and comment on state coastal management goals and policies. The director of the Port of Milwaukee serves on one of them—the Southeast Wisconsin Regional Planning Commission's technical advisory committee—in addition to serving on the state-level committee.

Operating ports in New Jersey, Pennsylvania, and California have no direct representation on advisory committees or councils and must, therefore, rely on other forums for expressing their views on coastal management policies. The Delaware River Port Authority, a promotional agency for Delaware River ports, is a nonvoting member on the Pennsylvania Advisory Council and indirectly represents the Philadelphia Port Corporation.

Public information documents and surveys. To involve the broader citizenry in developing coastal management policies, many coastal states distribute information documents to a wide audience. Wisconsin has effectively used such documents in its public participation program. The roles ports play on the Great Lakes are described in widely distributed brochures which the port director from Milwaukee assisted in producing. A survey conducted through a newspaper questionnaire prepared by the coastal management agency showed that ports were favored coastal users in those areas of the state for which responses had been processed (Lake Superior region). Prominent concerns identified by respondents included "promoting port development" and "state assistance for Great Lakes ports." State coastal program development in Wisconsin is proceeding with a thorough understanding of key port issues drawn from ports, independent consultants, and citizen participants.

In Texas, two widely distributed sets of documents addressing port issues have increased awareness of port-related issues in the legislature and among coastal users. The first of these, the *Coastal Management Program Hearing Draft and Appendices* (General Land Office, 1976), was mailed to interested parties prior to hearings in ten locations. Moreover, the Texas Coastal and Marine Council (1974, 1975, 1976, 1977)—an independent, legislatively created advisory group—has issued a series of reports dealing with ports and marine commerce on the Texas gulf coast.

In Washington, local governments were given almost complete responsibility for incorporating ports into local master programs with little guidance from the state coastal management agency. Local coastal management personnel relied primarily on direct public participation through citizen advisory committees. In addition local draft goals and policies were circulated for review, and public hearings were held.

In California, regional commissions circulated drafts of coastal plan elements for public review. Policies affecting ports in the south coast region first came to light through these documents. Ports were able to influence the South Coast Regional Commission's (SCRC) positions on port development, but attempts to intercede at the state commission level were ineffective.

Public hearings. Public hearings can be useful vehicles for obtaining public reaction to proposed coastal management goals and policies. In some cases, notably Wisconsin and Georgia, there was ample prior opportunity for ports to assist in policy development through reports and surveys, or representation on policy-making or advisory councils. But in Texas, formal hearings provided the first and only opportunity for ports to learn of and react to policies affecting them. The Brownsville hearing provided the only direct formal contact between the port and the Texas coastal management agency. The *Hearing Draft* (General Land Office, 1976) and its appendices had been mailed to all user groups prior to the hearings (held in ten locations), enabling users to submit their reactions in both written and oral form.

In Washington, public hearings were lengthy processes, sometimes running for over a year, during which detailed land- and water-use allocation decisions were debated intensely. In Seattle, for example, six redrafts of the local master program were produced before the city council finally approved the plan. Even then, issues such as the Port of Seattle holdings on the Duwamish River estuary, resulted in the rejection of portions of the master program. More hearings were held before the marsh island in question, previously designated a "conservancy" area, was redesignated "urban development" for port expansion purposes. The port's role in this case was resolute and aggressive. Another issue vigorously debated was a major development proposal for the harbor area of downtown Seattle's waterfront. Public hearings were used by numerous factions to fight detailed land- and water-use designations in one of the longest and most extensively reported public debates in Seattle's history.

Legislative involvement of ports in coastal management programs. California's draft policies of the South Coast Regional Commission (SCRC) alerted ports in the region to the need for incorporating port concerns into the coastal management policies. To increase their effectiveness, the ports united their efforts through the government relations committee of the California Association of Port Authorities (CAPA). The SCRC responded favorably to the port association's information. Unfortunately, when the regional plans were incorporated into the state plan, elements important to the ports were not included. The subsequent strategy adopted by the ports was to become directly involved in redrafting the implementing legislation. Again, using the same committee, they lobbied for an acceptable bill. The result was Chapter 8 of the California Coastal Act which gives four south coast region ports special authority to develop their own local coastal plans and to issue permits in conformance with their own state-certified plan.

In Washington, an initiative drive by the Washington Environmental Council (WEC) resulted in Shoreline Management Initiative 43 being placed on the ballot in 1971. A legislatively proposed alternative measure, Initiative 43B, was drafted with the substantial involvement of ports personnel, notably from the Port of Seattle. Initiative 43B, passed by the voters, placed more responsibility with local government for planning land and water uses in a smaller management area (200 feet inland versus 500 feet proposed in 43). Washington ports, which are special units of local government, appear to favor dealing with their local governments (counties and municipalities) rather than with a state agency (Department of Ecology) on matters of land- and water-use allocation.

Informal contacts between ports and coastal management agencies. There are many informal methods for sharing information. Staff contacts are frequent and ongoing among permitting agencies and port planning and engineering personnel. Shared professional values, membership in professional organizations, and familiarity with ongoing environmental and land- and water-use programs provide flows of information about each other's needs and regulatory authorities.

The political clout wielded by ports varies according to their size and economic importance to the region, the composition of their boards of commissioners, the balance between inland and coastal interests represented in the legislative bodies and, of course, the political affiliations of key port officials with state legislatures. At upper management levels, port directors and commissioners often have access to state agency directors and their legislative oversight committees. Such contacts complement formal communications through advisory councils, hearings, and coastal policy position papers. When their interests are threatened, as evidenced in the California Coastal Plan and Washington's shorelines initiative, ports can exercise this informal political power to influence legislation, either directly by port officials or through port associations and organizations representing commerce and development interests. Ignoring or discounting legitimate port concerns could result in last-minute amendments which could compromise the coherence and integration of coastal management program elements.

Regional trade and facility forecasting studies. Regional trade and facility forecasting studies may be used to coordinate future port facility development, to educate the public regarding the potential of ports, and to describe the current port facilities and their uses. Moreover, they provide information on new facility needs when a specific project proposal is addressed, although the validity of the information is often attacked by those opposing these developments. To date, regional studies have been completed in Washington, Wisconsin, San Francisco Bay, and Texas. Both the Washington Port Systems Study (1975), conducted by the Washington Public Ports Association (WPPA), and a Wisconsin study of Great Lakes ports (Mayer, 1975) illustrate the problems of aggregated data. They discuss regional trends only, without allocating future facilities to specific ports. In the Washington study, needs for new facilities are given by commodity type for each of four subregions in the state, but there is no mention of individual port expansion plans. Some ports disagree with this study methodology and projections used to develop the forecasts.

In response to legislative proposals to amalgamate port districts into a Washington State port authority and to counteract the threat to their members' autonomy, the WPPA commissioned a consultant to produce the port systems study. One of the study recommendations was that the WPPA establish a Cooperative Development Committee (CDC) through which a port may seek an evaluation of the need for new or expanded facilities relative to the projections in the ports systems study. A favorable evaluation results in a "certificate of need" being issued. In fact, the certification procedure has been used only once to date. As a mechanism for allocating expansion projects regionally, peer review such as the CDC certificate procedure is weak, since a decision is not binding on a member port.

In the San Francisco Bay area, the NORCAL-1 and NORCAL-2 studies (Northern California Ports and Terminals Bureau, 1975, 1976) assessed the short- and long-term future needs for port handling capacity in Bay area ports. The studies found, for example, that by the year 2000, NORCAL ports in the Bay area would need to handle one and one-half times as much break-bulk cargo, two and one-half times as much dry bulk cargo, and nine times as much container/LASH/ro-ro cargo. By the year 2020, these figures would triple. The study predicts expansion for particular ports, such as Richmond, but the factors leading to the expansion were known prior to the study. The study justifies the direction of port expansion already underway in the region.

Data collected for NORCAL are proving useful for the Bay Conservation and Development Commission (BCDC) study of ports. The BCDC is assisting the Metropolitan Transportation Commission in developing a regional ports plan for the San Francisco Bay. Phase 1 of the plan, dealing with cargo projections, requires a reconciliation of the port's view as stated in NORCAL-1 and NORCAL-2, and the U.S. Army Corps of Engineers projections done in a special study for that region. Phase 1 also evaluates the capacity of existing facilities and assesses alternative port configurations, which BCDC will use to update its 1969 San Francisco Bay Plan. The Bay Plan's current allocation for future port expansion was based on the port's statement of needs in 1967-68. The BCDC hopes that their current regional port study, conducted in conjunction with the ports, environmental groups and government agencies, will allow better allocation of shoreline space for port purposes.

The Texas Coastal and Marine Council's study of waterborne commerce, while not strictly a regional facility forecasting study, does assess the financial capability of individual ports to carry out proposed expansion plans. By assessng how much capital a port is likely to be able to raise in the near future, planners may be able to separate serious proposals from "puffing" and apply their planning resources to those areas most likely to develop.

The Corps of Engineers conducts studies on maintenance dredging and channel and harbor improvement projects which often contain information useful to coastal management programs. The studies discuss expansion plans of a port, the Corps' analysis of costs and benefits of the project, expected growth in trade, changes in technology, the size of ships, and other factors. Information contained in these studies may be useful for planning purposes, in identifying areas likely to grow, or for assessing impacts of a proposed project during permit review. Two case study ports, Grays Harbor and Los Angeles, are currently under consideration by the Corps for major channel and harbor improvement projects.

These Corps studies and projects often affect the regional allocation of port facilities. In Grays Harbor, for example, a decision was made to widen and deepen the Grays Harbor channel, but maintenance dredging will cease in Willapa Bay to the south. These two decisions preclude development of deep-draft port facilities in Willapa Bay and concentrate port development in Grays Harbor. In Los Angeles, the Corps' widening and deepening of the harbor and creation of new port lands resulted in continued competition between two contiguous ports, Los Angeles and Long Beach, rather than toward concentration of facilities. The Corps' analysis of the need for the harbor improvements in Los Angeles did not take a regionwide perspective, since the future of the Port of Long Beach, which shares the same bay and the opposite end of Terminal Island, was not thoroughly considered.

The Corps has long recognized the regional implications of civil works projects and the need for simultaneous review of many proposed projects before deciding which ones will receive funding. However, pressure from project proponents, and the narrow focus of the feasibility and engineering studies often preclude a regional analysis of port facility needs.

PORT PARTICIPATION IN IMPLEMENTING COASTAL MANAGEMENT PROGRAMS

Besides sharing information during states' coastal management program development, there are certain ways in which ports can participate directly in program implementation. In some cases port authorities have either been given, or have assumed, responsibilty for coordinating permit applications for their projects, or those of their lessees. Depending upon their statutory authority, ports can play an effective role in implementing the economic development goals of their states' coastal management programs. Finally, ports can encourage renewal of obsolete facilities on urban waterfronts. In only one case—in Southern California—have ports been delegated a regulatory role in coastal management.

Local Plan Implementation Role for Ports

Under Chapter 8 of the California Coastal Act, Southern California ports have been given authority to develop detailed, site-specific plans for managing lands within their own port districts. These plans are submitted to the State Coastal Commission and must include proposed land and water uses; proposed harbor alterations; an assessment of anticipated environmental impact, and mitigation proposals. The act contains policies that govern port development and the plans which are to be prepared.

Public and agency participation is required before a port plan is completed and public hearings must be held before the plan can be adopted by the port. Once the plan is certified by the State Coastal Commission, the port authority assumes responsibility to insure that all new developments within its jurisdiction comply with the certified plan. Certain projects can be appealed, such as those not directly related to shipping and energy facilities. If a project can be appealed, the commission must be notified during the planning and design phases. Ten days before construction begins, all interested persons, organizations, and agencies must be notified. Such an appeal mechanism should assure port compliance with state-certified plans.

The four California ports to which this special implementation authority is given have received funds from the coastal commission to develop port master plans. Conceivably the ports are eligible for grants to train their staffs to conduct coastal management planning activities. Furthermore, where port holdings present opportunities for public access to beaches or other areas of cultural, educational or aesthetic value, grants for estuarine sanctuaries and beach access are available.

Direct Participation in Estuary Management Studies

In Washington and Oregon, there are several examples of comprehensive estuary management studies growing out of the conflict between port needs for terminal expansion, channel improvement, and waterfront industrial development, and other competing land and water uses such as recreation, fisheries, and wildlife protection. The objective of these studies is to involve all the affected interests, including ports, in working toward the allocation of shoreline uses to accommodate all the diverse interests. Such studies are normally headed by a professional manager who is not affiliated with any of the participants.

After a state moratorium on dredge and fill projects was imposed, the Port of Portland, Oregon provided seed money for a management study of the lower Willamette River. The resulting management program allocating land and water uses is enforced by state and federal permit agencies, and—according to the consultant—dredge permits now are being approved in as little as 15 days.

The Grays Harbor Estuary Study Task Force provides an example of an ongoing, comprehensive, estuary management program which was modelled after the lower Willamette study. The study, which is coordinated by a private consultant, brings together representatives from local, state, and federal government agencies, environmental protection groups, businessmen, and citizens with responsibilities and interests in the Grays Harbor estuary. The Port of Grays Harbor is represented by its director. A technical team provides detailed environmental, land-use, and economic data to be used by the task force in developing an estuary management plan to guide future development. The port planner serves on the technical team, providing detailed information on port development and operations.

The principal impetus leading to the creation of the estuary study was excessive permit delays encountered in projects related to Corps channel realignment and deepening, and unresolved, incremental filling of tidelands. Through its membership on both the task force and the technical team, the port is able to address its needs on the Grays Harbor estuary in the presence of all affected parties, including regulatory agency representatives. The resulting management plan will bind all such parties to specific land- and water-use allocations and should facilitate timely processing of local, state, and federal permits required for site-specific projects.

In the Columbia River estuary, a similar project is underway. A bistate (Washington and Oregon) task force (CREST) is coordinating the interests of local governments and state and federal agencies in developing an estuary management program similar to that in Grays Harbor. Both the ports of Astoria (Oregon) and Ilwaco (Washington) serve on the CREST policy-making council.

In both these cases, ports have a role to play in coastal management programs after they have been implemented. The policies and shoreland allocation schemes developed by the Grays Harbor task force will refine the affected master programs in Washington. In Oregon, on the other hand, the CREST plan will implement the coastal policies set out by the Oregon Land Conservation and Development Commission (LCDC), the backbone of the Oregon coastal management program.

In neither of these studies do ports receive direct coastal management section 305 development funds or section 306 implementation funds. Instead, funds are allocated to the Grays Harbor Regional Planning Commission, to the local government units in Grays Harbor and on the Columbia River in Washington, and to local governments and the CREST organizations in Oregon.

In Tampa, Florida, an ad hoc committee composed of a variety of interest groups, including the port authority, meets regularly with the Corps of Engineers to decide upon the siting and configuration of dredge spoil disposal for sections of a major channel improvement project. The added costs of dredge spoil disposal due to environmental mitigation and enhancement requirements suggested by the ad hoc committee, are met through a tariff imposed by the Port of Tampa on exports of locally mined phosphate rock. The port avoids project delays using this strategy since they do not have to wait for Congress to approve mitigation funds.

The San Francisco Bay area's BCDC/Metropolitan Transportation Commission (MTC) regional ports plan is another example of direct port participation in estuary management studies. Local, state, and federal agencies and port authorities in the Bay area are conducting a three-phase study which will be used to update BCDC's coastal management program. The project is being managed by MTC's Seaport Policy Committee, utilizing section 305 funds. The first phase compares various regional port demand forecasts, notably NORCAL and Corps studies. Phase II assesses the needs for future facilities and compares their impacts on various environments within the Bay. Finally, in Phase III, a specific regional allocation plan for new facilities will be developed.

Environmental Permit Coordination

Port staff—through their contacts with their counterparts in regulatory agencies—can play an important role in coordinating required local, state, and federal permits for their lessees. For example, the Port of Brownsville acts as an agent for its industrial tenants and secures necessary permits. Each lease agreement requires the tenant to conform with all environmental regulations. Recently the port negotiated with the Texas

Water Quality Board on behalf of the Union Carbide Corporation, whose effluent discharge into a navigation channel failed to meet agency standards. The port, using pollution control bonds, has completed a major wastewater treatment facility for Union Carbide and the corporation is now in compliance with state and federal water quality standards.

The Port of Grays Harbor has played a similar role. A wood products-related chemical corporation, Ventron, with port encouragement and technical assistance, located a new facility in Grays Harbor County. Services provided by the port included site selection, arranging for provision of utilities and securing the necessary land-use and environmental permits. Within the harbor area, the Port of Grays Harbor has also prepared a site for the Kaiser Steel Corporation's offshore-oil-drilling-rig fabrication plant. The port secured the necessary permits for dredging, filling, and land-use change.

Providing services such as securing permits and insuring compliance with environmental regulations can be to the port's advantage because, to some degree, ports are responsible for the actions of their lessees. For example, when a Port of Los Angeles lessee resisted installing wastewater treatment facilities, both the port and the lessee were cited for the violation. A similar case occurred in Milwaukee where the C&O car ferry, a coal-burner fleet, violated air quality standards and incurred fines for the port and the steamship company.

If ports continue to provide these services for their lessees, they can play an important coordination role for a large segment of industrial coastal users, some of whom may be uncertain about a particular state's coastal management policies and procedures. Similarly, regulatory agencies can conduct their business with a single, informed agent, rather than dealing piecemeal with each lessee.

Achieving Economic Development Goals
of Coastal Management Programs

Port authorities are important promoters of regional economic development. In several case studies, the industrial enterprises which ports have helped attract have provided employment opportunities and trade beyond the port's own jurisdiction. Certainly the effect of trade increases will be felt in increased cargo movements through port facilities, but self-interest is not a port's only motive. A successful port director and port commissioners perceive their roles as broadly supportive of regional economic development and are strongly aligned with citizens' groups and planning organizations with similar goals—chambers of commerce, economic development agencies, and planning commissions.

Where coastal management programs identify selected coastal areas as having high economic development potential, port authorities usually are appropriate and aggressive proponents of development policies. In most of these cases, ports are identified as preferred users of coastal sites. Industrial activities that are not water dependent usually are discouraged or prohibited from locating on waterfront parcels. For example, the

Port of Brownsville steers general industrial tenants to upland sites, reserving land abutting the navigation channel for activities related to waterborne commerce.

States may be able to capitalize on this approach to help implement development aspects of coastal management programs. Depending upon the statutes under which it is organized, a port may own land, lease lands from the state, act as the state's agent and sublease to other harbor or tideland users, or act as an economic development agency encouraging industrial development both on and off lands it leases or owns.

None of the case study ports were solely concerned with cargo movement across port-owned facilities. Most of the ports were involved in promoting industrial development within their jurisdictions, even on sites they neither owned nor leased. In some cases, enabling statutes require ports to provide commercial fishery and recreational moorages in their facilities.

In Brownsville, the port director views his industrial development role as encompassing the entire lower Rio Grande Valley, including northeast Mexican communities like Matamoros. A major transportaion realignment proposal involving new road and railroad river crossings is being explored by the port and local authorities with the help of the U.S. and Mexican governments. If implemented, the route will funnel trade into the Port of Brownsville. Congested rail and road routes in central Brownsville would be bypassed and new terminal facilities built near the port. Moreover, major industrial parks, responsive to chronic unemployment and plentiful labor, are planned.

Similar proposals on a more modest scale have been undertaken or are planned for Grays Harbor, where a bypass highway, port expansion, and navigation channel realignment and deepening will improve the capacity and accessibility of this port. Within Grays Harbor County the port has also helped the Washington Public Power Supply System locate and secure the site upon which the Satsop Nuclear Power Plant will be built, pending federal approval.

Port Role in Urban Waterfront Redevelopment

As landlords or lessees of considerable waterfront property, ports can cooperate with coastal management agencies in another important way. Frequently, ports find themselves burdened with obsolete or underutilized waterfront properties in prime urban locations. Working together, ports and coastal management agencies can identify facilities needing rehabilitation. Urban waterfront that is not utilitized by ports can be redeveloped for either long-term or interim use to fulfill non-port related policies of coastal management programs. Many projects have been undertaken by ports, independently or in conjunction with local governments to restore these areas for non-port related commercial or public uses. In Seattle, finger piers that were once owned, leased, or operated by the port have been refurbished for use as specialty shops, waterfront parks and an aquarium. Similar ventures can be seen at Fisherman's Terminal in San

Francisco, Ports of Call in San Pedro Harbor, and Penn's Landing in Philadelphia. Although the Philadelphia development was conducted through the Penn's Landing Corporation, a state-backed nonprofit corporation, the port provided engineering and technical assistance.

MECHANISMS TO ADDRESS MULTIJURISDICTIONAL PORT-RELATED PROBLEMS IN THE COASTAL ZONE

Water bodies on which port facilities are located frequently present jurisdictional problems. Often, river estuaries form state boundary lines (Columbia River, Savannah River, Hudson River, etc.). More frequently an estuary, embayment, or lake lies within several local jurisdictions served by a single port authority, such as Grays Harbor. In other cases two or more port authorities are in close proximity (e.g., Los Angeles/Long Beach), compounding interjurisdictional relations.

Coastal management programs must provide mechanisms for coordinating programs that address regional land- and water-use issues in their states. Dredging projects for channel improvements and maintenance, dredge spoil disposal, and land- and water-use allocation affecting ports need to be dealt with on a water-body-wide scale to insure consistencies among local jurisdictions. While there is generally great resistance to multijurisdictional management programs, the case studies and other sources provided examples of organizational arrangements particularly suited to addressing these regional issues.

At the interstate level, states have an opportunity to develop unified policies to address problems and issues common to contiguous areas of two or more states. Section 309 of the Coastal Zone Management Act, as amended, provides for "interstate grants" to accomplish such interstate coordination. Either formal interstate agreements or compacts (e.g., river basin commissions or interstate compact commissions), or temporary ad hoc planning bodies may be used to achieve the intent of this policy. Funds may soon be available to supplement existing planning and implementation funds.

Multistate River Basin Commissions and Related Organizations

Where ports and coastal management issues span state boundaries, regional commissions and interstate compacts can provide a forum for cooperation. Two regional commissions, the New England River Basin Commission (NERBC) and the Great Lakes Basin Commission (GLBC), do provide support for coastal management programs. Through its member states, NERBC receives coastal management funds to provide staff support to the New England-New York Coastal Zone Task Force. NERBC also studies subjects of interest to coastal program officials, such as outer continental shelf related impacts in the coastal zone. The GLBC has established a standing committee on coastal management that also provides a forum for discussion and, where appropriate, resolution of interstate or regional issues. Recently the committee began to address such port-related topics as transportation of hazardous materials on the Great Lakes, vessel design standards, and shipboard waste handling. Coastal management agencies from all Great Lakes states are represented on the GLBC.

The Delaware River Port Authority (DRPA) operates under a bistate compact between New Jersey and Pennsylvania, and has been concerned primarily with bridges and high-speed transit between the two states. The DRPA also promotes trade for "Ameriports," the three deepwater ports on the Delaware River (Philadelphia, South Jersey, and Wilmington). DRPA has studied the potential of the region to develop support facilities for offshore oil exploration and production and the possibility of deepwater ports in Delaware Bay. These are important coastal management issues and demand a regional perspective. However, DRPA is not addressing two pressing regional issues relevant to the developed portion of the Delaware River: sites for disposing dredged material, and the need for a new container terminal.

In response to outer continental shelf oil and gas development, interstate coordination committees composed of Governors' representatives have been formed on the East and West Coasts. These committees were organized to coordinate and negotiate with large federal agencies to insure that state views are incorporated in agency decisions. Representatives of West Coast states formed the West Coast Oil and Ports Group to coordinate problems of the transportation and importation of Alaskan crude oil, and they have provided specific input to the Federal Energy Administration, Coast Guard, Bureau of Land Management, and other federal agencies. The Mid-Atlantic Governors' Coastal Resources Council has been active in developing state policy on issues of offshore oil and gas development. There have been no direct ties of either group to coastal management program development in the member states, but they may be useful models to apply to interstate port development issues in the future.

Ad hoc Interstate Planning

The Columbia River Estuary Study Team (CREST) in Washington and Oregon has representatives from local governments on both banks of the Columbia River, including the Ports of Astoria, Oregon, and Ilwaco, Washington. CREST is designed to address the land and water issues peculiar to the region and propose policies to local jurisdictions, including ports, implementing the coastal management programs of the two states.

A similar interstate land- and water-use study involving the Great Lakes ports of Duluth and Superior is being conducted by the Metropolitan Interstate Committee. The Department of Housing and Urban Development and the Office of Coastal Zone Management are funding this project under a pilot interagency coordination program because new facilities for increased dry bulk cargo movement, stalled maintenance dredging projects, and urban development pressures all require interstate, interagency coordination. Both the Wisconsin and Minnesota coastal management programs participate in this effort.

Intrastate Regional Planning Commissions

Intrastate regional planning commissions are proving to be an important coordination element for coastal management. Georgia has two regional planning groups—the Savannah/Chatham County Metropolitan Planning Commission (SCCMPC) and the Coastal Area Planning and Development Commission (CAPDC)—working to keep local governments informed of coastal management program developments and, conversely, to bring a local coastal perspective to the state personnel headquartered inland in Atlanta. State coastal management funds support one staff position in the SCCMPC and three in the CAPDC. As coastal management staff, four planners have participated in developing issue papers, including one dealing with ports and waterborne commerce.

Washington also provides an excellent example of the role a regional planning commission may play in program development. In Grays Harbor County the regional planning commission developed a model master program which all participating local governments subsequently adopted with minor revisions. Using the regional commission, local governments were able to simultaneously satisfy planning and public participation requirements of the Shoreline Management Act. The Grays Harbor Regional Planning Council is lead agency for the Grays Harbor Estuary Study.

Independent Advisory Commissions and Councils

Independent advisory commissions or councils, created at the state level and concerned with coastal and marine affairs in general, may be an appropriate forum for reconciling port and coastal management issues. Because of their unique structure, technical coordination committees, under the umbrella of such an organization, may be more effective than either a state line agency or a port effort.

The Texas Coastal and Marine Council is an independent advisory council, which has maintained good relations with the state legislature, the executive branch, and interest groups; at the same time, it has been instrumental in developing much of Texas' recent coastal legislation. The council is considering the merits of forming a technical coordinating committee to address problems common to the state's public ports: air quality and the nondegradation issue, requirements for donating land for wildlife preservation, dredge spoil disposal, and environmental permit procedures. The committee would include key port staff members from all Texas ports and representatives from selected state agencies.

In Washington, a similar group, the Oceanographic Commission of Washington (OCW), has been involved in technical and policy planning for oil transfer facilities and oil tanker movements on inland waters. It is, potentially, an organization which can address other port issues as well.

SUMMARY

Many forums are available for contact between port and coastal management personnel both during program development and program implementation. The effectiveness of each type varies, and is affected by organizational arrangements of the ports and coastal management programs. In general, however, when the interaction is frequent and ongoing, mutually agreeable coastal management programs result. When there is infrequent or ineffectual contact between port authorities and coastal management personnel, policy accords may never be achieved or may be hastily drawn up in legislatures or courts, undermining the legitimate objectives of both activities.

Because coastal management programs are developed at the state and local level, policies affecting the coastal environment and port, trade, and industrial development vary among coastal states. One state's policies may restrict port development while another's promote it, resulting in shifts in trade among ports. This may, in turn, affect total U.S. port capacity. Ports have traditionally argued for free competition among themselves, but if shifts in trade and changes in capacity resulting from coastal management programs become intolerable, it will be necessary to articulate national interests and policies in port development.

State coastal management programs are required to address the question of national interest; however, they have limited information and expertise for such a task. Although some federal agencies collect data on ports and trade, perform regional and national port studies, and review shipping rate structures, there is no single, coordinated national policy addressing port development to guide state coastal management program development. Unless national port interests are addressed, perhaps leading to national policies, port development patterns may be adversely affected differentially by decisions of state and local governments, federal resource agencies, and others.

3. PORTS AND THE DEFINITION OF THE COASTAL ZONE

The definition of the coastal zone under the federal Coastal Zone Management Act should be interpreted broadly to insure full and fair consideration of port development needs and multiple-use problems within the management program.

- Ports that are in reasonable proximity to coastal waters and port development activities that raise significant questions of compatibility with other important coastal users should be included in coastal management programs.

- Ports on channels or rivers somewhat inland from heads of estuaries, which regularly serve ocean or coastal trade, marine fishing, or recreational boating should be included in coastal management programs.

The federal Coastal Zone Management Act defines the coastal zone as extending inland to include shoreland uses which have a direct and significant impact on coastal waters. Most large-scale port development activities in coastal regions fall within this definition, but its ambiguities raise the possibility that some ports or port activities in coastal *regions* could be considered outside the legal definition of coastal *zone* in the federal act. For example, it can be argued that ports serving ocean-going vessels on rivers or channels, beyond tidal influence, are not in the coastal zone because port development activities do not affect coastal waters. It can also be argued that the coastal boundary in urban areas should be drawn at the bulkhead line because port activities inland of this line similarly do not affect coastal waters.

Coastal management program development efforts have not settled on a single, unified approach to defining the coastal zone. Of those programs which have been approved, two approaches are evident. In the first case, the coastal zone boundary is drawn a relatively short distance inland (i.e., 100-200 feet): port development proposed within this area is subject to special permitting procedures, while some inland port activities are not. In the second case, the boundary is drawn further inland (up to 1000 yards, for example, or to include whole coastal counties) but there is no special permitting procedure. Plans and controls which local governments have traditionally applied to port development activities—such as zoning—are augmented with state and regional coastal policies and procedures. This second approach includes more port development activities than the first but does not impose additional permit requirements.

These boundary definitions are not mutually exclusive. Some states employ both a narrow "permit zone" and a wider "planning area" in their programs in a two-tiered approach to defining the coastal zone.

4. PORT PARTICIPATION IN COASTAL MANAGEMENT PROGRAMS

Coastal management program personnel should actively solicit ongoing port participation in the development of coastal policies and plans.

- Port officials should serve on formally established advisory committees to insure regular and effective dialogue on policy issues concerning port development and other interests.

- Coastal ports should develop organizational units within their state or regional port associations so that they are at the same governmental level (i.e., state, county, or local) as the coastal management programs.

- Ports should provide relevant information to coastal planners regarding cargo characteristics and trends, facilities and port-controlled land uses, port administration, organization and financing, and major future plans and capital expenditure programs.

- If necessary, the status and trends of port development within a state or region should be assessed by independent experts, mutually acceptable to ports and the coastal management program, to provide information for program development. Ports should participate in designing such studies and reviewing the findings.

Ports should assist in refining or implementing appropriate elements of coastal management programs.

- Ports should play a lead role in implementing economic development objectives in coastal areas designated for that purpose.

- Ports should assist in developing a dredged material management program (see recommendation 9) and an obsolete facilties redevelopment program (see recommendation 8), coordinating permit requirements (see recommendation 6), and identifying research and environmental assessment needs.

- The California approach (Southern California port authorities are now developing and implementing port master plans, covering port and nonport related uses) should be evaluated to determine if port authorities, rather than local governments, are the appropriate governmental unit to handle this function.

Coastal management programs consider issues that are important to ports, such as future economic growth in coastal regions, the interconnection of transportation modes, and the relationship of commercial and industrial development activities to such uses as recreation, fisheries, and wildlife enhancement. The competing uses can only be balanced if the users—such as ports with a stake in the region—are fully involved in the program.

Port participation in coastal management program development has varied widely. Some ports often provided information and policy input, while others had no contact with coastal management program personnel. Some coastal management programs identified ports as key coastal users early in program development, generated special port studies, and made special initiatives to ports through public information programs. Other programs neglected ports, dealt with port issues late in the planning process, or dealt with port questions through an intermediary (such as a local government unit).

When ports and coastal management programs did interact, they became sensitive to each other's problems and responsibilities. Port officials recognized the broad planning and environmental mandates of coastal management programs and sought adequate attention to ports in them. Coastal management officials recognized the economic importance of ports and understood the competitive framework in which they operate. Continued interaction between the two groups should increase understanding and help them to avoid legal or political disputes.

Although there was some participation and mutual education of port and coastal management officials in almost all case study states, interactions during program development tended to remain at the broad policy level. Even then, ports largely reacted to policies that had already been drafted. Technical planning coordination on such issues as dredged material management, trade forecasts, and facility needs rarely occurred prior to policy formulation. Since most coastal management programs are still in the program development—rather than program implementation—phase, and the time frame for program development is short, the emphasis on broader policy matters is understandable. Detailed, refined planning is expected in most cases after the programs are approved, as is now occurring in Washington State and the San Francisco Bay region.

One explanation for ineffective or nonexistent interaction between ports and coastal management programs relates to the level of government at which the two activities are focused. In the case studies, communication between port authority and coastal management program officials occurred most smoothly if they were at the same level of government. When a program is developed at the state level, it is best for ports to develop a statewide view of port issues and to share information within port associations, informal multiport coordinating groups, or a state port authority. Similarly, programs developed at the local level dealt best with port issues when the port authority jurisdiction was also at the local level. Where the governmental levels of the two activities differed, special mechanisms for interaction between them were created—such as special port association committees or specially designated port representative seats on coastal management program committees.

In the case studies observed, the most effective ongoing interaction between ports and coastal management occurred when ports belonged to formal coastal management advisory or planning committees. The regular, face-to-face interaction allowed the people on the committee to identify critical issues and exchange useful information. It facilitated, as well, the development of mutual sensitivity and understanding of each other's programs and needs.

The boldest effort in the country to involve port authorities directly in coastal management programs is in California, where ports develop and implement master plans for their area, subject to state oversight and review. Public port authorities have traditionally been special purpose public agencies concentrating in marine commerce, economic development, and related transportation functions. In some cases, when required by law, recreational boating and commercial fishery needs have been accommodated by port authorities. California's requirement—that ports now consider public access and recreational and environmental values in reviewing activities that occur in their legal geographic boundary—is an example of a significant departure from traditional port functions.

5. DEVELOPMENT OF REGIONAL LAND- AND WATER-USE ALLOCATION PLANS

Proposed port development activities should be reviewed in accordance with a substate/regional use allocation plan, which should relate existing port facilities to regional needs, subject to coastal environmental constraints.

- A multiagency government task force or committee (led by the coastal management program and including all levels of government and port authorities) should develop the use allocation plan. Its objectives should be to agree on specific areas and locations for phased, longterm port development.

- The plan should include performance standards addressing conservation of waterfront land, avoidance of adverse environmental impact, provision of public access, and environmental mitigation features. More intensive use of existing port lands and locating port activities that do not require a shoreline inland should be urged to conserve waterfront land. Public access and environmental mitigation requirements should be required where port development preempts public use and identified environmental values are sacrificed for port development.

- The task force or committee should be assisted by citizen and technical advisory panels, and by independent consultants. technical assistance from the national level should be provided (See recommendation 7.)

- The plan should be implemented by incorporating it into each participating agency's existing review procedures.

- Where multiple-use problems involving port development occur in a water body common to two states (e.g., Duluth, Minnesota, and Superior, Wisconsin), a multiagency task force or committee approach should be taken. Existing river basin commissions and regional commissions might be used to assist this function.

- Development activities should be monitored for conformance with the allocation plan and its performance standards. The plan should be reviewed and updated periodically.

- Prior to and during the development of the land- and water-use allocation plan, port development activities should be reviewed on a project-by-project basis, augmented by interim performance standards adopted by the coastal management program with the participation of port representatives.

Because of increased user demand for shoreland space and interest in recreational development and environmental protection, governmental review of port development projects is complex and involves many different agencies. The problems of competing uses faced by these agencies involve complex environmental impact and land-use issues.

Development projects tend to be addressed on a project-by-project basis. Many resource conservation and land-use planning agencies now oppose this review approach. They argue that the key issues are the cumulative effect of the projects and the lack of any foreseeable limits on the encroachment of development activities into environmentally sensitive or recreationally important areas. They urge that plans be developed to determine long-term future uses of particular areas, and that this be done before decisions are made on major individual projects. Such approaches are now being developed by the San Francisco Bay Conservation and Development Commission and in Grays Harbor, Washington.

Coastal management programs must consider future uses in particular areas *and* significant environmental impacts. The federal Coastal Zone Management Act requires that permissible uses be identified and guidelines be developed for determining the priority of uses in particular areas. To date, coastal management programs have developed procedures for considering competing land- and water-use issues and broad decision-making policies, but very little planning has been done to accommodate specific uses in specific areas of the coast. This has inhibited the resolution of some multiple-use problems and caused two of the more experienced programs in the nation—Washington's and California's San Francisco Bay Conservation and Development Commission—to establish special task force studies to look into port development activities long after their respective programs had begun operating. Land- and water-use allocation schemes should benefit ports, since existing, uncoordinated environmental programs have frequently caused substantial delays or denials of proposed port development activities. In principle, mature coastal management programs should facilitate port development; policies will be clarified in advance, thereby removing much of the uncertainty of project approval.

6. RESOLVING PERMIT DELAY PROBLEMS

Coastal management agencies should develop a project review system to identify required permits and to comment on proposed projects before financial commitments are made.

Applications for development activities should be processed rapidly and reviewed thoroughly. Time limits should be specified for processing permit applications for small noncontroversial projects. Coastal management programs should initiate development of a rational permit review system among environmental and land-use agencies, to avoid duplication and encourage coordination.

Port authorities should assist their lessees to obtain necessary permits for facility development projects and meet land-use and environmental requirements.

Port facility development projects must be approved by local or state land-use planning agencies, state and federal environmental and resource management agencies, the Corps of Engineers, and others before they can be undertaken. The number of reviewing agencies has increased dramatically in recent years, and each project receives increasingly detailed scrutiny. Sequential review procedures often delay final resolution of port development project. Delays can be especially long where projects occur in sensitive environments, or are otherwise controversial.

Coastal management programs are required to closely coordinate their efforts with other governmental agencies. There is pressure from users and elected officials to avoid redundancy and streamline government permit processes. For this reason, coastal management programs should enhance their efforts to resolve the problems of duplication and delay in the review process.

7. INFORMATION EXCHANGE AND TECHNICAL ASSISTANCE

Port authorities and coastal management programs should continue to exchange information, including programs of technical assistance and continuing education. The Sea Grant Program's research and advisory services activities should assist (when appropriate) this information function. Exchange of personnel between port authorities and coastal management programs should be encouraged. Three important components of a technical assistance program should be included:

- Information and techniques to determine future port facility needs should be available to state and local land-use and environmental management personnel, including—

  projections of foreign trade,
  fleet characteristics,
  methods for calculating port capacity, and
  cargo-handling technology and related land-use requirements.

- Coastal management programs and the Corps of Engineers should sponsor planning workshops on regional dredged material management for development, environmental, and recreational interests. They should stress technical, economic, and planning aspects of the use or disposal of dredged material for commercial, environmental, or recreational development purposes.

- A national conference should be initiated by the federal Office of Coastal Zone Management on the potential for redevelopment of obsolete port facilities in urban waterfront areas. (See recommendation 8). It should involve interested governmental, industrial, and professional organizations and should consider potential use alternatives, planning and design factors, funding mechanisms (including strategies for combined public and private redevelopment ventures), and methods for coastal management program participation at local, state, and federal levels.

The federal Office of Coastal Zone Management should enhance its research and technical assistance activities, and Congress should act expeditiously to appropriate funds to carry out its legislative intent for this function. Port-related technical assistance should address the following:

- Port operations and cargo storage and handling practices as they relate to waterfront land use, and appropriate technologies and practices for efficient use of shoreland space.

- Monitoring the performance of coastal management programs and their effect on port development. Results would provide a basis for proposing coastal program modifications if inefficiencies or inequities become apparent.

- Needs identified by port and coastal management personnel polled frequently by the Office of Coastal Zone Management.

Information exchange between port and coastal management officials has varied considerably around the country, mostly focusing on broad policy issues, not technical matters. Until now, information exchange, in the form of technical assistance and detailed planning coordination, has occurred only with respect to particular project proposals.

The need for information exchange is likely to increase. Coastal management programs are maturing, and in future years will develop detailed plans and programs related to particular coastal user groups, such as ports. Port and shipping technology is changing and creating needs for new shorefront facilities, which must be reviewed and approved by coastal management programs and other agencies. Special problems such as dredged material management and redevelopment of obsolete waterfront facilities will require close planning coordination. Also, as competition for space in crowded coastal areas becomes more acute, port development needs and the needs of other user groups will have to be analyzed and trade-offs made in the preparation of shoreland allocation schemes. These future interactions will be more effective and result in better use of coastal resources if the respective participants are informed about each other's policies, operations, and objectives.

8. REDEVELOPMENT OF OBSOLETE PORT FACILITIES

Coastal management programs should give greater attention to the resolution of urban waterfront problems since they offer opportunities for improving the built environment, broadening the economic base of a region, and enhancing the recreational opportunities of a state. Using coastal management program funds, general purpose units of local government should identify obsolete or underutilized waterfront facilities in their jurisdictions that have potential for redevelopment to meet port or non-port uses on a permanent or interim basis. Redevelopment programs should address the following:

- Strategies for intergovernmental coordination, private sector cooperation, and port authority participation.

- Identification of potential funding sources, including federal, state, and local government and port authority capital improvement funds, or development of a new coastal conservation and development fund (see recommendation 10).

- Port policies that give consideration to the potential for redevelopment of waterfronts for non-port purposes, specifically those policies which address leasing or disposal of obsolete or underutilized facilities and surplus lands.

Ports are often plagued with obsolete or underutilized facilities that can no longer serve modern ships and cargo-handling equipment. Although they can sometimes be renovated or redesigned to meet modern shipping needs, in many areas these facilities are adjacent to congested urban areas and the back-up space and land transportation connections are inadequate. Further, urban waterfront areas are changing; expanded central business district activities, historic districts, and revitalized neighborhoods are out-of-character and incompatible with modern port terminal operations.

In many cities, obsolete waterfront facilities are being transformed to serve non-port functions. Parks, marinas, novelty and import retail trade, restaurants, promenades, housing, and office buildings are appearing where port, rail, and warehouse activities once were located. A combination of public urban renewal programs, public works projects, and private capital investment has supported most waterfront redevelopment and renovation. Port authorities have cooperated with government agencies and private investors by providing technical assistance, buildings, and surplus lands to aid redevelopment. However, the initiative for such projects has tended to come from outside the port and trade community. Because ports view this type of redevelopment as ancillary to their primary goal of serving marine commerce and associated industrial development, some ports allow non-port use of waterfront facilities on an interim basis only, thus reserving future use of the area for their own needs.

Coastal management programs have given priority, in these early years, to rural and urban fringe regions of the coastal zone, where many environmental and recreational issues are pressing. However, urban waterfront areas and redevelopment of obsolete facilities are beginning to receive attention, and policies for urban waterfront redevelopment are emerging. While coastal management funds may not be used for capital improvement projects, they can be used for planning waterfront programs.

9. MITIGATING THE ADVERSE EFFECTS OF DREDGING, DREDGED MATERIAL DISPOSAL, AND LANDFILL

Coastal management programs should require dredged material management plans within those estuarine regions of the state where channel improvement and maintenance activities occur. The plan should be developed by an interagency task force led by the coastal management program and appropriate port authorities, with independent consultants and advisory panels to assist them (see recommendation 5). It should identify potential uses of dredged material to serve multiple needs, including—

fish and wildlife habitat improvement
recreational development
landfill for port use
scientific and public education

• Use of dredged material should be determined by needs identified in the plan, giving weight to both environmental and recreational needs, as well as landfill and disposal needs. An information clearinghouse should be established to promote regional coordination of dredged or excavated material supply with use sites, both upland and coastal.

• Financing mechanisms appropriate for achieving the objectives of the plan should be identified, such as federal civil works funds, user charges imposed and collected by port authorities, state and local bonds, or a coastal conservation and development fund (see recommendation 10).

Major port development activities often require dredging for channel maintenance and improvement, disposal of dredged material, and creation of new landfill. The Corps of Engineers, through its civil works program, is responsible for channel improvements and dredged material disposal. Planning for dredged material use or disposal—traditionally the responsibility of the Corps, local sponsors (e.g., port authorities), fish and wildlife agencies, and state waterbottom management agencies—has related to specific projects and normally has not included local or regional land-use planning agencies, or coastal management programs. Although dredged material management has been viewed as a disposal problem rather than a resource management problem, research, experiments, and demonstration projects in recent years show great potential for using dredged material for marsh creation, erosion control, habitat islands, and aquaculture.

Where wetlands or water bodies are involved, state and federal fish, wildlife, and pollution control agencies watch development activities carefully to insure minimum damage to fish and wildlife resources. They may require that mitigating and compensating features be added to development projects to make up for any harm to resources or recreational uses. Requiring developers to dedicate natural areas to public use in exchange for the development area is one form of mitigation. There have been conflicts, however, over whether an agency can compel mitigation, how to measure the extent of environmental harm, how to fund additional costs, and how to determine the appropriate site and techniques for implementing the mitigation program.

Coastal management programs are beginning to develop mitigation policies in connection with dredge and fill activities. California requires mitigation by replacement for filled wetlands, and Oregon requires restoration of biological potential within estuaries. In other states, mitigation policies will likely be formulated as coastal management programs mature, since federal and state fish and wildlife agencies (with whom they must deal closely) regularly apply such mitigation requirements.

10. CAPITAL IMPROVEMENT PROJECTS TO ENHANCE THE COASTAL ENVIRONMENT

Coastal management programs should include the capability to finance selected capital improvement projects, which enhance the goals and objectives of the program and go beyond the specialized programs available through federal coastal management sources (estuarine sanctuary, public access acquisition, and energy facility impact assistance).

A state-level conservation and development fund should be established, drawing upon the example of the California State Coastal Conservancy (discussed below), to supplement private investment and traditional federal, state, and local capital improvement funding sources. Use of the fund should be limited to coastal enhancement projects, which are certified as consistent with the state's coastal management program. The fund could be used to provide the state's share of federally supported projects, to participate with private developers in redevelopment activities, to assist in land acquisition and retention, to help pay for rehabilitation of environmentally degraded coastal areas, or to add public-use features to development projects.

Most aspects of coastal management program implementation and administration—including regulatory procedures, planning, and coordination activities—can be funded by combined federal Office of Coastal Zone Management (80 percent) and state matching funds (20 percent). Although these funds cannot be used for capital improvements, in some cases there are opportunities to achieve specific coastal goals through capital improvements. The redevelopment of obsolete waterfront facilities (see recommendation 8) and aspects of dredged material management (see recommendation 9) are two examples of coastal program goals that require capital investment funding.

The federal Office of Coastal Zone Management has two specialized programs which do allow capital expenditures. The new Coastal Energy Impact Program (CEIP) provides loans and grants to local governments to help pay for local capital improvement projects necessitated by outer continental shelf oil and gas development. The CEIP also provides funds to ameliorate environmental and recreational losses resulting from coastal energy activities. Further, the federal office of Coastal Zone Management will pay up to 50 percent of the cost of acquiring and managing estuarine sanctuaries and acquiring access lands to coastal areas. These funds may, in limited instances, be available for port-related capital improvement activities—for example, assisting a port authority to finance a new facility that is necessary to serve outer continental shelf oil and gas activities, or acquiring land for redevelopment of old facilities or public access.

Although the Office of Coastal Zone Management and the Coastal Energy Impact Program capital improvement funds are limited by amount and purpose, there are other federal funds available for capital improvements that, while not oriented toward coastal activities, could be used for that purpose: land and water conservation funds for park acquisition, urban renewal funds for land acquisition in connection with redevelopment, and public works assistance funds. Further, the amount of federal funds available, and the purpose for which they can be used, vary greatly from year to year.

There are other potential sources for capital improvement financing. Funds for coastal improvement projects can be authorized through voter-approved bond issues, or by state legislature or city council appropriations. These tend to be allocated on a project-by-project basis. There has also been considerable private investment in coastal enhancement activities, much of it in urban waterfront areas where old piers and wharves have been restored for new commercial and recreational purposes.

California has adopted a coastal-oriented capital improvement program as a part of its coastal management activities. The state coastal conservancy is authorized to—

1. Acquire and protect coastal agricultural lands;

2. Restore, redesign, and improve land use that affects the coastal environment;

3. Enhance the natural and scenic values of coastal resources by correcting previous misuse—such as indiscriminate dredging and filling and improperly located or designed improvements;

4. Acquire lands within "buffer areas" to protect beaches, parks, natural areas, and fish and wildlife preserves;

5. Provide loans to allow significant coastal resource sites to be held and reserved for ultimate public use purposes;

6. Acquire public accessways to the coast.

Implementation of California's coastal conservancy law has just begun. It holds significant potential for port-related enhancement and restoration projects.

7 CASE STUDIES

Case studies of port authorities and coastal management programs proved to be the best vehicle for determining the most important land and water issues faced at present, the types of interaction between the two groups, and the policies emerging in coastal management programs that deal with port development issues. Six case study areas were selected for detailed analysis which summarize the activities of seven port authorities and seven coastal management programs. (One case study involved two states and two port authorities—the Philadelphia Port Corporation and the South Jersey Port Corporation in the Delaware River portion of Pennsylvania and New Jersey.)

In addition to the case studies, documents from four additional state or port authority areas were used: Port of Seattle, Washington; Massport, at Boston, Massachusetts; San Francisco Bay Conservation and Development Commission, California; and, the state of Oregon. Policies that are being developed in these areas were especially useful in rounding out the information base.

Case study information was compiled by researchers who visited each of the case study areas for three to five days, from September through December 1976. They collected key documents from port authorities and coastal management program offices, including statutes and regulations, plans and policy studies, annual reports, and other relevant studies and documents. They visited port facilities and coastal areas, especially those stretches of coast considered to be possible areas for future port development. They interviewed port directors and their aides, representatives of lessees or shipping companies, city or county planning officials, state and regional coastal management program staff, and some key federal agency personnel. The information summarized in the case study reports is current through the summer of 1977.

Each case study begins with a summary of the most important aspects of port and coastal management program development and how they interact. Port development and coastal management program development are then discussed in detail.

PORT OF MILWAUKEE/WISCONSIN COASTAL MANAGEMENT PROGRAM

Summary

The Port of Milwaukee is governed by a five-member Board of Harbor Commissioners under close city supervision. The city common council controls the port budget and must approve all plans for harbor improvements and industrial leases.

Although the Port of Milwaukee is one of the few ports on the Great Lakes which is free of ice year round, it is currently experiencing a decline in trade. General cargo movements are limited by the size of ships that can use the St. Lawrence Seaway. In addition, because of a single-rate

The Port of Milwaukee, looking north: center, Jones Island; right, outer harbor; and left, the V-shaped Municipal Mooring Basin. (Photo by Clair J. Wilson, courtesy of the City of Milwaukee, Board of Harbor Commissioners)

freight structure connecting sea transport with rail and truck service, ocean ports are used more and more to serve the interior states, thereby reducing trade with Great Lakes ports. The decline may reverse if the production of and trade in coal—the port's major export—increases.

Declining cargo requirements, limitations on the sewer system, and apparent city preferences for recreational development presently limit any major port development plans. Instead, finding alternative non-port uses for port facilities and sites and improving air and water quality around the port are issues that now involve the port and have implications for the state's coastal program.

The Wisconsin coastal management program is in its third year of development; its proposed program is now being circulated for review (Wisconsin Coastal Coordinating and Advisory Council, 1977).* At this time the state proposes to rely on existing local, regional, and state authorities, such as the Shorelands Act, which regulates shoreland uses in unincorporated county areas (Lauf, 1975), to regulate uses in the coastal zone.

Wisconsin has taken an aggressive role in dealing with port issues. First, background material on ports essential for decision making was compiled (Mayer, 1975). Information on ports has been widely disseminated and public opinion has been actively sought on the issue of future port development in Wisconsin.

Three alternatives for addressing port-related issues were postulated during the early stages of policy development. First, the coastal program

* It was formally approved in 1978.

might continue the state's present laissez-faire practice of not intervening or directing future port development patterns. Second, the program could actively promote the present system of port development, encouraging each port to maintain its current competitive position. Third, the state program could actively promote a plan for directing port growth. Under this last approach, one proposed policy would be to focus shipping activities in major ports and convert some smaller ports for recreational small-craft moorage. (Wisconsin Department of Transportation, 1976).

The coastal program presently under consideration fails to address port issues to the extent indicated by the preparatory work. The proposed coastal management policy stipulates only that the program will advocate "the role of Great Lakes ports both within the state and at the national level" (Wisconsin Coastal Coordinating and Advisory Council, 1977). The proposal also recommends that a state Citizens' Advisory Committee include representatives of shipping and port interests.

Although the Port of Milwaukee has not actively participated in the state coastal program, it could do so through its director's membership on two planning advisory committees. One of them, the Citizens' Advisory Committee, advises the Coastal Zone Coordinating and Advisory Council, thereby having a direct relationship to the coastal program. The port director also sits on a technical advisory committee to the Southeast Wisconsin Regional Planning Commission. Because that commission has been delegated some responsibility in developing Wisconsin's coastal program, the technical advisory committee indirectly affects it.

Port of Milwaukee, Wisconsin

Location and physical characteristics. Located on the west shore of Lake Michigan, the Port of Milwaukee is one of the few ports on the Great Lakes open to navigation throughout the year. Although there is traffic year round on Lake Michigan, interlake vessel movement ceases from about mid-December to mid-April because of ice conditions at the Straits of Mackinac. The port lies wholly within Milwaukee city limits and consists of two main groups of facilities:

1. An outer commercial harbor protected by a breakwater—known as Jones Island—is the municipal port area administered by the port's Board of Commissioners.

2. An inner commercial harbor is located on the three rivers which flow through the city; the confluence of the Milwaukee, Menominee, and Kinnickinnic Rivers with Lake Michigan occurs at the entrance to the inner harbor. This is an industrial and coal-receiving area, with many railroad yards.

The direct approach to the outer piers is one of the main assets of the Port of Milwaukee, and the Corps of Engineers has deepened the port's channels to full St. Lawrence Seaway draft of 28 feet.

Cargo characteristics. In 1975, the Port of Milwaukee handled approximately six million tons of cargo. The Municipal Harbor Terminal facilities handled about 41.1 percent of the total port commerce, while the balance was handled at private docks. Principal commodities are coal, cement, limestone, clay, sand and gravel, gasoline and nonmetallic minerals.

The Port of Milwaukee is presently in a state of decline, and is unable to use all its facilities to capacity (Figure 7.1). There is a problem finding new uses for old terminals.

There are three major factors affecting the Port of Milwaukee and the Great Lakes as a whole (Schenker and Smith, 1973):

1. Very large vessels cannot enter the St. Lawrence Seaway system and cannot call at Great Lakes ports.

2. The development of containerization eliminated many tons of general cargo from the Port of Milwaukee. The port was particularly affected by the development of the Port of Halifax, Nova Scotia, and shipment of containers inland by rail. General cargo that traditionally came from Europe and the Far East to Milwaukee now is off-loaded at Halifax and Seattle.

3. Shippers who once used all water transportation for goods now take advantage of the interstate highway system, thereby shifting cargo from the Great Lakes ports to coastal ports.

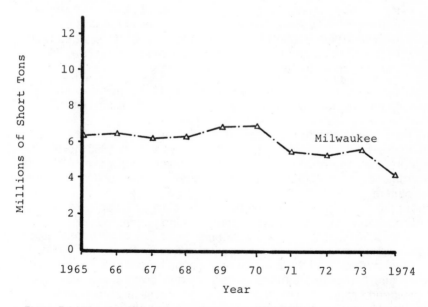

Figure 7.1 Milwaukee net total cargo tonnages, 1965-1974. Source: Corps of Engineers, 1974. *Waterborne Commerce of the United States.* Volume 4, p. 7.4a.

In addition, there are factors that especially have affected the Port of Milwaukee; coal shipments—the port's major commodity—have declined, automobiles once transported by water are now usually carried by rail, and oil pipelines have been constructed which greatly reduced the amount of oil transported through this port.

Port facilities. The Port of Milwaukee has both public and private dock facilities. There are specialized coal docks which handle large tonnages of lakeborne coal. Waterborne petroleum transshipment takes place at private terminals concentrated on Jones Island. The port is well-equipped to serve the general cargo trade with either municipally or privately owned terminals. Other port facilities include a car ferry terminal, cement and building material wharves, grain elevators, open docks, and a heavy-lift crane. Major port facilities are described below (Figure 7.2):

1. Petroleum terminal: Six oil companies have built modern terminals on leased harbor property on Jones Island. Waterborne petroleum receipts are 500,000 to one million tons per year; storage capacity is approximately 80 million gallons.

2. Municipal car ferry terminal: Milwaukee's first municipal port facility was placed in service in 1929; it was renovated and expanded in 1960. The facility handles more than 69,000 railroad cars and approximately 21,000 tourist automobiles each year.

3. Municipal heavy-lift facilities: Milwaukee has a reputation as the pioneer heavy-lift port on the Great Lakes. The largest crane on the U.S. side of the Great Lakes was put into service there in 1960; it can lift up to 200 tons. The city's 1,860-foot heavy-lift dock handles heavy bulk commodities such as steel, pig iron, scrap metal, and heavy machinery.

4. Continental Grain Company elevators: These privately owned grain elevators have a storage capacity of 3.5 million bushels.

Port administration. A hearing conducted by the Great Lakes Port Committee and subsequent study of port laws led, in 1958, to the basic statutory authority governing ports in Wisconsin. The statutes give local governments the authority to create a Board of Harbor Commissioners and generally outline the board's powers to develop, operate, and maintain a port. The statutes also emphasize the state philosophy of local control and foster a competitive atmosphere among commercial ports.

The Board of Harbor Commissioners of the City of Milwaukee is composed of five members, appointed by the mayor for three-year terms, subject to confirmation by the city common council. Board membership is honorary and carries no compensation. Salaried civil service staff execute policies and programs. The board can retain necessary administrative and engineering personnel, but its annual budget—both for operational purposes and for construction—is controlled by the common council.

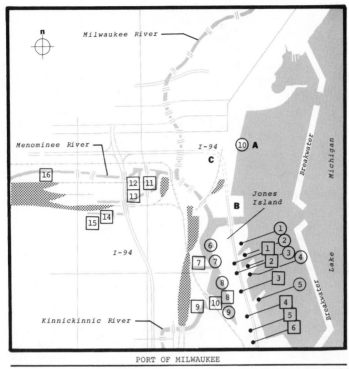

PORT OF MILWAUKEE

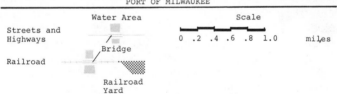

Streets and Highways

Water Area

Bridge

Railroad

Railroad Yard

Scale

0 .2 .4 .6 .8 1.0   miles

Figure 7.2 Port of Milwaukee. Port-owned facilities ◯ : (1) general cargo terminal No. 1; (2) general cargo terminal No. 2; (3) general cargo terminal No. 3; (4) general cargo terminal No. 4; (5) liquid cargo pier; (6) car ferry slip; (7) heavy lift dock; (8) bulk cargo dock; (9) municipal mooring basin; (10) municipal passenger pier.

Privately owned facilities ☐ : (1) American Oil Company; (2) Mobil Oil Corporation; (3) Shell Oil Company; (4) Texaco; (5) Wisconsin Petroleum terminals; (6) Phillips Petroleum; (7) Atlantic Richfield Company; (8) International Salt Company; (9) Milwaukee Solvay Coke Company; (10) Continental Grain Company; (11) Morton Salt Company; (12) Universal Atlas Cement; (13) Marquette Cement; (14) Huron Cement; (15) Penn Dixie Cement; (16) Great Lakes Coal and Dock Company.

Issue areas: **A**. unused passenger terminal; **B**. vacant 20-acre landfill; **C**. uncompleted freeway; **D**. Fishermen's Park.

Source: National Ocean Survey, 1972. Milwaukee Harbor, Wisconsin, Chart No. 743.

Under the Wisconsin statutes, the board is authorized to plan, construct, operate and maintain docks, wharves, warehouses, piers, and other port facilities for the needs of commerce and shipping. It is authorized to plan improvements of all waterways within the city, and to plan, construct and operate airports contiguous to the waterfront. Plans and projects for harbor improvement and industrial leases all must be approved by the council, but the board has exclusive authority over the day-to-day commercial operations of the public port.

The board also serves as the promotional agency for development of the commerce of the port, and has been successful in attracting industrial development. It advises the mayor and council with respect to transportation developments and serves as a legislative watchdog to guard against legislation—whether state or national—adverse to the economic and transportation interests of Milwaukee's waterfront.

Major planning and capital expansion programs. Because of the decline of the port, there are no major expansion plans at present; moreover, the City of Milwaukee has not indicated any interest in port expansion projects. Land for future port development is close to downtown and would conflict with expansion of the central business district.

Issues of current importance. Deteriorated dock facilities in the inner harbor and internal waterways require major redevelopment investment. The city is proposing a major redevelopment in the waterway area which will phase out obsolete port facilities in favor of barge traffic and land transportation links. However, urban renewal funds cannot be used for redevelopment because the city already owns the land. Another potential problem is that overlapping leases and lessee-owned improvements effectively preclude major aggregations of land for redevelopment.

Significant acreage of filled land, both north and south of the harbor area, remains vacant. Interim uses of these holdings include a Summerfest (fairground structures utilized for only two weeks per year), parking for a car convoy company, and a salt packaging plant. Other uses were discussed, but they were abandoned because the other leasehold arrangements considered by the city were unacceptable to private industry.

The port asserts that its vacant land should be reserved for commercial water-dependent activities and port use, not for recreational boating facilities. The county parks system services recreational needs at sites both north and south of the port's holdings.

Air and water quality standards are also issues within the port area. In the Menominee River Valley and the harbor, air quality is degraded and in the outer harbor inadequate sewage facilities preclude significant new connections to the sewer line.

Wisconsin's Coastal Management Program
Overview and implementing authority. Coastal management program development activities are currently being conducted by the Office

of State Planning and Energy. Through June 1976, program development funding totalled $1,197,315. The planning office is coordinating studies of potential policies, procedures, and implementing authorities to improve and enhance coastal management capabilities and to suggest specific actions to bring state and local efforts into line with requirements of the federal Coastal Zone Management Act. A comprehensive coastal management program proposal was issued in March 1977, and is being reviewed.

The coastal management program will rely on programs of the State Departments of Natural Resources, Transportation, Local Affairs and Development, Business Development, and the Public Service Commission. A state-level Coastal Management Council is proposed to oversee the programs. Although the coastal council would assume none of the responsibilities of existing state agencies, it would coordinate the programs and provide funds to each to improve management capabilities.

At the regional level, the proposed coastal program would fund the efforts of the three regional planning commissions to support public participation, technical assistance, and governmental coordination related to coastal issues.

Local planning and management at the city, county, and special district levels will continue as it is currently done. The state will intervene only when local governments request technical and financial assistance to resolve a coastal problem. When the state is already involved—as in shoreland and flood plain management—the coastal program would work to improve state standards and help the local governments to meet them.

Land and water use. Sources of input for establishing permissible and priority uses of Wisconsin shorelines come from local responses solicited by the regional planning commission, policy papers prepared by the state, and a group of university faculty. Priority issues identified by the state include air and water quality, shore erosion, protection of natural areas, public recreational access, port development, lake level regulation, Great Lakes fisheries, urban shore uses, economic development, power plant siting, and shoreland blight. The objectives of the Wisconsin program are to:

1. Advocate the wise and balanced use of the coastal environment;

2. Increase public awareness and participation in coastal resource decisions;

3. Coordinate existing government policies and activities;

4. Improve the implementation and enforcement of existing programs and policies;

5. Strengthen local government management capabilities.

Coastal zone boundaries. The proposed jurisdiction for the coastal program includes the state waters of Michigan, Lake Superior, Green Bay

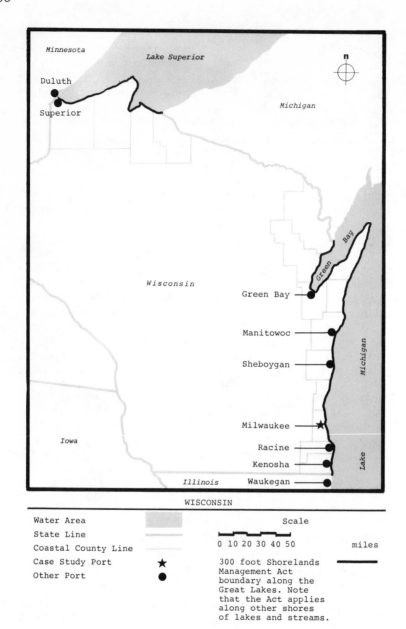

Figure 7.3 State of Wisconsin

and the total land area of the fifteen coastal counties (Figure 7.3). Within this broad area, specific areas will be identified for special management. At a minimum, the coastal zone boundary would incorporate within the fifteen coastal counties the management area of the present Wisconsin Shorelands Act. This statute includes all unincorporated lands 1,000 feet from lakes and 300 feet from streams or to the landward side of the flood plain, whichever is greater. (Lauf, 1975, p. 50).

Geographic areas of particular concern. In the proposed Wisconsin program, geographic areas of particular concern (GAPCs) delineate areas of significant scientific, natural, recreational, or historical value, areas especially suitable for water-related economic benefit, hazard areas, approved power plant sites, and areas requiring preservation or restoration. Designations will last between one and three years. At the end of the designated period these areas will be reassessed.

Before an area can be designated, geographic boundaries must be determined, management policies delineated, and implementation of policies authorized. Local governments, state agencies, interest groups, or private citizens can nominate an area to be a GAPC.

Public and governmental involvement. The proposed program was developed by the Coastal Zone Coordinating and Advisory Council. Council members represent state agencies, regional planning commissions, local governments, tribal governments, the University of Wisconsin, and public interest groups. Public viewpoints are expressed to the council through the Citizens' Advisory Committee, composed of citizens and public interest groups. Three regional planning commissions, which have jurisdiction on the Great Lakes, also participate in the coastal program. Each of these commissions is advised by a technical and a citizen advisory committee. Eleven public hearings were held in Wisconsin between May 10, 1977 and June 2, 1977 to solicit comments on the proposed management program.

The proposed program would establish an independently staffed, 27-member Citizens' Advisory Committee concerned primarily with monitoring the initial implementation of the program and with public education and participation.

State and local organizational arrangements. The plan submitted by the Coastal Zone Coordinating and Advisory Council calls for a strengthened state-local partnership and a state-level Coastal Management Council to make policy decisions and administer the program. The 29-member council would be composed of state legislators, local officials, citizens, tribal governments, and state agency representatives.

State-federal interaction and national interest. Wisconsin has a list of required contacts provided by the federal Office of Coastal Zone Management. These sets of contacts, in conjunction with the Great Lakes Basin Commission, provide the vehicles for communication, coordination, and substantive input between the Wisconsin program and appropriate federal agencies.

The state has asked federal agencies that own land in the coastal area to identify their land holdings and the management plans for those lands.

Existing review procedures, corresponding state permits, coastal management certificates of consistency and memoranda of understanding will be used to insure compatibility between the state coastal program and federal programs and activities.

DELAWARE RIVER AND BAY REGION

There are three major ports in the Delaware River and Bay region—Philadelphia, South Jersey (at Camden, across the river from Philadelphia) and Wilmington, Delaware. This region was chosen for study primarily because it represents a multiport and multistate region connected by a common water body. It provided an opportunity to analyze regional coordination and interaction on coastal land and water issues. Only the ports of Philadelphia and South Jersey were studied because it was believed that coordination and interaction problems of these two major ports would sufficiently illustrate regional problems.

There is only minimal coordination and interaction between the ports and the states on coastal land- and water-use issues, and no apparent attempts at a regional approach, in spite of the regional Delaware River Port Authority. For this reason, two regional agencies—the Delaware River Port Authority and the Delaware River Basin Commission—are only briefly discussed in this section. New Jersey and Pennsylvania ports and coastal management programs are presented in the following sections.

The Delaware River Port Authority (DRPA) was established as an interstate compact between Pennsylvania and New Jersey primarily to build and operate bridges across the Delaware River and to develop a mass transit system between Philadelphia and New Jersey communities. Legislation was proposed in 1967 and 1968 to enable the DRPA to assume ownership of and operate regional port facilities, but these efforts were frustrated by interests within each of the states. Its current port-related function is to assist individual port authorities promote the Delaware region in world trade circles.

The DRPA has been involved in coastal management program development in three ways. First, it has participated in the development of the Pennsylvania coastal management program by actively participating on the Coastal Steering Committee. Second, it has monitored New Jersey's coastal management efforts and has initiated contacts and forwarded proposals to coastal management program officials in that state. Third, it has conducted special studies of the region's potential to accommodate onshore service facilities for outer continental shelf oil and gas development. It has advocated use of existing or new facilities in the region for that purpose.

Port facilities along the Delaware River, looking north from the Walt Whitman Bridge. Right: Facilities of the South Jersey Port Corporation at Camden, New Jersey. Left: Facilities of the Philadelphia Port Corporation and private industry line the Pennsylvania side of the river. (Photo by Carlton Read, courtesy of the Delaware River Port Authority)

The Delaware River Basin Commission (DRBC), established by an interstate compact, involves Pennsylvania, New Jersey, Delaware, and New York. The commission works closely with federal and state agencies on many aspects of water resource and related land-use management; it controls water flow in the Delaware River, and reviews shoreland uses which may affect water quality. The DRBC, however, has only monitored the development of state coastal management programs in the region. Although it has not been actively involved in program development, it has produced water resource information and studies and made them available to coastal planners.

The Delaware River Basin Commission and Delaware River Port Authority have played only minor roles in port development and coastal management programs in Pennsylvania and New Jersey. Instead, these activities have been primarily carried out by individual ports and the states and their regional and local entities.

SOUTH JERSEY PORT CORPORATION/NEW JERSEY COASTAL MANAGEMENT PROGRAM

Summary

The South Jersey Port Corporation (SJPC) is a recently formed regional port authority of the state of New Jersey. Port facilities are located in Camden, across the Delaware River from Philadelphia. The major commodities shipped through SJPC facilities are lumber, plywood, and fresh fruit. Because of a depressed local economy, the City of Camden is working with the port to obtain public works funding to improve port facilities. The port has already revitalized two terminals and plans to develop an extension of a container terminal wharf.

Coastal planning in rural and recreation-oriented counties along the Atlantic Ocean is fairly well advanced because these areas are included in the jurisdiction of the state's Coastal Area Facility Review Act (CAFRA). It sets forth a timetable for developing policies and plans to control coastal development, and will constitute the heart of New Jersey's coastal management program. Since the areas where the major ports are located are not included under CAFRA's jurisdiction, the coastal management program is considering ways to expand CAFRA's scope or rely on other state authorities to control uses in these areas.

Only recently, in the third year of coastal program development, have urban areas and their shoreline problems been addressed. Explicit port policies may emerge when an economic analysis of port development being conducted by the State Department of Labor and Industry is completed. There are two proposed alternative strategies for implementing CAFRA that relate to port development:

1. Water access would be assured for water-dependent uses.

2. Industrial development would be preferred to other uses (such as residential or recreational uses) in the urbanized areas of North Jersey and the Delaware River.

As of early 1977, the coastal management program has had no contact with the South Jersey Port Corporation, but it has had limited contact with the Delaware River Port Authority concerning offshore oil development issues.

South Jersey Port Corporation, Camden, New Jersey

Location and physical characteristics. The port is located in Camden on the Delaware River, 125 miles from the ocean—an average voyage of about eight hours (Figure 7.4). The port's 279 acres account for all public port development on the eastern bank of the Delaware River below Trenton. The channel is sheltered from the effects of wind and sea conditions, and depth alongside docks ranges from 30 to 35 feet.

Cargo characteristics. In 1975, the South Jersey Port Corporation handled 1,136,464 tons of cargo, an increase of 13% over 1974

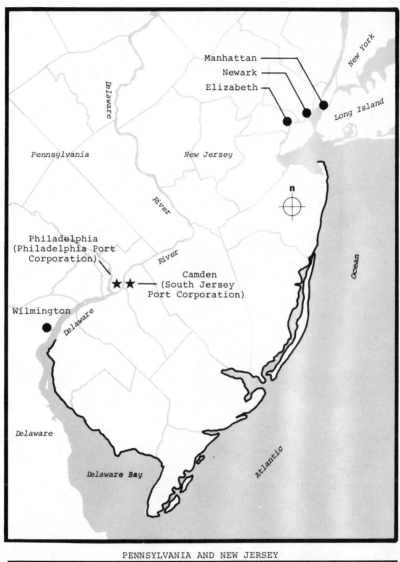

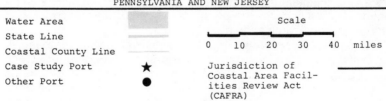

Figure 7.4 Pennsylvania and New Jersey coastal areas

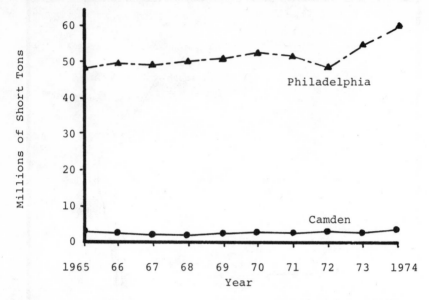

Figure 7.5 Philadelphia net total cargo tonnages, 1965-1974. Source: Corps of Engineers, 1974. *Waterborne Commerce of the United States.* Volume 1, p. 7.15a.

(Figure 7.5 gives net tonnages through 1974). Cargo includes such diverse items as fresh fruit, lumber, plywood, coil steel, bone, zinc, sponge, iron, cocoa, mushrooms, and a variety of metals. Lumber receipts declined in 1975 because of reduced residential construction.

Port facilities. The port has ten berths. Seven of them are located at Broadway Terminal, which has about 250,000 square feet of covered cargo storage and 25 acres of open storage area. At the Beckett Street Terminal there are three ship berths, 123,000 square feet of covered cargo storage, and 30 acres of open storage area (Figure 7.6).

Port administration. The South Jersey Port Corporation, created in 1968, is authorized to establish, acquire, construct, rehabilitate, improve, operate, and maintain marine terminals in the seven counties within its jurisdiction. In addition, the corporation may enter into lease agreements, issue bonds, and exercise the right of eminent domain.

The corporation reports directly to the Governor and state legislature; for administrative purposes it is under the State Department of Conservation and Economic Development. Seven corporation directors, appointed by the Governor with the consent of the Senate, represent different geographic areas. Three counties—Cape May, Cumberland, and Salem—are represented by one member; Camden and Gloucester Counties have three members, two of which must represent Camden; Burlington and

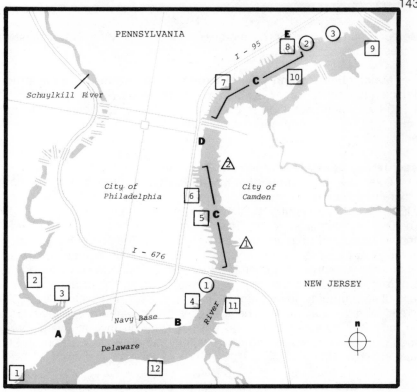

PHILADELPHIA / CAMDEN

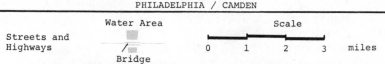

Figure 7.6 Philadelphia Port Corporation and South Jersey Port Corporation facilities. Philadelphia Port Corporation facilities operated by private lessees ◯ : (1) Packer Avenue Marine Terminal; (2) Tioga II Terminal; (3) Tioga Marine Terminal. South Jersey Port Corporation facilities △ : (1) Broadway Terminal; (2) Beckett Street Terminal.

Privately owned facilities ☐ : (1) Atlantic Richfield Company; (2) Gulf Oil; (3) Girard Point Terminal; (4) Greenwich Point, coal and ore piers; (5) Kerr-McGee Chemical; (6) Amstar Sugar; (7) National Sugar; (8) Port Richmond Terminals; (9) Hess Oil; (10) Cities Service, oil; (11) Phillips Petroleum; (12) Texaco.

Issue areas; **A**. regional dredged material disposal site; **B**. waterfront housing on Philadelphia navy base; **C**. obsolete and underutilized finger piers; **D**. Penn's Landing development (waterfront urban renewal); **E**. Port Richmond (obsolete railroad terminal)

Source: Delaware River Port Authority. *Ports of Philadelphia.*

Mercer Counties have three members, each county having at least one representative.

Major planning and capital expansion programs. Seventeen acres adjacent to Beckett Street Terminal were acquired by the port in 1975, and a 740-foot wharf extension is planned for this site to increase the terminal's capacity. Channel deepening adjacent to the wharf is planned as well.

New Jersey Coastal Management Program
Overview and implementing authority. The coastal management program is housed in the State Department of Environmental Protection (DEP), which has spent $1,624,125 on its development as of June 1976. The DEP also administers the Coastal Area Facilities Review Act (CAFRA), and wetlands and riparian statutes for the state. The combined jurisdiction of these various marine and shoreline programs may well constitute sufficient state authority to implement the coastal management strategy and program. The state is currently preparing case studies to analyze the extent of its authority to manage designated land and water uses in the industrialized coastal area. These studies cover waterfront redevelopment on the Hudson, liquefied natural gas facilities on the Delaware, dredge spoil disposal, major housing construction and a chemicals port and tank farm in Jersey City.

Land and water uses. *Interim Land Use and Density Guidelines for the Coastal Area,* prepared by DEP (1976), provides interim policy guidance for administering CAFRA. Precedents established in administering CAFRA and the policies in the state's wetlands and riparian statutes are additional sources for identifying permissible and priority uses of the New Jersey coastal area. Further definition of statewide coastal land- and water-use policies are reflected in policy alternative papers, compiled by DEP (1976), and in the environmental inventory mandated by CAFRA.

Uses considered priority issues by the state coastal program include large-scale residential and commercial development, high quality and readily accessible recreation areas, energy related development, power plants, and waste disposal. Wetland and shellfishery preservation, beach erosion, and navigation channels are also priority issues.

Coastal zone boundaries. The state coastal management office is considering a multitiered approach to delineating the coastal boundary. Currently, all counties with shorelines and river banks subject to tidal influence are in the planning boundary, but the state plans to establish a more specific regulatory boundary, to complement the broader planning boundary. The regulatory boundary would consist of the coastal water areas, the legislatively and judicially defined inland boundaries of CAFRA, and the inland boundaries of the riparian and wetland laws for those areas outside CAFRA's jurisdiction.

A second and more inclusive boundary alternative would be to define the area by a system of roads and rights-of-way, which extend inland from the jurisdictional limit of the riparian and wetlands laws. This boundary would be determined by criteria used by DEP to delineate the initial CAFRA boundary. The inland boundary could range from several thousand feet to a number of miles from coastal waters.

The state's third alternative would be to consider the entire geologic coastal plain—a very large region in the southeast portion of the state—as part of the coastal zone. This, however, would be a difficult alternative to justify and administer.

Geographic areas of particular concern. The state uses environmental and socioeconomic factors to identify geographic areas of particular concern (GAPCs). The interim land use and density guidelines categorize 25 land and water features of the CAFRA area into preservation, conservation, and development areas. Some policy alternative papers also identify certain important geographic areas, such as aquifer recharge areas, historic districts, dunes, and depressed urban areas. Designating depressed urban areas as GAPCs could imply an active economic development program. A GAPC could also be the area around a nuclear power plant, which would indicate that low-density development would be advisable.

Public and governmental involvement. The Department of Environmental Protection (DEP) uses various methods of encouraging public and governmental involvement—largely associated with the implementation of CAFRA. Proposed CAFRA procedural rules were widely circulated in May 1975 and March 1976. The state held two public meetings in 1975 to introduce the coastal management program, and public hearings are required during the CAFRA permit process. Since 1975, smaller meetings have been held with builders, county planning directors, environmental leaders, and state agencies to seek other opinions about land-use and density guidelines. Additional opportunity for involvement is possible for site-specific decisions.

State and local organization arrangements. The Office of Coastal Management, (under DEP's Division of Marine Resources) will likely remain responsible for the coastal program. They will have a coastal planning group and a coastal information system for the program. The organizational requirements of alternative levels of decision-making, with some delegation of state authority to local agencies, is being studied.

State-federal interaction and national interests. Various federal agencies are given the opportunity to comment on draft CAFRA regulations in informal meetings, and are included in public agency advisory conferences. Federal agencies have been asked about their interests in coastal areas and opinions on outer continental shelf related development in the CAFRA area. Affected and interested federal agencies are notified of coastal permit applications.

PHILADELPHIA PORT CORPORATION/PENNSYLVANIA COASTAL MANAGEMENT PROGRAM
Summary

The Philadelphia Port Corporation was formed through the cooperative efforts of the City of Philadelphia, the Commonwealth of Pennsylvania, and the Chamber of Commerce of Greater Philadelphia. City officials play an active role in the port corporation, which manages city-owned port facilities.

Port facilities are located on the Delaware River within the Philadelphia city limits, 125 miles inland from the Atlantic Ocean. Although the distance from the ocean is considerable, the area is subject to tidal influence and is included in the planning area of the Pennsylvania coastal management program.

Petroleum and petroleum products—the major cargos, by tonnage, in the region—pass through many oil refineries' private docks. New public port growth is being spurred by growing container traffic; but although finger piers have been converted to quay-type berths for container traffic, there are still many piers that are unsuitable for container shipping and are currently underutilized. The city is studying the potential for a new major container facility. Another problem is the need for new dredge spoil disposal sites.

Pennsylvania divides its coastal management efforts between the Lake Erie coast and the Delaware River shoreline. This case study examines only the Delaware River shoreline. The proposed coastal boundary extends upstream to a point north of Philadelphia, offshore to the middle of the Delaware River, and inland using census tracts to a maximum of three miles in rural areas and one-half mile in urban areas.

Pennsylvania Department of Environmental Resources' Division of Outdoor Recreation is primarily responsible for the coastal management program. Research and planning for the Delaware River segment have been subcontracted to the Delaware Valley Regional Planning Commission, whose staff has expertise in urban coastal zone problems. The mechanisms for implementing a coastal management program are undecided at this point, although the chief of the Division of Outdoor Recreation has indicated that new statutory authorities will probably not be necessary.

Draft policies for managing the Delaware River shoreline have been proposed. They were developed with input from the Delaware River Port Authority, a nonvoting member of the Pennsylvania Coastal Management Steering Committee, but the Philadelphia Port Corporation has not been directly involved. Nevertheless, there is informal information exchange between the port and coastal planning staff through the Philadelphia Planning Department.

The draft policies acknowledge the necessity of port expansion. Specifically, they support research and planning, encourage improvement of services, and note the need to rectify deficiencies in port infrastructures. They also reflect the need to revitalize obsolete finger piers. Locating dredge spoil disposal sites is addressed, but there are no criteria for establishing these sites.

Philadelphia Port Corporation

Location and physical characteristics. The Port of Philadelphia is located in the geographic and marketing center of the North Atlantic Seaboard and competes with the aggressive and modern ports of New York/ New Jersey and Baltimore (Figure 7.4). The main channel is dredged to 40 feet up to Newbold Island, north of Philadelphia; five deepwater areas are provided for the anchorage of four to five ships in the river.

Cargo characteristics. Between 1965 and 1974, Philadelphia's net total cargo increased by 12 million tons, to a total of 60 million tons (Figure 7.5). Petroleum and petroleum-related products moving through private terminals account for a large share of the increased tonnage. In 1972, more than 72 percent of the import cargo, measured by bulk tonnage, represented crude oil and petroleum products bound for the region's refineries. New container facilities, however, are largely responsible for the rapid growth of the Philadelphia Port Corporation. Containers handled by Philadelphia facilities totalled 86,148 20-foot equivalents in 1975; in 1970 fewer than 14,000 were handled.

Port facilities. Figure 7.6 shows the location of Philadelphia's port facilities. Since the formation of the Philadelphia Port Corporation in 1965, Tioga Marine Terminal has been built to handle a variety of general cargo, including unitized bulk, ro-ro ("roll on, roll off") containers, and break-bulk cargo. This terminal has five marginal berths and two slip berths (one for ro-ro's and one for barges).

Packer Avenue Terminal, which has five marginal berths, has been modernized and now has container and ro-ro facilities. Other port terminals include the Tioga II at Pier 179N, which handles general cargo, lumber, steel products, chemicals, and petroleum products; Pier 96, which handles general cargo, including steel and automobiles; Northern Terminal, which handles general cargo, containers, and unitized cargo, including ro-ro; four central waterfront piers south and two north of Penn's Landing; Greenwich Point Ore and Coal Piers; and Port Richmond Terminal Complex owned by the Reading Co.

Port administration. The Philadelphia Port Corporation was formed March 8, 1965, by the City of Philadelphia, the Commonwealth of Pennsylvania, and the Chamber of Commerce of Greater Philadelphia. An interesting proviso in its mandate calls for transferral of the corporation to the

Delaware River Port Authority when and if it and Philadelphia's mayor and council, the Governor, and the Chamber of Commerce president, believe that DRPA is capable of assuming the corporation's functions and responsibilities.

The port corporation's mandate is to promote waterborne commerce; to acquire, maintain, and modernize existing facilities; and to design, construct, maintain, and modernize new facilities. Although the port manages the leasing of facilities, the lessees operate them. Longer-term planning is done by the city's planning and commerce departments. All public facilities are owned by the city, not the port corporation.

The corporation's Board of Directors, which meets quarterly, is composed of 33 members:

1. Nine city directors (department and committee heads)

2. Nine Chamber of Commerce members

3. Two representatives of the Commonwealth of Pennsylvania

4. Two Delaware River Port Authority representatives

5. Eleven public directors (business and financial leaders)

An executive committee of 13 meets more frequently and manages most of the port's affairs.

Major planning and capital expansion programs. The city's Department of Commerce let a contract for a port facilities study in 1976, which is to be a cooperative effort among concerned regional port and government agencies. The request for proposals to do the study required a regional perspective for the analysis but required that Philadelphia be the site for any recommended port development. The study is addressing the need for additional container capacity in the region.

Issues of current importance. Sites are needed for the disposal of dredged material but suitable sites are difficult to find. The current disposal site may be phased out shortly and much of the remaining shorelands near Philadelphia are already developed.

Containerized cargo has changed the facility requirements of the port. New uses are needed for obsolete finger piers and new facilities for handling container cargo may be necessary.

Pennsylvania Coastal Management Program (Delaware River Segment)
Overview and implementing authority. The overall state coastal management program is in the Department of Environmental Resources, but the Delaware River segment is being developed by the Delaware Valley Regional Planning Commission under contract with the state. As of June 1976, total funding for coastal management activities in Pennsylvania was $1,000,500.

The roles of local and state agencies in the implementation of the coastal zone program have not been clarified. Present authority consists of a combination of state and local powers. The Navigation Office for the Delaware River, Department of Transportation, establishes bulkhead and pierhead lines along the river outside first class cities. Philadelphia, a first class city, regulates bulkhead and pierhead lines within city limits. Interstate authorities, such as the Delaware River Basin Commission and the Delaware River Port Authority have additional powers.

Existing statutes, administrative regulations, judicial decisions, executive orders, and interagency agreements are being studied to determine if a legal framework and organizational structure to implement coastal management policies, which would meet the federal Coastal Zone Management Act requirements, can be fashioned without new legislation. The Department of Environmental Resources will likely be the lead agency to implement the coastal management program. A strong local role is expected because of an historic home-rule preference in Pennsylvania government.

Land and water uses. Several multiple-use issues have been identified along the Delaware River. Many issues arise because the region is highly urbanized and industrialized. Waste treatment, disposal of polluted dredge spoil, renewal of deteriorated waterfronts, and navigational conflicts have been given priority.

Draft policies address most of these issues, although standards and criteria for permissible uses and priorities have not yet been developed. Specific guidelines have been proposed for special interest recreational facilities and the siting of coastal-dependent uses.

Coastal zone boundaries. Offshore, the coastal zone boundary extends to the middle of the Delaware River. For planning purposes, the upstream boundary extends to the extent of tidal influence—at the rapids near Morrisville, about 30 miles north of Philadelphia. The inland boundary has not yet been adopted, but presently includes three or four census tracts near the Delaware River or tidal waters. In the more sparsely populated areas, it extends inland up to three miles; in the Philadelphia area, it extends inland approximately one-half mile.

Geographic areas of particular concern. Both natural and development opportunity areas have been selected as geographic areas of particular concern, presented at a series of public meetings, and finalized. Because this is an urban area, only a few sites are suitable for natural designations; these include Tinicum Marsh, Little Tinicum Island, Van Sciver Lake, and various creek inlets. Examples of development opportunity designations are the Philadelphia International Airport and Port Richmond, an 80-acre waterfront industrial site which is currently underutilized.

Public and governmental involvement. Local governments are involved through the coastal zone steering committee. Voting members of the committee are from the Delaware County Planning Commission, Bucks County Planning Department, Philadelphia Planning Commission, and one representative from local governments within Bucks County and Philadelphia County. Advisors to the committee are from the Delaware River Basin Commission, Delaware River Port Authority, Chamber of Commerce for Greater Philadelphia, Academy of Natural Science, Army Corps of Engineers, League of Women Voters (Philadelphia), and representatives from three coastal management advisory committees and Philadelphia Electric Company. A coastal management newsletter, *Tidings,* is published quarterly and widely distributed.

State and local organizational arrangements. The State Department of Environmental Resources contracts coastal program development activities with the Delaware Valley Regional Planning Commission. Since it is a contract, the work is done at a staff level without being reviewed by the commissioners, who represent local and regional political interests. More active local participation can be anticipated once an implementation scheme for the coastal management program is proposed.

Coordination of relevant state agencies has been handled by the coastal management subcommittee of the state's Water Resources Coordinating Committee. Members are from the Departments of Commerce, Agriculture, Community Affairs, Environmental Resources, Planning and Development, and Transportation, the Fish and Game Commission, and Public Utility Commission.

State-federal interaction and national interests. Coordination with federal agencies occurs through the circulation of reports for review and comment. The Federal Regional Council has focused on intergovernmental aspects of coastal management, including methods for addressing regionwide implications of state coastal management programs.

The state is developing procedures to identify and assess federal interest in regional facility siting. Facilities of regional benefit that involve national interests are being defined, and procedures that will insure that there are no unreasonable or arbitrary restrictions and exclusions placed on them are being studied.

GEORGIA PORTS AUTHORITY/
GEORGIA COASTAL MANAGEMENT PROGRAM
Summary

The Georgia Ports Authority is a state authority, whose major port facilities are located in Savannah, 26 miles up the Savannah River from the Atlantic Ocean. Savannah is within the planning boundary of the state's coastal management program. Because this port has undertaken extensive construction of container facilities in the past ten years, it is one of the major container ports on the South Atlantic coast. Although no major new developments are proposed at this time, acreage is available for future development. The port owns 900 acres near the Garden City terminal and can accommodate two additional container berths.

Georgia's coastal program is nearing final stages of development, although no coastal management policies have yet emerged. But important land- and water-use issues have been identified, background papers on each issue have been developed, and the various ecosystems along the Georgia coast have been analyzed. The Coastal Zone Advisory Council, appointed by the Governor, reviews and recommends coastal policies, procedures, and mechanisms. The lead agency for developing the program is the state's Office of Planning and Budget.*

It has not yet been decided if new legislation will be enacted to regulate coastal uses or if existing legislation, such as the Marshlands Protection Act will be sufficient. A decision on this matter will help determine the inland coastal boundary for regulatory purposes. For planning the inland boundary includes Georgia's eight coastal counties.

The Georgia Ports Authority intends to play an active role in the development of coastal management policies. Its director is a member of the Coastal Zone Advisory Council, chairman of the council's sub-committee on ports and waterborne commerce, and a member of its subcommittee on industrial development. Because the port authority is a state authority, its director works on this council as an equal with other state agency heads.

Georgia Ports Authority at Savannah

Location and physical characteristics. The port at Savannah, 26 miles up the Savannah River, enjoys a geographic advantage in relation to other South Atlantic ports (Figure 7.7). It is well located in relation to industrial areas in north Georgia, Tennessee, and South Carolina. The Savannah River provides inland waterway access into these areas, and the Savannah River Basin is an area of considerable industrial growth potential.

Cargo characteristics. In 1974 the port at Savannah handled about 9 million tons of cargo (Figure 7.8). Petroleum and petroleum products are its principal commodities, however, the port also handles large tonnages of general cargo. Clay, pulp, and paperboard are major general cargos.

Port facilities. The Georgia Ports Authority has provided new facilities—such as its new $9 million bulk materials facility—at the port of Savannah to increase its traffic and improve its competitive position (Figure 7.9). One feature of this multiproduct terminal is a large storage warehouse which covers nearly five acres. Cargo received at the terminal can be stored in compartmented areas to be later reclaimed and shipped. Chemicals, ores, and other dry-bulk cargos are handled.

* Lead agency responsibility was moved to the state's Department of Natural Resources in 1978.

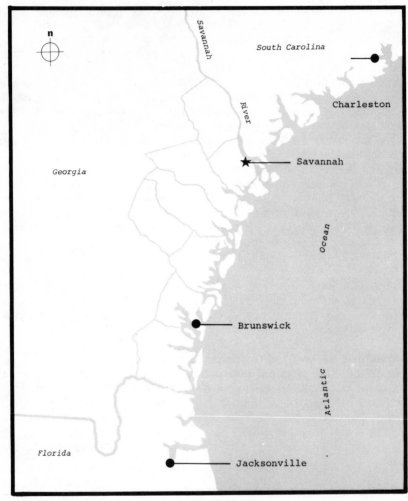

n

Savannah

South Carolina

River

Charleston

Georgia

Savannah

Ocean

Brunswick

Atlantic

Florida

Jacksonville

GEORGIA

Water Area

State Line

Coastal County Line

Case Study Port ★

Other Port ●

Scale

0 10 20 30 40 50 miles

Coastal counties
shown comprise the
Coastal Area Plan-
ning and Develop-
ment Commission
(CAPDC)

Figure 7.7 Georgia coast

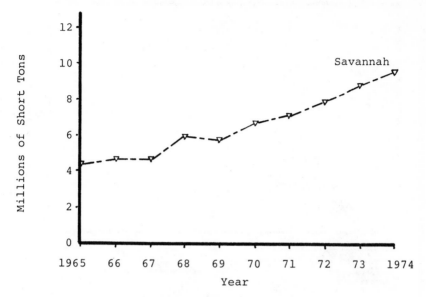

Figure 7.8 Savannah net total cargo tonnages, 1965-1974. Source: Corps of Engineers, 1974. *Waterborne Commerce of the United States.* Volume 2, p. 7.28a.

The port has entered the container race on the South Atlantic coast with its new $4.5 million container terminal. It features a 16-acre paved marshalling yard and a modern container crane.

Another important facility is a $1.1 million "Lighter Aboard Ship" (LASH) terminal, which has enabled Savannah to become the first South Atlantic coast port to begin LASH operations. The LASH vessels are large mother ships that can carry up to 83 barges; each measures approximately 62 feet by 31 feet, has a draft of 13 feet, and weighs 80 tons. Each barge has a capacity of 19,600 cubic feet and 370 tons.

The Georgia Ports Authority at Savannah operates general cargo berths at its Ocean Terminal. These include liquid cargo berths, one container-general cargo berth, and two dry-bulk berths.

There are also private docking terminals in Savannah. The Seaboard Coast Line Railway currently operates four berths; three are shed berths and one is an open berth. The Georgia International Trading Corporation operates six general cargo berths. Additional docks and loading facilities are operated by private oil companies, and a new facility to handle bulk kaolin is scheduled for construction by Southeastern Maritime Company.

The Georgia Ports Authority currently provides more than three million square feet of warehousing space at its two terminals. There is additional warehousing space at private terminals run by Seaboard Coast Line Railway and the Georgia International Trading Corporation.

Waterfront property is available for the expansion of port facilities in Savannah. The two-hundred-acre Ocean Terminal has limited space, but

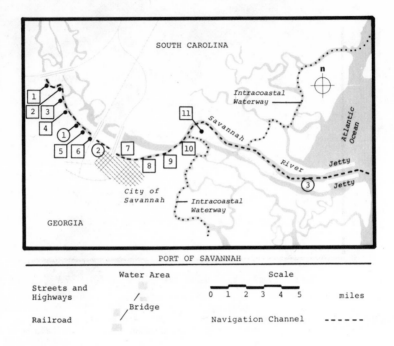

Figure 7.9 Port of Savannah. Georgia Ports Authority facilities ◯ : 1) Garden City Terminal; (2) Ocean Terminal; (3) LASH Terminal.

Privately owned facilities ☐ : (1) Continental Can Company; (2) Atlantic Creosoting Company; (3) Savannah Sugar Refining Company; (4) Chevron Asphalt Company; (5) American Oil Company; (6) Union-Camp Corporation; (7) Southeast Maritime Company, kaolin terminal; (8) Seaboard Coast Line, railroad terminal; (9) Flintkote Company; (10) American Cyanimid Company; (11) Liquefied natural gas (LNG) transfer and storage facility.

Source: Savannah District, Corps of Engineers, October 1974. Plate I, Recommended plan of improvement.

the Garden City Terminal has acquired approximately 900 acres for the port's future needs. The new container terminal and the new bulk-handling facility have enough open land between them to construct two additional container berths when the need arises.

Port administration. The Georgia Ports Authority is a public corporation with statewide jurisdiction. It is the exclusive public port authority in the state with the exception of the Brunswick Port Authority which operates in Glynn County, in the southern portion of the state. Both authorities have jurisdiction in the Brunswick area, but only the Brunswick Port Authority actually operates facilities there.

The Georgia Ports Authority may acquire, hold, and dispose of property, but it does not have the power to condemn land. State land can be

155

Three major facilities of the Georgia Ports Authority on the Savannah River, look-ing southeast down the river. Left: part of the storage shed of the bulk-handling facility. Center: Georgia Ports Authority Container Central. Upper center: Ware-houses of the Garden City Terminal. (Photo courtesy of the Georgia Ports Author-ity)

conveyed to the port authority by other agencies of state government. Port development can be financed by general obligation or revenue bonds.

The port authority may contract for the lease and use of its facilities. Projects may include other facilities to aid commerce, including rail terminals, airports, seaplane bases, highways, and bridges. Moreover, the port authority can contract with municipalities or counties to lease, oper-ate, or manage property in or adjacent to any seaport.

Georgia Ports Authority has the authority to provide a wide range of industry-related facilities, such as those used "in the manufacturing, pro-cessing, assembling, storing or handling of any agricultural or manufac-tured produce or products or produce and products of mining or industry, if the use and operation thereof, in the judgement of the Authority, will result in the increased use of port facilities, the development of the system of State docks, or, in connection therewith, promote the agricultural, in-dustrial and natural resources of the State." (Georgia Statutes, Chapter 98.2) These facilities must, however, be located on or near port property.

In 1966, Georgia Ports Authority membership increased from five to seven members. Although a clause was added in 1973 that the members should be appointed by the Governor from the state at large, in practice one director comes from each port location and two from the state at large. Appointments are for four-year terms.

The Georgia Ports Authority has a close working relationship with the Savannah Port Authority (SPA). The SPA, founded in 1925, is a regional governmental entity distinct from the Georgia Ports Authority at Savannah despite the similarity in names. Although it has the authority to develop and operate facilities, it functions primarily as an industrial promotion authority, issuing revenue anticipation bonds to foster individual development, recommending harbor regulations to the city, and issuing wharf permits for developments between the shore and bulkhead line. The SPA also facilitates trade negotiations for the Georgia Ports Authority, promotes the port facilities, and lobbies at the national and local level for harbor improvements.

Major planning and capital expansion programs. Land acquisition for developments between 1986 and 1996 and a new bulk cargo terminal and associated canal dredging are currently being planned.

Georgia Coastal Management Program
Overview and implementing authority. Georgia's coastal management program is being developed by the state's Office of Planning and Budget. Funding through June 1976 totalled $944,895. Technical studies have been performed and an advisory council has met, but no formal proposal has been developed as yet.

Present marshlands management authority exists in the Coastal Marshlands Protection Act of 1970 which regulates dredging, draining, removal, or other alterations of coastal marshlands through a permit system administered by the Coastal Marshlands Protection Committee within the Department of Natural Resources. The type and extent of additional implementing authority needed for a coastal management program is still being addressed.

Two planning agencies, the Brunswick-Glynn County Joint Planning Commission and the Chatham County-Savannah Metropolitan Planning Commission, and one coastwide regional planning agency, the Coastal Area Planning and Development Commission, have active planning programs. They address numerous coastal problems, including sand dune protection, flood plain zoning, marsh conservation, and storm drainage and protection.

Land and water uses. Permissible land and water uses have not been designated as yet. Background material has been prepared, however, on several coastal uses, on the value and vulnerability of key coastal resource ecosystems, and on ecosystem capability.

The coastal management program will address a number of concerns: the protection of fragile natural resources, comprehensive regional planning for coastal areas, inadequate water treatment facilities and saltwater intrusion into underground aquifers, and a need for intergovernmental coordination and cooperation in decision making.

Coastal zone boundaries. For planning purposes, Georgia has established an inland boundary which includes the eight coastal counties. Six alternatives have been defined for the management boundary, based on natural characteristics such as topography, drainageways, and wetlands vegetation:

1. Coastal watershed—the area drained by the five major rivers running into the Atlantic Ocean;
2. Geologic coastal Georgia—all lands and waters in the coastal watershed located between the coast and the 100-foot contour;
3. Primary geologic division—all lands and waters in the coastal watershed located between the coast and the 50-foot contour;
4. Coastal wetlands within the 50-foot contour—all waters and wetlands within the boundary of the primary geologic division;
5. Tidal wetlands—all waters and wetlands influenced by tides;
6. Tidal marsh—all waters and marshes.

The final boundary determination—perhaps a combination of these alternatives—will be made when economic, political, and physical studies are completed.

Geographic areas of particular concern. Studies identified the following types of areas as possible geographic areas of particular concern: unique physical features, important natural areas, developments dependent on coastal waters, conflicts in use due to organization, areas of significant hazard if developed, coastal aquifers and watersheds, sand areas, and valuable natural habitats.

Public and governmental involvement. Georgia has both a technical committee and an advisory council to achieve formal public and governmental involvement in coastal management. The technical committee is comprised of representatives of nine state agencies, the attorney general's office, and three regional coastal agencies. The Governor's Coastal Zone management Advisory Council has 26 members—local and state officials and citizens—who review and recommend coastal management policy, procedures, and mechanisms.

Three regional planning agencies are under contract to prepare general coastal planning and management principles, GAPC recommendations, future land use plans, and public participation activities.

State and local organizational arrangements. It has not been decided as yet which agency or agencies will implement a coastal management program and what methods will be used to control land and water uses. A combination of direct state control and state standards to guide local implementation is anticipated.

158

State-federal interaction and national interest. The Office of Planning and Budget has had direct contact with the Federal Regional Council and with individual federal agencies. Specific strategies or policies for state-federal interaction have not yet been developed.

PORT OF BROWNSVILLE/TEXAS COASTAL MANAGEMENT PROGRAM

Summary

The Brownsville Navigation District is a state-created authority that operates port facilities and promotes industrial development on its extensive land holdings. These holdings generally border a 17-mile navigation

The Port of Brownsville from the end of the ship channel (in foreground) to the Gulf of Mexico, 17 miles to the east. (Photo courtesy of the Brownsville Navigation District)

channel from the Gulf of Mexico to the waterfront near Brownsville.

Close proximity to Mexico has a significant impact on the port's commodity mix. As northern Mexico and the port itself have become industrialized, cotton exports have given way to bulk commodities, petroleum, and petroleum products. Fifty-five percent of the cargo shipped through the port originates in or is destined for Mexico.

One of the port's primary functions is to promote industrial development. The port has devised its own procedures for siting new development, guiding those that do not need waterfront property to upland areas. The port helps its lessees obtain requisite permits and is a leader in maintaining local air and water quality standards.

Hearings were held on the Texas draft coastal management program during the summer and fall of 1976, and in 1977 legislation was passed that enacted its salient features. Existing authorities are integrated through the Natural Resources Council, an interagency policy-level council. Regulations within the coastal zone will rely on an assessment of development impacts by a network of state agencies rather than on land- and water-use plans developed and implemented at the local level.

Coastal boundaries in the legislation explicitly define a variety of land and water areas. In general, these areas include the nearshore areas of the Gulf of Mexico, beaches, barrier islands, sand dune complexes, and areas which have measurable amounts of seawater. Areas to be designated geographic areas of particular concern will be identified based on the needs of statewide, rather than local, interests.

Interactions between Texas ports and the coastal program have been minimal. Although the attorney for the Port of Corpus Christi sits on the Land Office Advisory Council, the highly competitive nature of Texas ports makes it unlikely that any one port district would represent port interests of the entire state. There have been informal contacts between the Brownsville Navigation District and the coastal program, however. The port offered testimony at the public hearing held in Brownsville on the Texas draft coastal management program.

Port of Brownsville

Location and physical characteristics. The city of Brownsville is located on the Rio Grande River at the southernmost tip of Texas (Figure 7.10). The Port of Brownsville is about five miles northeast of the city proper and 17 miles from the Gulf of Mexico. It is reached through a dredged channel across dry land that extends from the Gulf of Mexico through Brazos Santiago Pass, across Laguna Madre and then through the Brownsville Ship Channel. The entrance channel is 38 feet deep and 300 feet wide, and the 17-mile ship channel is 36 feet deep and 200 feet wide. Inland of the small boat basin the channel widens to 500 feet, ending in a turning basin 1,000 feet wide and 3,500 feet long. In addition to the turning basin, there is a small boat basin that is 15 feet deep, with 10,800 feet of dock space which provides port facilities for up to 400 shrimp boats that operate in the Gulf of Mexico.

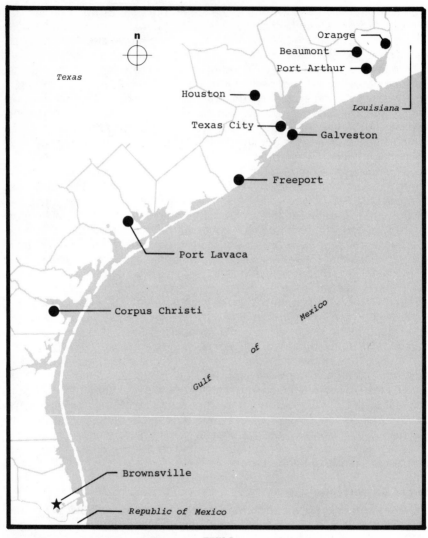

Figure 7.10 Texas coastal area

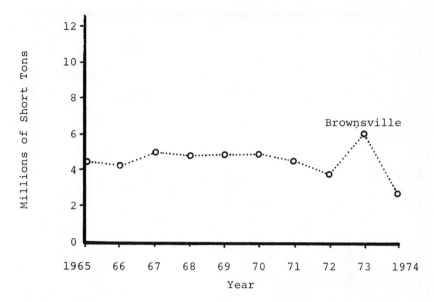

Figure 7.11 Brownsville net total cargo tonnages, 1965-1974. Source: Corps of Engineers, 1974. *Waterborne Commerce of the United States.*

Geographically, the port's location serves the lower Rio Grande Valley and a large industrial and agricultural area of northeastern Mexico.

Cargo characteristics. Only a short time ago, agricultural products—primarily cotton—were the principal commodities handled by this port. Rapid development of industry throughout the lower Rio Grande Valley and northern Mexico has resulted in a shift from general cargo to bulk commodities, liquid petroleum, and petroleum products. Figure 7.11 shows net total cargo tonnages from 1965 to 1974.

Principal products handled by the Port include shrimp, citrus fruits, sorghum, soybeans, gasoline, diesel fuel, crude oil, fluorspar, scrap iron, steel, machinery, various ores, and chemicals. Approximately 55 percent of the tonnage is import or export trade with Mexico.

Port facilities. Brownsville's main turning basin has dock facilities for eight general cargo ships, three tanker vessels, one bulk commodity ship, and berthing space for twelve barges. Figure 7.12 shows the location of the major facilities at the port, which include a public grain elevator with a storage capacity of 3,750,000 bushels and a loading rate of 12,000 tons per hour. A bulk materials handling facility adjacent to the elevator can receive, deliver, and store up to 30,000 tons at a rate of 300 tons per hour. The turning basin offers 7,000 lineal feet of wharves, with 530,000 square feet of transit shed space. An additional 1,250,000 square feet of public warehouse space is located nearby. The Brownsville Navigation District

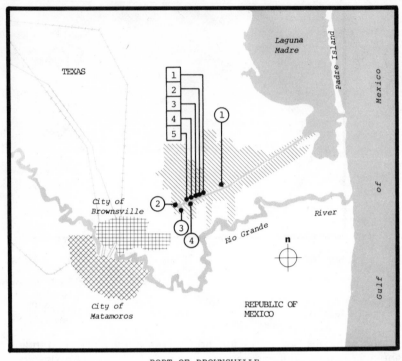

PORT OF BROWNSVILLE

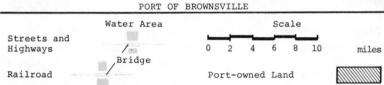

Figure 7.12 Port of Brownsville. Port-owned facilities ◯ : (1) fishing harbor; (2) transit sheds; (3) barge slips; (4) grain elevator.

Privately operated facilities ☐ : (1) Union Carbide; (2) Humble Oil; (3) Premier Oil; (4) Pemex Oil; (5) Texaco.

Source: Brownsville Navigation District. *The Port of Brownsville.*

also owns and operates about 60 acres of paved open area for storage of commodities that do not require protection from the weather. Cold storage facilities are available near the main turning basin and at the fishing Harbor. The port's land holdings include 42,000 acres of industrial land, much of it adjacent to the waterway.

Port administration. Two provisions in the state constitution (Article II, section 52, and Article XVI, section 59) first established navigation districts in Texas. State statutes also provide an enabling act for the creation of subsequent navigation districts; Brownsville Navigation District operates under the codified general enabling act.

A comprehensive review of constitutional and statutory law affecting the formation and administration of navigation districts in Texas appears in the *Texas Coastal Management Program 1975 Hearing Draft* (Texas General Land Office, 1976).

The Brownsville Navigation District is governed by a Board of Navigation and Canal Commissioners consisting of three elected representatives from Cameron County, where Brownsville is located. Each commissioner serves a six-year term; one term expires every two years. A port director/general manager and financial and legal counsel report to the board.

There are six key staff positions for the internal operation of the port: administration and finance, engineering and planning, operations/harbormaster, traffic and trade development, grain elevator, and special projects/public relations. All development planning and environmental regulation compliance is handled by the engineering and planning division.

The Port of Brownsville is empowered to maintain and develop waterways and ports within Cameron County. Specifically, the port has the power of eminent domain to acquire land on which to develop wharves, docks, and grain elevators and to develop and maintain other kinds of facilities for navigation and commerce in the port and on its waterways. Acquisition of land is permitted for industrial development as well. The port has certain police powers over its facilities so long as these powers are not in conflict with municipal police powers operating within the port's jurisdiction. The port can set rates for the use of its facilities to defray costs of construction, operation, and maintenance of facilities for other parties, thus enabling the port to function as an industrial developer.

In its role as an industrial developer, the port acquires and prepares land for its industrial lessees, provides utility and infrastructure investments, and secures land-use and environmental quality permits. These services are available only to lessees of port-owned land, since state law precludes port-sponsored improvements on land not controlled by the port. A clause in each lease requires that the lessee satisfy all state and federal environmental regulations. Thus, the port acts as an advocate for its lessees with respect to federal, state, and local regulations, subject to the contractually guaranteed good faith of the lessee in meeting those standards.

Fiscal powers of the port include a statutorily authorized maintenance and operation tax, not to exceed 20 cents per $100 valuation, which needs only initial electoral approval; tax bonds, requiring voter approval and limited to 40 years to maturity; and, revenue bonds pledged by revenue from all of the district's facilities, again limited to not more than 40 years to maturity.

It is important to note that Texas' state courts have held that the "acquisition of land for industrial development by navigation districts is for a public use" (Buchanan, 1973) and that a navigation district has broad administrative authority to condemn and acquire lands for industrial development.

Major planning and capital expansion programs. Future plans include continual upgrading of waterfront facilities and utility connections, several new major facilities (including a water treatment plant and new barge docks), and enlargement of the turning basin.

Issues of current importance. Processed waste from Union Carbide Corporation's chemical plant located on port-owned land north of the waterway has, until recently, been piped into a natural lagoon system (San Martin Lagoon). After small levels of discharge from the lagoon system were detected in the waterway, the port and Union Carbide negotiated with public and governmental interests to find an economical means of meeting pollution control requirements. The Texas Department of Water Resources (TWR) required Union Carbide to construct evaporation/aeration ponds to achieve federal, 1985 zero-discharge requirements. On November 10, 1976, a $6 million wastewater processing facility was officially opened for operation. While opinion is still divided on the necessity of this investment, the port publicly shares credit with Union Carbide for this unique, low-energy-consuming wastewater treatment system.

Shrimp processing waste treatment and disposal at the fisheries harbor, an issue of environmental importance, is being resolved by construction of a wastewater treatment plant.

Texas Coastal Management Program

Overview and implementing authority. The development of the Texas coastal management program is the responsibility of the General Land Office. A final program document, *Texas Coastal Management Program Hearing Draft and Appendices* (General Land Office, 1976), has been in the process of public and governmental review for the past year. The Texas legislature passed key laws early in the summer of 1977 aimed toward establishing sufficient implementing authority to meet requirements of the federal Coastal Zone Management Act. As of June 1976, program development funding for Texas totalled $3,405,171.

The new laws are modelled after those proposed in the *Texas Coastal Management Program*. The Natural Resources Council Act (1977) established a 16-member Natural Resources Council (NRC) chaired by the Governor or his alternate and composed of representatives of state agencies and offices. The council, which operates as a top-level advisory council to the Governor and legislature, must propose a state natural resource data management system. Under the Coastal Coordination Act (1977), the NRC must recommend procedures for permit application review to the Governor, in order to simplify and reduce permit requirements in the state. A specific systematic activity analysis, discussed in detail in the coastal management program draft, must be part of the recommended permit application review procedures. The act urges (but does not require) other state agencies to incorporate the activity analysis procedures into their permit reviews. Finally, the coastal Wetlands Acquisition Act (1977) was passed authorizing the identification and ultimate acquisition of ecologically important coastal wetlands.

In addition to the new legislation discussed above, Texas has existing resource management programs which add additional potential implementation devices. Two of these programs are notable. First, the state land office has broad authority over management of public submerged lands, up to the mean high-water mark, to insure their use in the public interest. In addition, the public's historic right of access to Texas beaches are protected under legislation in existence since 1959.

Before Texas' coastal management program can be approved, it must be determined whether the laws discussed above are sufficient to allow the control of land and water uses in the coastal zone as prescribed in the federal Coastal Zone Management Act. Federal and state officials still do not agree whether the proposed coastal management program and the laws discussed above adequately meet the federal legal requirements.

Land and water uses. The Texas coastal management program's goal is to coordinate state natural resource program policies and activities to balance environmental, economic, and social considerations. Proposed uses will be systematically reviewed to identify environmental, economic, and social effects. Land- and water-use policies are found in existing state laws; permissible coastal land and water uses, however, will be determined on the basis of performance standards. Those uses which have a "direct and significant impact" on coastal resources will be identified by an analysis of the capability of coastal resources to support various uses. This analytical system, once established, will provide the basis for reviewing new projects.

Coastal zone boundaries. For initial planning purposes, 28 Texas coastal counties are considered the state's coastal area. Within these counties are such major urban centers as Houston-Galveston, Beaumont-Port Arthur, Victoria, Corpus Christi, and Brownsville. The Coastal Coordination Act of 1977 (section 4 [b]) redefines the coastal area as "nearshore areas in the Gulf of Mexico; tidal inlets and tidal deltas; bays; lagoons containing a measurable concentration of seawater; oyster reefs; grassflats; spoil deposits in or immediately adjacent to water containing a measurable amount of seawater; channels, the waters of which contain a measurable amount of seawater; coastal lakes; tidal streams; beaches; barrier islands; wind tidal flats; tidal marshes; washover areas; sand dune complexes on the Gulf shoreline; and river mouths up to the farthest point of intrusion by a measurable amount of seawater."

Geographic areas of particular concern. Identifying geographic areas of particular concern (GAPCs) will let public and private interests know that there are important state interests in particular areas. Stringent regulatory requirements imply that permits will be harder to get in those areas. The state currently has programs to regulate, study, enhance, develop, and preserve those areas.

Public and governmental involvement. Many state agencies have assisted in the inventory of coastal resources and the preliminary identification of GAPCs. The Inter-agency Council on Natural Resources and the Environment, comprised of representatives from state agencies that have natural resource interests, reviews the technical studies. Regional councils of governments have conducted public information meetings and have provided data and comments on technical studies. Briefings have been held for local officials on the coastal management program, and a 40-member advisory committee held public hearings in various coastal locations to solicit input. Extensive public hearings were held on the *Hearings Draft* of the program before it was submitted to the legislature. Additional public information and education efforts have included distribution of the film, *Faces of the Coast* (Hart Sprager, 1976), to civic groups and businesses, publication of a newsletter, and distribution of technical reports and brochures.

State and local organizational arrangements. Texas proposes to use existing state-level controls to regulate coastal land and water uses. The numerous programs and requirements are to be streamlined and rationalized through a systematic activity analysis to be developed by the new Natural Resources Council (discussed above). Regional and local responsibilities remain with existing regional organizations and local governments.

State-federal interaction and national interests. Texas has worked with a special coastal task force of the Federal Regional Council (FRC) and has worked directly with individual federal agencies to enable them to participate in developing the state's coastal management program. Federal agencies assisted the state in identifying federal lands within the coastal area, cataloging national interests, and identifying GAPCs.

PORT OF LOS ANGELES/CALIFORNIA COASTAL MANAGEMENT PROGRAM

Summary
The Port of Los Angeles is physically removed from the main part of the city of Los Angeles. A narrow strip of land was annexed from neighboring jurisdictions to link the port with the city. The port's facilities extend into San Pedro Bay, where dredge and fill activities of the past 100 years created the harbor. The Port of Los Angeles facilities abut those of the Port of Long Beach. The port's major commodities include petroleum, petroleum products, and container cargo. Present plans anticipate siting a

liquid natural gas (LNG) facility on part of a proposed 1,034-acre fill. Material for the fill would come from a proposed Corps of Engineers project to deepen the port's channel to 45 feet.

The California Coastal Act, adopted in August 1976, is based on the coastal plan developed by state and regional coastal commissions during an interim period between 1972 and 1976. This act, and companion laws enacted at the same time, established a comprehensive coastal management program in the state, which is implemented by the California State Coastal Commission and local governments. The commission, which is part of the state's resources agency, has fifteen members representing state agencies, regional commissions, local government, and the public. Local governments have primary responsibility for developing detailed management plans that are consistent with the Coastal Act and issuing permits for activities in the coastal zone after the local program is certified by the State Coastal Commission. The commission can review selected local permit decisions as well.

Jurisdiction under the new Coastal Act extends, generally, three miles offshore to 1,000 yards inland. In designated resource areas, the boundary may be extended inland to the first parallel ridgeline or to five miles, whichever is less. The coastal boundary defined by the act excludes the San Francisco Bay area, which is regulated under a separate coastal program (Figure 7.13).

A special chapter of the Coastal Act addresses port development problems that apply to the ports of San Diego, Hueneme, Long Beach, and Los Angeles. Except for certain resource areas within their jurisdictions—such as wetlands, estuaries, and recreational areas—these four ports comply only with the special coastal regulations set forth in the chapter dealing with ports.

Each of the four ports cited above must prepare and adopt a port master plan which is consistent with state port policies relating to the commercial fishing industry, diking, filling, and dredging, tanker terminals, and port-related developments. Ports must provide for public participation in preparing these plans. Traditional port development plans are likely to be certified as consistent with state coastal policies. Special development problems—such as the proposed siting of a liquid natural gas (LNG) facility at the Port of Los Angeles—are reviewed under broader policies and will not be easily resolved.

Once a port's plan is certified by the state, the port must insure that all new developments within its jurisdiction comply with the master plan. Only selected activities or developments may be appealed to the State Coastal Commission, such as those relating to energy, fisheries and recreation, and sensitive environments.

During the preparation of the coastal plan, and during the debate

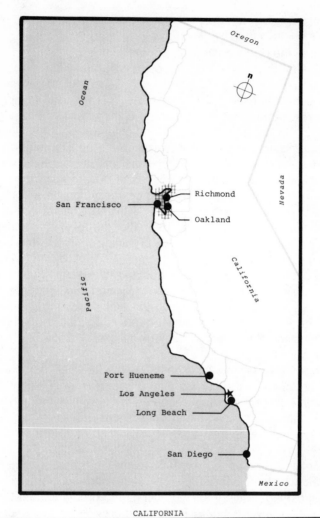

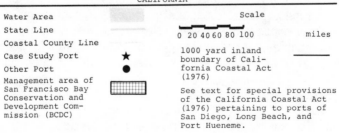

CALIFORNIA

		Scale
Water Area		
State Line		0 20 40 60 80 100 miles
Coastal County Line		
Case Study Port	★	1000 yard inland boundary of California Coastal Act (1976)
Other Port	●	
Management area of San Francisco Bay Conservation and Development Commission (BCDC)	▦	See text for special provisions of the California Coastal Act (1976) pertaining to ports of San Diego, Long Beach, and Port Hueneme.

Figure 7.13 State of California.

The Port of Los Angeles, looking northeast along the main channel. In the foreground are the West Channel/Cabrillo Beach areas and the Union Oil supertanker
terminal. At far right center, across the main channel, is the commercial fish harbor on Terminal Island. Just out of view on the right is the Port of Long Beach.
(Photo courtesy of the Port of Los Angeles)

preceding the passage of the Coastal Act, port interests were represented
by a special governmental coordination committee of the California Association of Port Authorities (CAPA), which the Port of Los Angeles belongs
to. Port officials actively participated with this committee, and presented
testimony about the coastal plan at public hearings. Many of their suggestions were incorporated into regional recommendations for the coastal

plan, although they were not included in the final state-level draft. Ports continued lobbying after the plan was distributed, and eventually coastal policies that recognized ports as special coastal users were adopted, and special provisions tailored to their needs and problems were included in the Coastal Act.

Port of Los Angeles

Location and physical characteristics. The Port of Los Angeles is a manmade harbor, 40 to 51 feet deep in the outer harbor and 35 feet deep in most of the inner harbor, which includes the main channel. The port encompasses portions of the Terminal Island, Wilmington, and San Pedro districts of Los Angeles, comprising about 6,752 acres of water and land. It is connected to Los Angeles by a narrow nine-mile-long strip of land extending through other jurisdictions.

Cargo characteristics. Although petroleum and petroleum products represent approximately two-thirds of the total tonnage that passes through the Port of Los Angeles, general cargo and containers are important commodities (Figure 7.14 shows net tonnages for 1965-1974.) The port's primary business is with the large metropolitan and regional markets of Southern California.

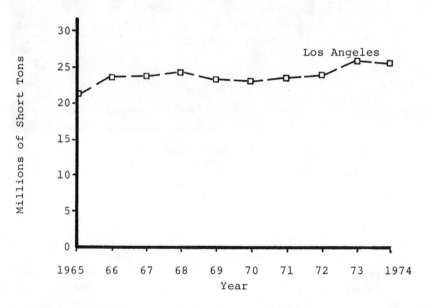

Figure 7.14 Los Angeles net total cargo tonnages, 1965-1974. Source: Corps of Engineers, 1974. *Waterborne Commerce of the United States.* Volume 4, p. 7.45a.

Port facilities. The Port of Los Angeles offers a wide variety of facilities to handle many types of cargo (Figure 7.15). General cargo facilities include 32 berths and 17 transit sheds. Container facilities include seven berths at four terminals served by seven modern gantry cranes. The port is also equipped to handle ro-ro ships and LASH operations. Thirteen waterfront facilities are specially equipped to receive petroleum products, providing more than 13,000 lineal feet of berthing space with a storage capacity in excess of 11 million barrels. The port also has specialized terminals to handle imported automobiles, lumber and wood products, dry bulk commodities, and chemicals, as well as large facilities for commercial fishing boats and seafood processing.

Port administration. A tidelands grant from the state of California has enabled the city to foster port development, which is managed through the Harbor Department. A five-member Board of Harbor Commissioners, appointed by the mayor with city council approval, oversees port development and operations. The port operates on its own revenues and to date has not required any tax revenues.

Major planning and capital expansion programs. Planning and development efforts are described in the port's comprehensive master plan. Major improvements are being considered: dredging the main channel and inner harbor to 45 feet; filling an additional 1,034 acres on Terminal Island; constructing a 45-acre container terminal at berths 127-129; siting an LNG terminal on new landfill; and building a tanker terminal in the outer harbor. The Corps of Engineers is conducting a feasibility study of the channel improvements.

Issues of current importance. The port is confronted with two particularly pressing needs. First, a deeper harbor is needed to accommodate increasing ship drafts; most of the inner harbor, including the main channel, is only 35 feet deep—too shallow for container ships and bulk and oil carriers. The port is working with the Corps of Engineers on a proposal to deepen the channel to 45 feet. Second, land-use analyses and cargo forecasts indicate a need for an additional 1,000 acres of land to serve port needs by 1990. This land could be created by a landfill on Terminal Island, using spoils from the harbor dredging project. Preliminary planning for this project is underway.

California Coastal Management Program
Overview and implementing authority. In August 1976, the California legislature passed comprehensive coastal legislation based on a coastal plan submitted by an earlier, interim coastal commission. A new State Coastal Commission, housed in the Resources Agency, is administering the program, and state regulations are being finalized to guide local governments and port authorities in developing detailed local implementation programs. California's coastal management program has been sub-

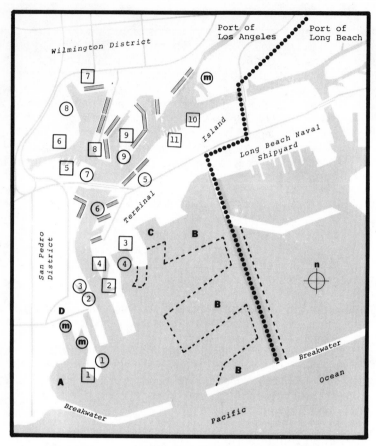

PORT OF LOS ANGELES

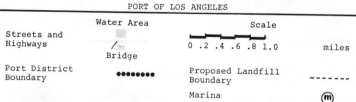

	Water Area	Scale	
Streets and Highways			
	Bridge	0 .2 .4 .6 .8 1.0	miles
Port District Boundary	●●●●●●●●	Proposed Landfill Boundary	- - - - - - -
		Marina	(m)

Figure 7.15 Port of Los Angeles. Port-owned facilities ○ : (1) transit sheds bulk loader; (2) fishermen's slip; (3) municipal fish markets; (4) fish harbor; (5) Indies Terminal; (6) Terminal Island docks; (7) Catalina Terminal; (8) Los Angeles container terminal; (9) grain and tallow terminal.

Privately-owned facilities □ : (1) Union Oil supertanker terminal; (2) Bethlehem Steel shipyards; (3) canneries; (4) Mobile Oil; (5) Todd Shipyards; (6) Phillips Petroleum; (7) distribution and auto service; (8) Union Oil; (9) Shell Oil; (10) Matson container terminal; (11) auto and ship graveyard.

Issue areas: **A**. proposed Cabrillo Beach small-boat harbor; **B**. proposed 1034-acre landfill on Terminal Island; **C**. proposed LNG terminal; **D**. Union Oak tank farm controversy.

Source: Port of Los Angeles, 1975. *Comprehensive Master Plan 1990.*

mitted to the federal Office of Coastal Zone Management for approval:*
program development funding through June 1976 totalled $4,241,946.

Local governments are responsible for developing local coastal management programs and port authorities must develop master plans for
their jurisdictions. These programs or plans, once certified by the State
Coastal Commission, are implemented through a permit system. Local
coastal management programs must include relevant portions of local
general plans, zoning ordinances, zoning maps, and means of implementing the Coastal Act policies. In sensitive areas, local programs must include ordinances, regulations, or programs for protecting resources. A
port master plan, for land and water use within its jurisdiction must comply
with special policies in the Coastal Act concerning port expansion in urban areas, dredge and fill activities, pollution prevention, protection of
commercial fishing facilities, and port-related developments.

The State Coastal Commission, with the assistance of temporary
regional commissions, performs three major functions:

1. It assists, reviews, and approves the preparation of local
   coastal programs and port master plans to insure that these
   programs will achieve the objectives and policies of the
   Coastal Act.

2. It reviews permit decisions made by local governments and
   ports. Before programs or plans are certified, this review is extensive; after certification, reviews are limited to development—in key geographic areas—of energy-related development, waste treatment facilities, roads and buildings not
   related directly to port activities, and fisheries and recreation
   facilities.

3. It coordinates the comprehensive coastal management program with state agencies that perform related resource management functions—such as the Bay Conservation and Development Commission, fish and game, water resources, air
   resources, energy, and others.

Land and water uses. Three types of performance standards for
judging all coastal developments are included in the Coastal Act:

1. Those dealing with general developments in all coastal areas;

2. Those dealing with a specific use or impact;

3. Those dealing with the protection of a particular resource.

Coastal uses of greater than local importance will be defined admin-
istratively by the State Coastal Commission and should be considered by
local governments in preparation of their coastal programs.

Legislative priorities were also established in the Coastal Act, and

* Final approval came late in 1977.

because its ultimate goal is to preserve and protect natural resources, priority in environmentally sensitive areas is given to uses that are consonant with resource protection. Uses of these areas are limited to those that are dependent upon some natural attribute of the area. Maintaining prime agricultural land is another legislatively mandated priority.

Outside of agricultural and ecologically sensitive areas, priority is given to coastal-dependent uses and to public recreation. Even where coastal areas are suitable for private development, certain priorities exist. For example: visitor-serving commercial recreation development has priority over private residential, general industrial, and general commercial development; development with public access to the coast has priority over other general developments; and visitor-serving commercial recreation and private residential developments that include low and moderately priced facilities can have priority over exclusive and expensive facilities.

Coastal zone boundaries. The California legislature authorized coastal boundaries "extending seaward to the state's outer limit of jurisdiction, including all offshore islands, and extending inland generally 1,000 yards from the mean high tide line of the sea." In eighteen significant coastal areas identified by the State Coastal Commission, the inland boundary "extends inland to the first major ridgeline paralleling the sea or five miles from the mean high tide of the sea, whichever is less" (Coastal Act 30103a). In urban areas, the coastal zone is usually less than 1,000 yards. Landward boundaries may be adjusted up to 100 yards to avoid bisecting a single lot or to conform to physical features. The area under the jurisdiction of the San Francisco Bay Conservation and Development Commission is excluded from the Coastal Act.

Geographic areas of particular concern. California has several categories of geographic areas of particular concern (GAPCs). (Table 3.2, page 37, outlines them.) The first category subsumes all the others—it is the state's entire coast. (This designation indicates that the state recognizes the need for special regulatory powers throughout the coastal zone.) The second category consists of significant estuarine habitats, and recreational areas which have extended inland boundaries. The third category consists of sensitive coastal resource areas containing geographic settings and resources that may require specific management policies. These areas must have been identified by the State Coastal Commission by September 1, 1977 and action must have been taken by the legislature within two years or the designation is removed. Additional GAPCs include those under the commission's permit jurisdiction: all coastal areas that do not have a certified local plan, areas where local decisions are subject to appeal (generally the off-shore area to 300 feet inland), and areas immediately adjacent to bays and wetlands.

Public and governmental involvement. The California coastal management program is derived from a citizen-initiated interim program, which voters approved in 1972. Between 1972 and 1976, the six regional coastal commissions and the State Coastal Commission established by the initiative worked with individuals, groups, and agencies to develop policies to submit to the legislature. (The final document was titled the California Coastal Plan.) Nearly 20,000 individuals were included on the commission's mailing lists. Public meetings were held to inform the public about the coastal plan while it was being prepared. About 10,000 people actively participated in 259 public hearings held in the six coastal regions. Before the coastal plan draft was finalized and submitted to the legislature, additional formal hearings were held. Finally, the legislature held public hearings on the proposed Coastal Act.

The regional and state-level coastal commissions offered federal, state, and regional agencies the same opportunities they offered the public to participate in developing the coastal plan. Often, regional commissions solicited these agencies' technical expertise when preparing technical reports. The Coastal Act includes special provisions for coordination with other state agencies which are spelled out in some detail.

Regulatory actions also provide an avenue for public participation. The legislation gives regional coastal commissions limited authority to issue coastal development permits, which must be issued during meetings open to the public. Decisions about proposed developments that are made by local governments (under certified plans) may be appealed to the State Coastal Commission. Hearings on these appeals are also open to the public.

State and local organizational arrangements. Cooperation among all public agencies—state, regional, and local—and the State Coastal Commission is mandated by the California Coastal Act. Three state bodies—the Resources Agency, Business and Transportation Agency, and the State Lands Commission—have ex officio representatives on the commission. The roles of eight more state agencies are explicitly coordinated with the commission in the statute. These agencies deal with fish and game, air and water quality, energy resources, forestry resources, state lands, planning and research, and the San Francisco Bay coastal program. With the exception of the last two agencies, the commission is authorized to recommend changes in administrative regulations, rules, and statutes to these agencies. It can also recommend coordinating measures to those agencies dealing with parks and recreation, navigation and ocean development, mines and geology, and oil and gas.

State-local coordination is specified in the implementation procedures of the Coastal Act. Local governments will develop coastal programs which conform to Coastal Act policies and State Coastal Commission guidelines. The commission is expected to assist local governments in exercising their responsibilities.

State-federal interaction and national interests. Federal agencies met with the State Coastal Commission and participated in the public hearings on the California coastal plan. The commission included many federal agency suggestions in its revisions of the preliminary coastal plan. A notable addition was a section entitled, "National Interest on the Coast." Policies in the Coastal Act relating to agricultural lands, recreational uses, and energy development are based on national interest arguments. In addition, two federal employees—one from the Department of Interior, the second from the Environmental Protection Agency—worked on the commission staff to help develop the plan.

Specific state-federal interaction procedures are called for in California's coastal management program. The state will monitor federal activities in the coastal zone by using existing procedures—such as environmental impact statement review, Corps of Engineers public notices, and A-95 review (a formal process whereby local and state agencies review federally funded projects for consistency with existing projects and policies). Memoranda of understanding between the State Coastal Commission or local coastal agency, and federal agencies will be requested for federal actions that are consistent with the coastal management program and would otherwise require a coastal management permit. Federal agencies which do not use memoranda of understanding must adopt another procedure to notify the appropriate coastal management agency of a proposed federal policy.

PORT OF GRAYS HARBOR/WASHINGTON COASTAL MANAGEMENT PROGRAM

Summary

The Port of Grays Harbor is a port authority established under state law with countywide jurisdiction. Its facilities are located in the cities of Aberdeen and Hoquiam, situated on the shallow Grays Harbor estuary, which opens directly into the Pacific Ocean. The estuary is relatively undeveloped and contains valuable fish and wildlife resources.

Lumber and wood products are the major commodities shipped through the port and reflect a local dependence on the timber industry. The port is a prime income generator. It promotes both trade and industrial development for the area, which is in an economically depressed region of the state. Current development plans include completion of a fill site for a proposed offshore-oil-rig fabrication plant and promotion of a Corps of Engineers project to deepen the channel to 40 feet.

Washington's coastal management program is based on the Shoreline Management Act (SMA) enacted by the legislature in 1971 and confirmed by the voters in 1972; the program was approved by the federal Office of Coastal Zone Management in June 1976. The Shoreline Management Act places primary responsibility on local government for inventorying the shores, developing master programs, and issuing permits for activities in the coastal zone, according to guidelines developed by the

State Department of Ecology (DOE). Local government permit decisions may be appealed to the Shoreline Hearings Board by the Department of Ecology, the state Attorney General's Office, or any aggrieved person.

The first tier boundary of the Washington coastal zone corresponds to those of the Shoreline Management Act. Generally, jurisdiction extends 200 feet upland from the ordinary high-water mark and includes bays, swamps, flood plains, etc. A second tier, established for planning and co-ordination purposes, extends to coastal county lines.

The Shoreline Management Act gives high priority to port uses, al-though its final guidelines, prepared by the Department of Ecology (1972), require that statewide needs be considered before shorelines are allo-cated for port uses. Further, the guidelines encourage planning among jurisdictions, to avoid unnecessary duplication of port facilities, and re-quire that local governments assess the effect of structures on scenic views before issuing permits, provided this requirement does not endan-ger the public or hamper port operations.

The Shoreline Management Act and guidelines prescribe policies for dredge and fill activities, which identify ports as a priority use for which landfill in coastal areas is authorized. Dredging to provide landfill material is prohibited. When dredging is undertaken for navigational purposes, up-land disposal is preferred to disposal in the estuary.

The Port of Grays Harbor was an early participant in coastal manage-ment. As a member of the Grays Harbor Regional Planning Commission, it assisted in the development of preliminary shoreline management guide-lines. They were subsequently used to develop final statewide guidelines under the Shoreline Management Act.

There are some conflicts over future development of the port. The local shoreline master program policies were found to be too general to resolve port development needs, given the policies of federal and state fish and wildlife protection agencies. Because of these conflicts, the state designated Grays Harbor as a geographic area of particular concern. Port officials and representatives from all levels of government have partici-pated in the Grays Harbor Estuary Task Force, which is guiding refinement of the local master programs.

Port of Grays Harbor, Washington

Location and physical characteristics. The Port of Grays Harbor is located on the Pacific coast of Washington on the Grays Harbor estuary of the Chehalis River (Figure 7.16). Port facilities are located 14 miles from the Pacific Ocean in the cities of Aberdeen and Hoquiam. The port offers year-round harbor accessibility, through a maintained channel 350 feet wide and 30 feet deep. The greatest advantages of the port's location are that it is close to timber-cutting regions and it saves about one day's sail-ing time to Japan compared with the Puget Sound ports of Seattle and Ta-coma.

Cargo characteristics. Principal commodities of this port are forest

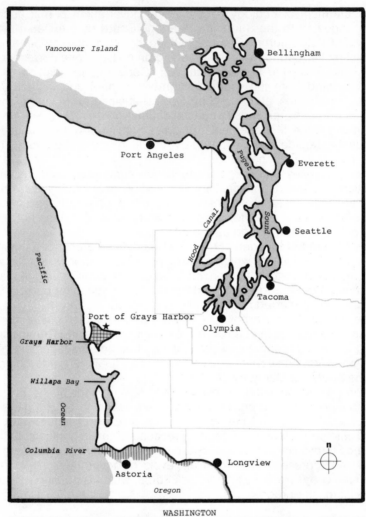

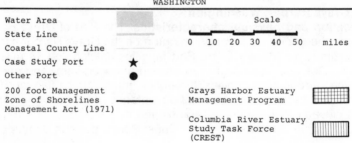

Water Area	
State Line	
Coastal County Line	
Case Study Port	★
Other Port	●
200 foot Management Zone of Shorelines Management Act (1971)	

Scale

0   10   20   30   40   50   miles

Grays Harbor Estuary Management Program

Columbia River Estuary Study Task Force (CREST)

Figure 7.16 Washington coastal area

products—logs, lumber, pulp, paper, shingles, shakes, and plywood. Other commodities include petroleum products and general cargo. Waterborne commerce moving through the Port of Grays Harbor and private docks totalled 2,565,793 tons for the year 1975, a seven percent reduction from the 2,759,334 tons handled in 1974 (Figure 7.17). This reduction in waterborne commerce resulted from adverse economic conditions in both the United States and Japan that affected the demand for forest products in both countries.

Port facilities. Two port-owned terminals are available for handling logs and lumber and for liquid bulk transfer. (Figure 7.18 shows the location of facilities.) One of the terminals is equipped with two 25-ton gantry cranes and one 40-ton container crane modified for loading logs. Large backup space (unpaved) for log sorting and storage is available.

Privately owned port facilities in the region include Anderson-Middleton log wharf and storage yard, with floating crane barge; ITT-Rayonier pulpmill, with wharf for pulp export; Anderson-Middleton sawmill, with wharf for sawn lumber export; and Weyerhaeuser pulpmill and log and chip transfer facilities.

The port also operates a regional airport, industrial development area, and a marina at Westport.

Port administration. The Port of Grays Harbor was formed by Grays Harbor County in 1911 to develop waterways, marine terminals, airports,

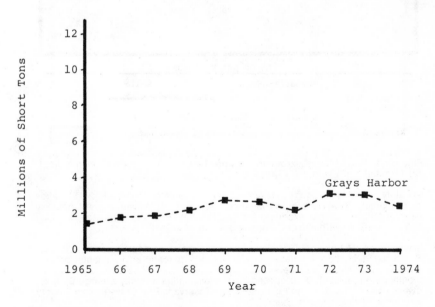

Figure 7.17 Grays Harbor net total cargo tonnages, 1965-1974. Source: Corps of Engineers, 1974. *Waterborne Commerce of the United States.* Volume 4, p. 7.54a.

and to promote business and industrial development in the county. Policies are established by a three-man commission, elected by county voters, and administered by the port staff. The port area is under the taxing jurisdiction of two municipalities—Aberdeen and Hoquiam.

Major planning and capital expansion programs. The Corps of Engineers, with the cooperation of the port authority, is planning the development of a 40-foot draft channel to allow larger ships into the harbor area. The port also plans to fill the finger pier at Terminal 1 to create a quay-type berth.

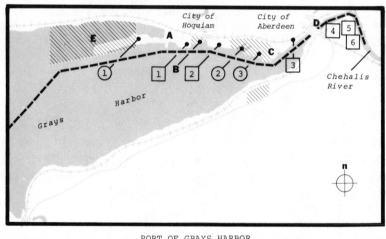

PORT OF GRAYS HARBOR

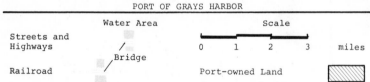

Figure 7.18 Port of Grays Harbor. Port-owned facilities ◯ : 1) Bowerman Airfield; (2) Terminal 1; (3) Terminal 4 (logs).

Privately owned facilities ☐ :)1) Anderson and Middleton log wharf; (2) ITT Rayonier pulpmill; (3) Anderson and Middleton sawmill; (4) Weyerhaeuser Company sawmill and wood-chip exporting facility; (5) Weyerhaeuser Company Bay City Mill No. 1; (6) Weyerhaeuser Company Bay City Mill No. 2.

Issue areas: **A**. new ITT Rayonier sawmill (environmental permit delays); **B**. Kaiser Steel site (national energy priorities supercede environmental protection); **C**. new Boise-Cascade sawmill (water dependency questions and environmental permit delays); **D**. proposed hotel site (conflict with city zoning); **E**. port-owned, future industrial land classified as conservancy by Grays Harbor County Shoreline Master Program.

Source: WPPA, 1975. *Port System Study.*

Grays Harbor, looking west down the Chehalis River toward the Pacific Ocean. Port of Grays Harbor terminals 1 and 4 are shown (indicated by arrows) adjacent to the urban areas of Aberdeen and Hoquiam. The bottom of the photo is approximately the upstream limit of navigation. (Photo by Jones Photo Co., courtesy of the Port of Grays Harbor)

A new 45-acre site has been diked and filled. Kaiser Steel Corporation holds an option on the land to develop an offshore-oil-rig assembly yard, although they have not yet exercised it. In the event that the site is not developed by Kaiser, it may be used by another water-dependent industry.

Bowerman field, a regional airport adjacent to the main channel, is planned as an industrial development park. A recent agreement with fish and wildlife agencies may pave the way for moving the airport to an inland location and developing the airport land for industry.

Issues of current importance. Future development depends on the port being able to resolve fundamental differences of view with fish and wildlife agencies and interests that have arisen over the Corps of Engineers channel project, the Bowerman field development, and other projects. Through the Grays Harbor Estuary Task Force, a general outline for staged industrial growth in the estuary—with stated limits on the growth allowed over the next 50 years—was initially developed in August 1977, although final approval is still pending and the methods of implementation have yet to be worked out.

Washington Coastal Management Program

Overview and implementing authority. The Washington coastal management program, administered by the State Department of Ecology, received federal approval in June 1976. The heart of the program is the Shoreline Management Act, augmented by the State Environmental Policy Act, Environmental Coordination Procedures Act, and other specific programs with which the state has established a coordinating network.

The state also conducts specialized studies to enhance program implementation—such as a coastal atlas, outer continental shelf impact studies, and guidelines for water uses. Further, the state coordinates program activities with state and federal agencies. Over the past four years, $4,745,730 has been allocated for program development and implementation.

The Shoreline Management Act focuses management responsibility at the local level. Master programs are prepared by local governments, pursuant to state guidelines, and are reviewed and approved by the state: they classify shoreline areas and identify uses or performance standards applicable to each classification. Local governments also administer a substantial development permit system (permits are needed for most development activities). Permit decisions can be appealed to the Shoreline Hearings Board (SHB) by the applicant, State Attorney General, Department of Ecology, or citizens' petition. Well over 300 appeals have been heard by the SHB since the act was passed, providing an effective review of local government decisions regarding shoreline development.

Land and water uses. The Shoreline Management Act establishes the process, policies, and guidelines to define permissible land and water uses. It permits all "reasonable and appropriate uses" which do not adversely affect public health, the land and its vegetation and wildlife, state waters, and aquatic life.

Local governments were required to address 21 land and water activities in the development of master programs. These activities were placed within a framework of environments on the basis of existing development, biophysical capabilities and limitations, and local goals. Environments were usually classified as natural, conservancy, rural, and urban, as recommended in the state guidelines.

Shorelines designated in the legislation as "shorelines of statewide significance" are subject to additional constraints. Preference is given to projects which "(1) recognize and protect statewide interests over local interests; (2) preserve the natural character of the shoreline; (3) result in long-term over short-term benefits; (4) protect the resources and ecology of the shoreline; (5) increase public access to publicly owned areas of the shoreline; (6) increase recreational opportunities for the public in the shoreline; (7) . . . other elements . . . deemed appropriate or necessary." (*Revised Code of Washington* 90.58.020).

Coastal zone boundaries. Washington's coastal management area has two tiers. The primary tier, the "resource boundary," is that area included in the Shoreline Management Act. It encompasses the state's marine waters and their associated wetlands, and a minimum of 200 feet upland from the ordinary high-water mark. The second tier, the "planning and administrative boundary," extends inland to include all of the area within the 15 coastal counties.

Geographic areas of particular concern. The following criteria are used by the state to identify areas of particular concern: (1) areas with a resource whose environmental value is of greater than local concern or significance, (2) areas recognized as being of particular concern by state or federal legislation, administrative and regulatory programs, or land ownership, (3) areas with potential for more than one major land or water use or with a resource sought by ostensibly incompatible users.

With these criteria Washington identified ten major areas of particular concern:

1. The Nisqually River estuary
2. Hood Canal
3. The Snohomish River estuary
4. Skagit and Padilla Bays
5. The Strait of Juan de Fuca and areas in northern Puget Sound which are under consideration as a terminal for oil imports.
6. The Dungeness estuary and spit complex
7. Grays Harbor
8. The Willapa Bay estuary
9. The Pacific coastal dune area
10. The continental shelf

Most of these areas were identified as "shorelines of statewide significance" in the Shoreline Management Act.

Public and governmental involvement The state program originated from the involvement of concerned citizens. In response to an initiative proposed by the Washington Environmental Council, the legislature passed an alternative management program—the Shoreline Management Act of 1971—and enacted it effective June 4, 1971, as an emergency law. In November 1972, voters selected the legislative alternative over the initiative. The State Department of Ecology and other interested parties carried on an active campaign to inform the electorate of the issues involved in the two management proposals.

The Shoreline Management Act authorized the State Department of Ecology to develop guidelines for local governments to follow in preparing master programs. Public hearings were held before the state guidelines were adopted (Department of Ecology, 1972). Local governments were required to appoint broadly based citizen advisory committees with members representing both commercial and environmental interests. (Failure to encourage citizen participation was considered contrary to the act.) In addition, local governments were to define goals and draft policy statements, encourage participation of government agencies, describe results of the meetings, and provide information to the public about policy statements and program developments. Program development often extended over an 18-month period and required anywhere from 5 to 40 public meetings. In this lengthy process, more than 2,000 citizens were directly involved in developing the shoreline program in Washington. Further, before local master programs could be adopted, a formal public hearing had to be held.

In some cases, public hearings are also held with respect to the issuance or denial of coastal development permits. Local governments must publish notices of proposed developments in a local newspaper within the county before they can issue permits.

State and local organizational arrangements. The Shoreline Management Act details the relationship between local governments and the State Department of Ecology (DOE). Although the DOE reviews local management programs and local decisions on shoreline permits, and provides local government with some financial and technical support for these shoreline management responsibilities, direct interaction is generally informal. More formal contact is maintained in Puget Sound where local government planners and DOE representatives meet periodically.

State-level organizational arrangements are handled in two ways. Coordinating committees operate where regular ongoing contact between agencies is necessary. In addition, six coastal coordinator positions have been established in the state agencies that have most contact with the coastal and shoreline program. Staff members filling these positions review shoreline development permit applications and master program adoption and amendments, and insure use of agency expertise in coastal management program development and refinement.

State-federal interaction and national interests. During the development of the shoreline management guidelines in 1971-72 (prior to passage of the federal Coastal Zone Management Act) federal agencies were invited to review and comment on the draft guidelines. A special state-federal task force was set up to review master programs in the early years of the Shoreline Management Act. Early in 1975, when the coastal management program was beginning to take shape, a questionnaire was sent to federal agencies to receive their input on coastal problems and management responsibilities. These responses were considered as the program was refined. There was also considerable consultation and discussion between state and federal officials during 1975 and 1976, when Washington's program was being considered for approval.

With approval of the program, primary attention has shifted to methods for implementing the federal consistency provisions. Washington has issued operational guidelines and general policies detailing the implementation of the four classes of federal activities which must be consistent with the state coastal management program. The state relies considerably on the A-95 review process and other existing permit mechanisms to achieve this review. Consistency determinations are made, for the most part, by evaluating a proposed federal action against the Shoreline Management Act, DOE's final guidelines, and local master programs.

ENDNOTES

Chapter 1

American Association of Port Authorities (AAPA). 1976. Public seaport considerations.

Borland and Oliver. 1972. *Port expansion.*

Coastal Zone Management Act of 1972 (CZMA) as amended.

Commission on Marine Science, Engineering and Resources (COMSER). 1969. *Science and Environment.*

Frankel, Ernst. 1973. *The future of Atlantic ports.*

Mayer, H.M. 1975. *Wisconsin's Great Lakes ports.*

National Research Council. 1976. *Port development in the United States.*

Schenker, Eric and Henry Brockel, eds. 1974. *Port planning and development as related to problems of U.S. ports and the U.S. coastal environment.* Cambridge, Massachusetts: Massachusetts Institute of Technology.

Schenker, Eric, H.M. Mayer, and Henry Brockel. 1976. *The Great Lakes Transportation System.* Madison, Wisconsin: The University of Wisconsin Sea Grant College Program. WIS-SG-76-230.

U.S. Department of Commerce, Maritime Administration, NORCAL. 1975. *Trade outlook.*

_____1976. *Port requirements.*

_____1976. *Methodology for estimating capacity.* Volumes I and II.

U.S. Department of Transportation. 1977. *National transportation trends.*

Washington Public Ports Association (WPPA). 1975. *Port system study.* Volume I and Volume II, parts 1-6.

Chapter 2

AAPA. 1976. *Public seaport considerations.*

Gross, R.O. 1968. *Studies in maritime economics.*

Hille, Stanley J. and James E. Suelflow. 1968. *The economic impact of the Port of Baltimore to Maryland.* College Park, Maryland: Department of Business Administration, University of Maryland.

Marcus, Henry S. et al. 1976. *Federal port policy in the United States.*

U.S. Department of Commerce, NORCAL. 1975. Trade outlook.

_____1976. *Port requirements.*

_____1976. *Methodology for estimating capacity.* Volumes I and II.

WPPA. 1975. *Port system study.* Volume I and Volume II, parts 1-6.

Chapter 3

Brewer, William. 1976. Federal consistency and state expectations.

California Coastal Act. 1976. *Public Resources Code,* division 20, section 30000 et seq.

California Coastal Zone Conservation Act of 1972. (Proposition 20) as amended by Chapters 28 and 1014 (1973). *Public Resources Code,* division 18, section 27000 et seq.

Coastal Area Facilities Review Act. 1973. *New Jersey Public Laws,* Chapter 985.

Coastal Coordination Act. *Texas Laws 1977.* (65th Legislature, regular session) Chapter 758, pp. 1900-1902.

Coastal Wetlands Acquisition Act. *Texas Laws 1977.* (65th Legislature, regular session) Chapter 758, pp. 1902-1906.

Coastal Zone Management Act of 1972 (CZMA) as amended.

COMSER. 1969. *Science and environment.* Volume I, part III.

Dredged Materials Act. *Texas Laws 1977.* (65th Legislature, regular session) Chapter 759, pp. 1906-1908.

Englander et al. 1977. Coastal zone problems.

Keifer, Robert. 1975. NOAA's marine sanctuary program.

Marine Protection, Research, and Sanctuaries Act of 1972. (Ocean Dumping Act) 33 *United States Code* 1413, Title III.

National Council on Marine Resources and Engineering Development. *Marine science affairs.* Annual report of the President to Congress, 1967-1971.

Natural Resources Council Act. *Texas Laws 1977.* (65th Legislature, regular session) Chapter 756, pp. 1895-1899.

Shoreline Management Act of 1971. *Revised Code of Washington* (RCW). Chapter 90.58.

U.S. Department of Commerce, Office of Coastal Zone Management (OCZM). 1976. Threshold papers, 1-7.

U.S. Department of Interior, Bureau of Sport Fisheries and Wildlife. 1970. *National estuary study.*

U.S. Federal Water Pollution Control Administration. 1969. *The national estuarine pollution study.*

U.S. Senate, Committee on Commerce. Report on S. 3507, Report No. 92-753 National Coastal Zone Management Act of 1972. Washington, D.C.: Government Printing Office.

Washington Department of Ecology. 1972. Final guidelines, Shoreline Management Act of 1971. *Washington Administrative Code* (WAC), 173-16-010 and 173-16-020. Olympia, Washington:

_____1976. *Washington State coastal zone management program.* Olympia: DOE

Chapter 4

California Coastal Act.

California Coastal Zone Conservation Commission. 1975. *California coastal plan.* San Francisco: CCZCC.

California Coastal Zone Conservation Act of 1972. (Proposition 20)

California LNG Terminal Act of 1977. *Public Resources Code,* division 2, chapter 10.

Clark, John. 1974. *Coastal ecosystems.*

Coastal Area Facilities Review Act.

Coastal Coordination Act.

Coastal Wetlands Acquisition Act.

Delaware Valley Regional Planning Commission. 1976. *Coastal zone management program, draft policy framework.* Philadelphia: DVRPC.

Dredged Materials Act.

Englander et al. 1977. Coastal zone problems.

Georgia Coastal Marshlands Protection Act. *Georgia Code.* Chapter 45-1 as amended.

Goodwin, Robert F. 1976. Shoreline management and marine recreation.

_____1977. Marina siting and design.

_____1978. Marinas under the Shoreline Management Act.

188

Grays Harbor Regional Planning Commission. 1975. *Shorelines management master program.* Aberdeen, Washington: GHRPC.

Massachusetts Executive Office of Environment Affairs. 1977. *Massachusetts coastal zone management program.* Volume I. Boston: MEOEA.

McAteer-Petris Act. *California Government Code.* Chapter 1162, statutes of 1965 as amended. Title 7.2 San Francisco Bay Conservation and Development Commission.

Montagne-Bierly and Associates and Wilsey and Ham. 1978. *Grays Harbor estuary management plan.* Preliminary draft. Aberdeen, Washington: Grays Harbor Regional Planning Council.

Rivkin Associates, Inc. 1976. *Guiding the coastal area of New Jersey: The basis and background for interim land use and density guidelines.* Trenton, New Jersey: Department of Environmental Protection.

Roy Mann Associates, Inc. 1975. *Aesthetic resources of the coastal zone.*

San Francisco Bay Conservation and Development Commission. 1969. *San Francisco Bay plan* and *Supplement.* Sacramento, California: Office of State Printing.

Seattle Department of Community Development. 1976. *Seattle shoreline master program.* Seattle: SDCD.

_____1977. *The State Environmental Policy Act, how it works in Seattle.* Seattle: SDCD.

Swanson, Gerald C. 1975. Coastal zone management administrative perspective.

Texas General Land Office. 1976. *Texas coastal management program, hearing draft and appendices.* Austin, Texas: GLO.

_____1976. *Texas coastal management program, public hearing transcripts, Brownsville, August 9, 1976.* Austin, Texas: GLO.

Tobin, Caroline. 1977. Central waterfront redevelopment as an aspect of coastal zone management. In *Report of the advanced coastal management seminar 1976-1977,* Marc Hershman, ed. Seattle: Institute for Marine Studies, University of Washington.

U.S. Department of Commerce, NORCAL. 1975. *Trade outlook.*

_____1976. *Port requirements.*

_____1976. *Methodology for estimating capacity.* Volumes I and II.

U.S. Department of Defense, Army Corps of Engineers. 1959. *Future development of the San Francisco Bay area, 1960-2020.* Washington, D.C.: Government Printing Office.

_____1977. Regulatory program of the Corps of Engineers. 33 Code of federal regulations, parts 320 et seq. *Federal Register.* Volume 42, p. 37122, July 19, 1977.

U.S. Department of Interior, Fish and Wildlife Service. 1975. Review of fish and wildlife aspects of proposals in and affecting navigable waters. *Federal Register.* Volume 40, p. 55810, December 1, 1975.

WPPA. 1975. *Port system study.* Volume I and Volume II, parts 1-6.

Washington State Energy Facility Siting Act. *Revised Code of Washington.* Chapter 80.50 amended (1977).

Washington State Environmental Coordination Procedures Act. Revised Code of Washington. Chapter 90.62.

Washington State Environmental Policy Act. *Revised Code of Washington.* Chapter 43.21 amended (1976).

Washington State Shoreline Management Act of 1971.

Washington State Department of Ecology. 1972. *Final guidelines.*

_____1976. *Washington State coastal zone management program.*

Weir, Robert. 1976. Impacts of coastal dredging in San Pedro Bay, California. In *Time stressed coastal environments: Assessments and future action.* Proceedings of the Second Annual Conference of the Coastal Society, November 1976. Arlington, Virginia: The Coastal Society.

Chapter 5

Mayer, H.M. 1975. *Wisconsin's Great Lakes ports.*

Texas Coastal and Marine council et al. 1974. *Analysis of the role of the gulf intracoastal waterways in Texas.* College Station, Texas: Texas A & M University, Sea Grant Program. TAMU-SG-75-202.

Texas Coastal and Marine Council. 1975. *Texas coastal legislation.* Second edition. Austin: TCMC.

_____1976. The Texas port book. Draft. Robert R. Richards, ed. College Station: Texas A & M Sea Grant.

_____1977. Report to the 65th Legislature. *Marine commerce.* Pursuant to SR 269/HSR 82. Austin: TCMC.

Texas General Land Office. 1976. *Texas coastal management program hearing draft and appendices* and *Public hearing transcripts, Brownsville, August 9, 1976.*

Washington State Shoreline Management Act of 1971.

Wisconsin Coastal Coordinating and Advisory Council. 1976. Coastal management questionnaire. Madison, Wisconsin: WCCAC.

WPPA. 1975. *Port system study.* Volume I and Volume II, parts 1-6.

U.S. Department of Commerce, NORCAL. 1975. *Trade outlook.*

_____1976. *Port requirements.*

_____1976. *Methodology for estimating capacity.* Volumes I and II.

Chapter 7*

Port of Milwaukee/Wisconsin Coastal Management Program Case Study

Sources

Bay-Lake Regional Planning Commission et al. 1976. *A report on local perception of issues of concern to citizens of Wisconsin's coastal counties.* Madison, Wisconsin: Wisconsin Coastal Coordinating Council.

Center for Great Lakes Studies. 1975. *Analysis of international Great Lakes shipping and hinterland.* The University of Wisconsin-Milwaukee.

Gandre, D.A. 1968. Changes in the degree of utilization of land devoted to handling waterborne commerce at Wisconsin ports. *Land economics.* 44(4):509-514.

Howard, Needles, Tammen, and Bergendoff. 1976. *Menominee River Valley ingress and egress improvements, engineering analysis and feasibility study.* Prepared for the City of Milwaukee.

*Key documents were collected for the case studies from port authorities and coastal management programs. These included statutes and regulations, plans and policy studies, annual reports, and other relevant studies and documents. These documents are listed here, along with the names of people interviewed for the study, by case study.

190

Lauf, Ted. 1975. Shoreland regulation in Wisconsin. *Coastal Zone Management Journal.* 2(1):47-59.

Mayer, H.M. 1975. *Wisconsin's Great Lakes ports.*

Schenker, Eric. 1971. *Present and future income and employment generated by the St. Lawrence Seaway.* Madison: The University of Wisconsin Sea Grant Program. A Sea Grant reprint Wis-SG-71-313.

Schenker, E. and M. Bunamo. 1971. *The Great Lakes container dilemma.* Madison: The University of Wisconsin Sea Grant Program. A Sea Grant reprint Wis-SG-71-304.

Schenker, E. and D. Smith. 1973. The economic merits of extending the St. Lawrence Seaway navigation season. Madison: The University of Wisconsin. A Sea Grant reprint Wis-SG-73-335.

Schenker et al. 1976. Great Lakes transportation system.

Water Resources Act. Wisconsin Statutes. Section 59.971.

Windsor Publications, Inc. 1973. Port of Milwaukee, Wisconsin. Prepared for The Board of Harbor Commissioners, City of Milwaukee, and Port of Milwaukee, Wisconsin.

Wisconsin Coastal Coordinating and Advisory Council. 1977. *Wisconsin coastal management program proposal: Draft for public review,* and *appendices, draft for public review.* Madison: Wisconsin Coastal Management Program. 102 pp.

_____1976. Coastal management questionnaire. Madison.

Wisconsin Coastal Management Program. 1974. *Bibliography of Wisconsin coastal management program publications.* Madison: State Planning Office.

Wisconsin Department of Transportation. 1976. *Wisconsin's Great Lakes ports: Alternative state policy options.* Prepared for the Wisconsin Coastal Management Development Program.

U.S. Department of Commerce. Office of Coastal Zone Management and Wisconsin Coastal Management Program. 1977. *State of Wisconsin coastal management program and draft environmental impact statement.* Washington, D.C.: Office of Coastal Zone Management.

Yanggen, Douglas A. and Jon A. Kusler. 1968. Natural resource protection through shoreland regulation. *Land Economics.*

Interviews

H.C. Brockel, University of Wisconsin-Milwaukee. Former Director, Port of Milwaukee.

Erving F. Heipel, County Landscape Architect, Parks Commission, County of Milwaukee.

Harlan E. Klinkenbeard, Director, Southeastern Regional Planning Commission.

Ronald C. Kysiak, Director of Economic Development, Department of City Development, City of Milwaukee.

Harold Mayer, Professor of Geography, University of Wisconsin-Milwaukee.

Al Miller, Program Administrator, Wisconsin Coastal Management Program, Office of State Planning and Energy.

Eric Schenker, University of Wisconsin, Milwaukee.

John Seefeldt, Director, Port of Milwaukee.

Phil Winkel, Wisconsin Department of Transportation.

Gene Wouk, Sea Grant Marine Advisory Program, University of Wisconsin, Madison.

South Jersey Port Corporation/New Jersey Coastal Management Program Case Study*

Sources
Coastal Area Facilities Review Act.

Coastal Wetlands, New Jersey Conservation and Development. *New Jersey Statutes Annotated,* section 13:9A-1 et seq. (West) 1976.

Control of Waterfront and Harbor Facilities Development. *New Jersey Statutes Annotated,* section 12:5-1 et seq. 1968 and 1976.

Delaware River Basin Compact. *New Jersey Statutes Annotated,* section 32:111. (West) 1963 and 1976.

Delaware River Basin Commission. 1974. *Administrative manual, Part II, Rules of practice and procedure,* and *Part III, Basin regulations—water quality.* Trenton, New Jersey: DRBC.

_____1975. *Annual report.* Trenton: DRBC.

_____1975. *Twelfth water resources program.* Trenton: DRBC.

_____1975. *Water management of the Delaware River Basin.* Trenton: DRBC.

Delaware River Port Authority. Undated. Collection of port aerial photos. *Ameriport, Ports of Philadelphia.* Camden, New Jersey: DRPA.

_____No date. *Ports of Philadelphia. Waterfront facilities, Philadelphia . . . America's industrial center.* Camden: DRPA.

Delaware River Port Authority Interstate Compact. *Purdon's Pennsylvania Statutes Annotated.* Volume 36, section 3503-3509.

Echevarria, John. 1976. Riparian law and coastal zone management. Staff discussion paper, draft ⧧ 2. Trenton: Department of Environmental Protection (DEP).

Economic Development Research Unit, New Jersey Department of Labor and Industry. 1975. *Economic inventory: Economic characteristics of the population and economic structure.* Trenton: DEP.

_____1976. *Economic issues and problems in the northeastern region of the New Jersey coastal zone.* Trenton: DEP.

New Jersey Department of Enviromental Protection. 1976. *Alternatives for the coast.* Trenton: DEP. 87 pp.

_____1976. *The Jersey Coast.* No. 1, July and No. 2, September. Trenton: New Jersey Office of Coastal Zone Management, DEP.

Prior, James T. 1976. New Jersey—Seaport to the world. *New Jersey Business.* June. pp. 45-52.

Rivkin Associates, Inc. 1976. *Guiding the coastal area of New Jersey.*

South Jersey Port Corporation enabling legislation. New Jersey Chapter 60, Laws of 1968.

South Jersey Port Corporation. 1975. A port on the move, 1975 annual report. Camden: SJPC.

Interviews
Willard Cooper, Delaware River Port Authority
John Dale, Office of Economic Research, Department of Labor and Industry
John P. Gaffigen, Manager, Marketing Services, Delaware River Port Authority
William Handkowski, Mayor's Office, City of Camden
Hannah Kahn, Office of Economic Research, Department of Labor and Industry
James R. Kelly, Director, World Trade Division, Delaware River Port Authority

*Includes sources and interviews relating to the Delaware River Port Authority and Delaware River Basin Commission.

David Kinsey, Chief, Office of Coastal Zone Management, DEP
Edward Linky, Office of Coastal Zone Management, DEP
Robert Pettegrew, Executive Director, South Jersey Port Corporation
Seymour D. Selzer, Branch Head, Program Planning, Delaware River Basin Commission
Andrea Topper, Office of Coastal Zone Management, DEP
John Weingart, Office of Coastal Zone Management, DEP

Philadelphia Port Corporation/Pennsylvania Coastal Management Program Case Study

Sources

Delaware Valley Regional Planning Commission. 1976. Coastal Zone Management Program, Draft Policy Framework.

_____1975. Problems and issues within and affecting the coastal zone. Philadelphia: DVRPC.

_____1976. *Tidings,* Pennsylvania Coastal Zone Management Program Newsletter for the Delaware River. Published quarterly. Philadelphia: DVRPC.

_____1975. *Transportation systems in the coastal zone.* Philadelphia: DVRPC.

Hammer, Green, Siler Associates and W. B. Saunders and Co. 1965. *The Delaware River Port.* 137 pp. plus appendices. Prepared for the Commonwealth of Pennsylvania State Planning Board and State Department of Commerce.

_____Navigation commission for the Delaware River. *Purdon's Pennsylvania Statutes Annotated.* Volume 55, Chapter 1, section 1-16.

Penjerdel Corporation. 1976. *Delaware valley transportation. Facts and facilities.* Philadelphia: The Penjerdel Corporation, Philadelphia Chamber of Commerce.

Penn's Landing Corporation. *Penn's Landing, Philadelphia urban waterfront.* Phildadelphia: City of Philadelphia and Old Philadelphia Development Corp., Penn's Landing Corporation.

Philadelphia Port Corporation. 1976. *Annual report.* Philadelphia: Philadelphia Port Corporation.

_____1973. Composite copy of the original articles of incorporation of Philadelphia Port Corporation, as amended in 1966 and 1972.

_____1972. By-laws, Philadelphia Port Corporation (as amended).

_____1975. *Summary listing of lift facilities. Port of Philadelphia.*

Interviews

Dave Baldinger, Environmental Analyst, Philadelphia Planning Department.
Harry J. Fisher, Assistant to Executive Director and Corporation Secretary, Philadelphia Port Corporation.
Jim Martin, Penn's Landing Corporation.
John Nagel, Philadelphia City Planning Commission.
Michael Wolf, Delaware Valley Regional Planning Commission.

Georgia Ports Authority/Georgia Coastal Management Program Case Study

Sources

Carruth, Gordon. 1976. Urban development. Issue paper presented to Georgia's Coastal Zone Management Advisory Council. Atlanta: Georgia Office of Planning and Budget.

_____1976. Waterborne commerce. Issue paper presented to Georgia's Coastal Zone Management Advisory Council. Atlanta: Georgia Office of Planning and Budget.

Chatham County-Savannah Metro Planning Commission. 1975. *Chatham's coast: Goals and issues for the future.* Savannah: CC-SMPC.

Clifton, David S. and Larry R. Edens. 1973. *The economic impact of Georgia's deepwater ports.* Atlanta: Industrial Development Division, Engineering Experiment Station, Georgia Institute of Technology.

Coastal Area Planning and Development Commission. 1976. Coastal Georgia annual report. Brunswick, Georgia: CAPDC.

_____1976. *Year two work program.* Brunswick: CAPDC.

Dean, Lillian et al. 1975. *The value and vulnerability of coastal resources.* Atlanta: Department of Natural Resources.

Georgia Ports Authority. *Georgia Anchorage.* Bimonthly publication.

Georgia State Department of Natural Resources. 1975. *Activities in Georgia's coastal waters. Past trends and future prospects.* Atlanta: DNR.

Georgia State Department of Natural Resources, Office of Planning and Budget. No date. *Inventory and analysis of legal authority relevant to state control of coastal zone land and water uses.* Atlanta: DNR.

_____No date. *Methodology for assessing environmental impacts.* Atlanta: DNR.

_____1975. *User's information for coastal resources maps.* Atlanta: DNR.

_____1975. *Year 1—Coastal zone management program: Summary of coastal resource data and implications for coastal zone management.* Atlanta: DNR.

Hindes, James. 1976. An overview. Issue paper presented to Georgia's Coastal Zone Management Advisory Council. Atlanta: Office of Planning and Budget.

Howard, Roger D. 1976. *Environmental regulations for Georgia industry.* Atlanta: Bureau of Industry and Trade. (In particular, see *Georgia Code,* Chapter 45-1. Coastal Marshlands Protection Act of 1972, Appendix 7.)

Kusmik, Joe. 1976. Industrial development. Issue paper presented to Georgia's Coastal Zone Management Advisory Council. Atlanta: Office of Planning and Budget.

State Port Authority. *Georgia Statutes,* Chapter 98.2

Interviews

Gordon A. Carruth, Planner, Chatham County-Savannah Metropolitan Planning Commission.

Rick Cothran, Coastal Representative, Office of Planning and Budget.

William B. Dawson, Assistant Manager, Brunswick Port Authority.

James H. Dodd, Office of Planning and Budget.

Mike Gleeton, Director of Planning, Coastal Area Planning and Development Commission.

Tom Hilton, Coastal Area Planning and Development Commission.

Jim Hindes, Office of Planning and Budget.

O.A. Kelly, Superintendent of Operations, Georgia Ports Authority.

Joe Kusmik, Associate Regional, Coastal Zone Management Planner, Savannah Office, Coastal Area Planning and Development Commission.

William H. McGowan, Executive Director, Emeritus, Savannah Port Authority.

James Newsome, Jr., Director of Operations, Georgia Ports Authority.

Bob Reimold, Marine Extension Agent, University of Georgia, Sea Grant Program, Brunswick, Georgia.

B. Sanford Ulmer, Executive Director, Savannah Port Authority.
Dee Willis, Office of Planning and Budget.
James R. Wilson, Chief, Resources Planning Section, Office of Planning and Research, Department of Natural Resources.

Port of Brownsville/Texas Coastal Management Program Case Study

Sources

Brownsville Navigation District. No date. The Port of Brownsville (brochure).

Buchanan, G. Sidney. 1973. Texas navigation districts and regional planning in the Gulf Coast area. *Houston Law Review.* 10(3):533-597.

Coastal Coordination Act.

Coastal Wetlands Acquisition Act.

Dredged Materials Act.

Espy, Huston, and Associates, Inc. 1976. *A study of the placement of materials dredged from Texas ports and waterways.* Two volumes. Austin: General Land Office.

Ferguson, Henry V. 1976. *Port of Brownsville: A history.* Brownsville: Springman-King Press.

Harland, Bartholomew and Associates, 1975. *Land use plan, Brownsville, Texas.* Prepared for the City of Brownsville, City Planning Department.

Hart Sprager, R.P.C. Consultants. 1976. *Faces of the coast.* A film produced for the Texas General Land Office, Austin.

Natural Resources Council Act.

Richards, Robert R. 1976. *Public port financing in Texas.* Prepared for Texas Coastal and Marine Council. College Station, Texas: Texas A&M University, Center for Marine Resources.

Texas Coastal and Marine Council. 1975. *Texas coastal legislation.*

_____1976. *The Texas port book.*

_____1977. *Marine commerce.* Austin: TCMC.

Texas Coastal and Marine Council et al. 1974. *Analysis of the role of the gulf intracoastal waterways in Texas.* College Station, Texas: Texas A&M University, Sea Grant Program. TAMU-SG-75-202.

Texas General Land Office. 1976. *Texas coastal management program, hearing draft and appendices.*

_____1976. *Executive summary, hearing draft.*

_____1976. *Public hearing transcripts, Brownsville, August 9, 1976.*

Interviews

Al Cisneros, General Manager and Port Director, Port of Brownsville.

Steve Frishman, Publisher, *South Jetty,* Port Aransas, Texas.

Jep Hill, Assistant Director, Texas Coastal Management Program.

Ersel G. Lantz, Director of Engineering and Port Development, Port of Brownsville.

Mario Moreno, Director, City Planning Department, Brownsville.

Fred W. Rusteberg, Special Assistant to the General Manager, Port of Brownsville.

Port of Los Angeles/California Coastal Management Program Case Study

Sources

Board of Harbor Commissioners, Port of Los Angeles. 1975. *Comprehensive master plan 1990.* Port of Los Angeles, California.

_____1975. *Port of Los Angeles.* Port of Los Angeles, California.

California Coastal Act.

California Coastal Commission. 1977. *Local coastal program manual.* Sacramento: CCC.

_____1977. *Local coastal program regulations.* Sacramento: CCC.

_____1977. *Permit and port planning regulations.* Sacramento: CCC.

California Coastal Zone Conservation Act of 1972 (Proposition 20).

California Coastal Zone Conservation Commission. 1975. *California coastal plan.*

_____1974. *Transportation element.* Draft and final. Long Beach: South Coast Regional Commission.

Swanson, Gerald C. 1975. *Administrative perspective.*

U.S. Department of Commerce, NORCAL. 1975. *Port requirements.*

_____1975. *Trade outlook.*

_____1976. *Methodology for estimating capacity.* Volumes I and II.

U.S. Department of Commerce, Office of Coastal Zone Management. 1977. *State of California coastal management program and revised draft environmental impact statement.*

Interviews

Joseph D. Carrabino, Engineering Management Science Corporation.

Fred Crawford, Director, Port of Los Angeles.

Paul Grandle, Manager, Mechanical and Structural Engineering, Union Oil Company, Los Angeles.

Lee Hill, Environmental Division, Port of Los Angeles.

Glen Hughes, Legislative Aide to Los Angeles Port Director.

Carl Hurst, Head, Environmental Division, Port of Los Angeles.

Frank Lambardi, Assistant Director, City of Los Angeles, Planning Department.

Larry Leopold, Marine Resources Specialist, Sea Grant Office, University of Southern California, Los Angeles.

Dave Metz, Sea Grant Office, University of Southern California, Los Angeles.

Dave Smith, Chief Planner, South Coast Regional Commission, Los Angeles.

Mike Tharp, Planner, City of Los Angeles Planning Department.

Port of Grays Harbor/Washington Coastal Management Program Case Study

Sources

Borland and Oliver. 1972. *Port expansion.*

Grays Harbor Regional Planning Commission. 1975. *Shorelines management master program.*

Greenacres Consulting Corporation. 1973. Forest tributary to the Port of Grays Harbor. Prepared for the Commissioners of the Port of Grays Harbor.

McCrea, Maureen and James H. Feldmann. 1977. Interim Assessment.

Port of Grays Harbor, Commissioners. *Port of Grays Harbor annual report* 1970 through 1976. Aberdeen, Washington.

Public Port District Act. *Revised Code of Washington.* Chapter 53.08.

Shoreline Hearings Board practice and procedure. *Washington Administrative Code,* 371-08-125.

U.S. Department of Defense, Army Corps of Engineers. 1976. *Grays Harbor and Chehalis River, and Hoquiam, Washington, channel improvement for navigation.* Feasibility report. Seattle District.

Washington Department of Ecology. 1972. *Final guidelines*.
_____1976. *Coastal zone management program*.
Washington State Shoreline Management Act of 1971.
WPPA. 1975. *Port system study*. Volume I and Volume II, parts 1-6.

Interviews
Pat Dugan, Planning Director, Grays Harbor Regional Planning Commission.
Stan Lattin, Director of Planning, Port of Grays Harbor.
Rod Mack, Division Head, Department of Ecology, State of Washington.
Henry E. Soike, General Manager, Port of Grays Harbor.

BIBLIOGRAPHY

COASTAL ZONE MANAGEMENT BIBLIOGRAPHY

The references in the bibliography are selected for several purposes. First, references include general information on coastal zone management. Second, references relate to the federal Coastal Zone Management Act, particularly general references and more detailed analysis of the different aspects discussed in the text of this volume. Third, selections are included which have implications for ports in the management of the coastal areas.

Armstrong, John M. and Earl H. Bradley Jr. 1971. Status of state coastal zone management programs. *Marine Technology Society Journal,* 6(5):7-16 and 6(6):7-14.

Armstrong et al. 1974. *Coastal zone management: The process of program development.* Sandwich, Massachusetts: Coastal Zone Institute. 327 pp.

Ashbaugh, John and Jens Sorensen. 1976. Identifying the "public" for participation in coastal zone management. *Coastal Zone Management Journal.* 2(4): 383-410.

Baram, Michael. 1976. *Environmental law and the siting of facilities: Issues in land use and coastal zone management.* Cambridge, Massachusetts: Ballinger Publishing Co. 255 pp.

Berger, Anne H. 1975. *Methods of control of land and water uses in the coastal zone.* Office of Coastal Zone Management, National Oceanic and Atmospheric Administration, U.S. Dept. of Commerce, Washington D.C. NTIS # PB 249 799. 44 pp.

Brahtz, J.P. Peel (ed.). 1970. *Coastal zone management, multiple use with conservation.* New York: John Wiley and Sons. 160 pp.

Bish, Robert L. 1975. *Coastal resource use: Decisions on puget sound.* Seattle, Washington: University of Washington Press. 198 pp.

Blumm, Michael C. and John B. Noble. 1976. The promise of federal consistency under section 307 of the Coastal Zone Management Act. *Environmental Law Reporter,* 6:50047-50065.

Bowden, Gerald. 1976. Legal battles on the California coast: A review of the rules. *Coastal Zone Management Journal.* 2(3):273-296.

Bradley, Earl H. Jr. and John M. Armstrong. 1972. *A description and analysis of coastal zone and shoreland management programs in the United States.* University of Michigan Sea Grant Program.

Brewer, William. 1976. Federal consistency and state expectations. *Coastal Zone Management Journal,* 2(4):315-326.

Clark, John. 1974. *Coastal ecosystems.* Washington, D.C.: The Conservation Foundation.

_____1976. *The Sanibel report: Formulation of a comprehensive plan based on natural systems.* The Conservation Foundation. 305 pp.

_____1977. *Coastal ecosystem management. A technical manual for the conservation of coastal zone resources.* New York: John Wiley & Sons, Inc. 919 pp.

Commission on Marine Science, Engineering and Resources (COMSER). 1969. *Science and environment.* Panel reports, Volume I, section III. Washington, D.C.: Government Printing Office.

Detwyler, Thomas R., ed. 1971. *Man's impact on the environment.* New York: McGraw Hill. 731 pp.

Devanney, J.W. III et al. 1976. *Parable Beach: A primer in coastal zone economics.* Cambridge, Massachusetts: MIT Press. 100 pp.

_____1970. *Economic factors in the development of a coastal zone.* Cambridge, Massachusetts: MIT Press.

Ditton, Robert B. and Mark Stephens. 1976. *Coastal recreation: A handbook for planners and managers.* Executive summary and full report with appendices. Prepared for U.S. National Oceanic and Atmospheric Administration, Office of Coastal Zone Management.

Ditton, Robert, John Seymour and Gerald C. Swanson. 1977. *Coastal resource management: Beyond bureaucracy and the market.* Lexington, Massachusetts: Heath & Co.

Ducsik, Dennis. 1974. *Shoreline for the public: A handbook of social, economic, and legal considerations regarding public recreational use of the nation's coastal shoreline.* Cambridge, Massachusetts: MIT Press. 182 pp.

_____1974. *Coastal zone management: An introductory course syllabus.* Cambridge, Massachusetts: MIT Sea Grant Program. MIT-SG-75-1. 144 pp.

Englander, Ernie, Jim Feldmann and Marc Hershman. 1977. Coastal zone problems: A basis for evaluation. *Coastal Zone Management Journal,* 3(3):217-236.

Environmental Information Center. 1976. *State laws and regulations: A guide to environmental legislation in the fifty states and the District of Columbia.* New York. E.I.C. 42 pp.

Fuller, Dale B. et al. 1977. Managerial applications of a four-year regional program in remote sensing. *Coastal Zone Management Journal,* 3(2):183-196.

Goodwin, Robert F. 1976. Shoreline management and marine recreation industry, in *Recreation 76' Conference Proceedings,* ed. Robert F. Goodwin. Pullman, Washington: Cooperative Extension Service, Washington State University WSG-WO-76-1.

_____1977. Marina siting and design, in *Shorelines '77: Performance and prospects,* ed. Robert F. Goodwin. Seattle, Washington: Washington Sea Grant. WSG-WO-77-3.

_____1978. Marinas under the Shoreline Management Act, in *Moorage Workshop Proceedings,* ed. Caroline C. Tobin and Robert F. Goodwin. Seattle, Washington: Northwest Marine Trade Association.

Great Lakes Basin Commission. 1977. *Energy facility siting in the Great Lakes coastal zone: Analysis and policy options.* Prepared as U.S. Commerce Department, Office of Coastal Zone Management Technical Assistance Document. 524 pp.

Heikoff, Joseph M. 1977. *Coastal resources management: Institutions and programs.* Ann Arbor, Michigan: Ann Arbor Science Publishers, Inc. 287 pp.

Hershman, Marc J. 1972. The federal Coastal Zone Management Act of 1972. *Louisiana Coastal Law,* ≠8. Baton Rouge, Louisiana: LSU Sea Grant Legal Program.

_____1975. Achieving federal-state coordination in coastal resources management. *William and Mary Law Review,* 16:747-772.

Hershman, Marc J. and John Folkenroth. 1975. Coastal zone management and intergovernmental coordination. *Oregon Law Review,* 54:13-33.

Hite, James C. and James M. Stepp, eds. 1971. *Coastal zone resource management.* New York: Praeger Publishers. 169 pp.

Hite, James C. and Eugene A. Laurent. 1972. *Environmental planning: An economic analysis and applications for the coastal zone.* New York: Praeger Publishers. 155 pp.

Hood, Donald W. 1971. *Impingement of man on the oceans*. New York: Wiley Interscience. 738 pp.

Irland, Lloyd C. 1976. Federal river basin planning in the coastal zone: The Long Island Sound Study. *Coastal Zone Management Journal*, 2(3):247-272.

Jaworski, Eugene and C. Nicholas Raphael. 1976. The confined dredge spoil disposal program in the Great Lakes. *Coastal Zone Management Journal*, 3(1):91-96.

Johnson, Ralph. 1977. Law of the coastal zone. Unpublished text available through the University of Washington School of Law, Seattle, Washington.

Keifer, Robert. 1975. NOAA's marine sanctuary program. *Coastal Zone Management Journal*, 2(2):177-188.

Ketchum, Bostwick H., ed. 1972. *The water's edge*. Cambridge, Massachusetts: MIT Press. 363 pp.

Koppelman, Lee E., Project Director. 1976. *Integration of regional land use planning and coastal zone science. A guidebook for planners*. Prepared for the Office of Policy Development and Research, Department of Housing and Urban Development, Long Island, N.Y.

Laist, David. 1976. *Coastal facility guidelines: A methodology for their development with environmental case studies on marinas and power plants*. Washington, D.C.: Office of Coastal Zone Management, National Oceanic and Atmospheric Administration, and U.S. Department of Commerce.

Langlois, Edward. 1975. Port authorities view state coastal management programs. *Coastal Zone Management Journal*, 2(2):171-176.

Lauf, George F., ed. 1967. *Estuaries*. Washington, D.C.: American Association for the Advancement of Science, Publication No. 83. 757 pp.

Mandelker, Daniel R. and Thea A. Sherry. 1974. The National Coastal Zone Management Act of 1972. *Urban Law Annual*. pp. 119-137.

McCrea, Maureen and James H. Feldmann. 1977. Interim assessment of Washington State shoreline management. *Coastal Zone Management Journal*, 3(2): 119-150.

Meta Systems. 1975. *An operational framework for coastal zone management planning*. Meta Systems, NTIS Report ≠ PB 239 519. 284 pp.

Moss, Mitchell L. 1976. The urban port: A hidden resource for the city and the coastal zone. *Coastal Zone Management Journal*, 2(3):223-246.

Natural Resources Defense Council. 1976. *Who's minding the shore? A citizen's guide to coastal management*. Washington, D.C.

Odum, Howard T., B.J. Copeland and E.A. McMahan, eds. 1974. *Coastal ecological systems of the U.S.* Four volumes. Washington, D.C.: Conservation Foundation. 1977 pp.

Odum, William E. and Stephen S. Skjei. 1974. The issue of wetlands preservation and management: A second view. *Coastal Zone Management Journal*, 1(2): 151-164.

Pope, R.M. and James G. Gosselink. 1973. A tool for use in making land management decisions involving tidal marshland. *Coastal Zone Management Journal*, 1(1):47-65.

Power, Garrett. 1975. Watergate Village: A case study of a permit application for a marina submitted to the U.S. Army Corps of Engineers. *Coastal Zone Management Journal*, 2(2):103-124.

Real Estate Research Corporation. 1976. *Business prospects under coastal zone management*. Chicago, Ill.: U.S. Department of Commerce, Office of Coastal Zone Management Technical Assistance Document. 18 pp.

Robbins, J. Michael and Marc J. Hershman. 1974. Boundaries of the coastal zone: A survey of state laws. *Coastal Zone Management Journal,* 1(3):305-332.

Rosentraub, Mark S. and Robert Warren. 1975. Informal utilization and self evaluating capacities for coastal zone management agencies. *Coastal Zone Management Journal,* 2(2):193-223.

Roy Mann Associates, Inc. 1975. *Aesthetic resources of the coastal zone.* U.S. Department of Commerce, Office of Coastal Zone Management Technical Resource Document, NTIS ≠ PB 247-927. Cambridge, Massachusetts: Roy Mann Associates, Inc. 199 pp.

Russell, Clifford S. and Allen V. Kneese. 1973. Establishing the scientific, technical, and economic basis for coastal zone management. *Coastal Zone Management Journal,* 1(1):47-65.

Sabatier, Paul. 1977. State review of local land use decisions: The California Coastal Commissions. *Coastal Zone Management Journal,* 3(3):255-290.

Sorensen, Jens C. 1971. *A framework for identification and control of resource degradation and conflict in the multiple use of the coastal zone.* University of California, Berkeley, Department of Landscape Architecture.

Stang, Paul, ed. *Boundaries of the coastal zone.* Office of Coastal Zone Management, National Oceanic and Atmospheric Administration, and Department of Commerce, Washington, D.C. NTIS ≠ PB 249-594.

Swanson, Gerald C. 1975. Coastal zone management from an administrative perspective: A case study of the San Francisco Bay Conservation and Development Commission. *Coastal Zone Management Journal,* 2(2):81-102.

U.S. Department of Defense, Army Corps of Engineers. 1971. *Shore management guidelines.* Washington, D.C.

U.S. Department of Commerce, 1976. Maritime Administration. *Untangling dredging regulations.* (Western Region) San Francisco, California, 45 pp.

U.S. Department of Commerce. National Oceanic and Atmospheric Administration. Office of Coastal Zone Management. *State coastal zone management activities, 1974.* NTIS ≠ PB 249 753. 124 pp.

_____1975. *The federal consistency provisions of the coastal zone management Act of 1972: A preliminary analysis.* Washington, D.C.: The Office of Coastal Zone Management. 26 pp.

_____1975. Results of a survey of state coastal zone management needs. Washington, D.C.: Office of Coastal Zone Management. 21 pp. with appendix.

_____1976. *Living coastal resources. A coastal zone management technical assistance document.* NTIS ≠ PB 258 477. Washington, D.C.: Government Printing Office. 34 pp. with appendices.

_____1976. *State coastal zone management activities, 1975-1976.* Washington, D.C.: Office of Coastal Zone Management. 153 pp.

_____1976. *National Coastal Zone Management Act of 1972 Threshold Papers: No. 1: Boundaries. No. 2: Land and water uses. No. 3: Geographic areas of particular concern (Draft). No. 4: Public and governmental involvement (Draft). No. 5: State-federal interaction and national interest. No. 6: Organization. No. 7: Authorities.* Washington, D.C.: The Office of Coastal Zone Management.

U.S. Department of Interior, Bureau of Sport Fisheries & Wildlife, U.S. Bureau of Commercial Fisheries. 1970. *National estuary study,* 7 Volumes. Washington, D.C.

U.S. Federal Water Pollution Control Administration. 1969. *The national estuarine pollution study, a report to the Congress.* Three Volumes. Washington, D.C.: Government Printing Office.

U.S. General Accounting Office. 1976. *The coastal zone management program: An uncertain future.* Report to the Congress by the Comptroller General of the United States. GGD-76-107.

U.S. Senate, Commerce Committee, *National Coastal Zone Management Act of 1972.* Senate Commerce Committee report on S. 3507, Report No. 92-753. Washington, D.C.: Government Printing Office.

U.S. Senate, Committee on Commerce and National Ocean Policy Study. 1976. *Legislative history of the Coastal Zone Management Act of 1972, as amended in 1974 and 1976 with a section-by-section index.* Washington, D.C.: Government Printing Office. 1,117 pp.

Urban Land Institute. 1976. *The economic benefits of coastal zone management: An overview.* U.S. Department of Commerce, Office of Coastal Zone Management Technical Assistance Document. Urban Land Institute Research Division. 29 pp.

Walker, Richard A. 1974. Wetlands preservation and management on Chesapeake Bay: The role of science in natural resource policy. *Coastal Zone Management Journal,* 1(1):7-103.

Warren, Robert, Louis F. Wechsler, and Mark S. Rosentraub. 1977. Local-regional interaction in the development of coastal land use policies: A case study of a metropolitan area. *Coastal Zone Management Journal,* 3(4).

Weyl, Peter K. 1977. Pollution susceptibility: An environmental parameter for coastal zone management. *Coastal Zone Management Journal,* 3(3):255-290.

Zile, Zigurds L. 1974. A legislative-political history of the Coastal Zone Management Act of 1972. *Coastal Zone Management Journal,* 1(2):235-275.

Statute

Coastal Zone Management Act of 1972 (CZMA) as amended, 16 *United States Code* section 1451-64.

Rules

Estuarine sanctuary guidelines. (CZMA Section 312). 15 Code of Federal Regulations, Part 921. *Federal Register,* Volume 39, p. 19924. June 4, 1974.

State coastal zone management programs: development and approval. (CZMA sections 305 and 306). 15 Code of Federal Regulations, Part 923. *Federal Register,* Volume 43, p. 8378. March 1, 1978.

State coastal zone management program. (CZMA Section 306 (c) (1), 307 (b), 307 (h), dealing with federal-state coordination.) 15 Code of Federal Regulations, Part 925. *Federal Register,* Volume 40, p. 8546, February 28, 1975.

Coastal zone management program development grants, allocation of funds to states. (CZMA Section 305 (e)). 15 Code of Federal Regulations, Part 926. *Federal Register,* Volume 40, p. 11863, March 14, 1975.

Coastal zone management program, administrative grants, allocation of section 306 funds to states. 15 Code of Federal Regulations, Part 927. *Federal Register,* Volume 40, p. 23275, May 29, 1975.

Coastal zone management program development grants, outer continental shelf. (CZMA Section 305). 15 Code of Federal Regulations, Part 928. *Federal Register,* Volume 40, p. 23275, May 29, 1975.

Federal consistency with approved coastal zone management programs. (CZMA Section 307 (c) and (h), 316, and 317). 15 Code of Federal Regulations, Part 930. *Federal Register,* Volume 42, p. 43586, August 29, 1977.

Coastal energy impact program. (CZMA Section 308). 15 Code of Federal Regulations, Part 931. *Federal Register,* Volume 43, p. 7546. February 23, 1978.

Coastal zone management interstate grants. (CZMA Section 309). 15 Code of Federal Regulations, Part 932. *Federal Register,* Volume 42, p. 19856, April 15, 1977.

Coastal zone management research and technical assistance. (CZMA Section 310 (a)). 15 Code of Federal Regulations, Part 933. *Federal Register,* Volume 42, p. 4046, January 21, 1977.

Annual Reports and Conferences

Coastal Society. *The present and future of coasts.* Proceedings of First Annual Conference. Bethesda, Maryland: The Coastal Society (P.O. Box 34405). November 1975. 278 pp.

_____. *Time-Stressed coastal environments: assessment and future action.* Proceedings of Second Annual Conference, November 17-20, 1976. Arlington, Virginia: The Coastal Society. 1976.

Coastal Zone Management. Annual report for fiscal year 1973. Washington, D.C.: Government Printing Office. May 1974.

Council of State Government. *Proceedings of the conference on organizing and managing the coastal zone.* Annapolis, Maryland, June 13-14, 1973. Council of State Governments. Washington, D.C. 1973. 331 pp.

Marine Technology Society, Coastal Zone Marine Management Committee. *Tools for coastal zone management,* Proceedings of the Conference, February 14-15, 1972, Washington, D.C. 1972. 213 pp.

New England River Basins Commission. *Proceedings, the coastal zone options for state action.* New England River Basins Commission, Boston, Massachusetts. 1970. 60 pp.

Report to the congress on coastal zone management, July 1973-June 1974. Public Law 92-583. Washington, D.C.: Government Printing Office. May 1975.

Report to the congress on coastal zone management. July 1974-June 1975. Public Law 92-583. Washington, D.C.: Government Printing Office. April 1976. NTIS # PB-257-520 ($4.50).

Report to the congress on coastal zone management. Fiscal Year 1976. Public Law 92-583. April 1977. 73 pp.

U.S. Senate Committee on Commerce. *The coastal imperative: Developing a national perspective for coastal decision making.* Proceedings of the second national conference on coastal zone management. United States 93rd congress, 2nd Session, 1974.

U.S. Department of Commerce, National Oceanic and Atmospheric Administration, and Office of Coastal Zone Management. *Proceedings of the third national conference on coastal zone management.* Spring 1975. Office of Coastal Zone Management, Washington, D.C., 1976.

Bibliographies

Jenks, Bonnie, Jens Sorensen, and James Breadon. 1976. *Coastal zone bibliography citations to documents on planning, resource management and impact assessment. 2nd Edition, Sea Grant Publications* # 49. La Jolla, California: University of California, Institute of Marine Resources.

Heikoff, Joseph M. 1975. *Shorelines and beaches in coastal management: A bibliography.* Monticello, Illinois: Council of Planning Librarians. 63 pp.

Laird, Beverly L., Rosemary Green, Maurice P. Lynch, and William J. Hargis, Jr. D. 1975. *Documents related to the coastal zone: An annotated bibliography.* Special Report No. 40 in Applied Marine Science and Ocean Engineering, Virginia. Gloucester Point, Virginia: Institute of Marine Science.

U.S. Department of Commerce, National Oceanic and Atmospheric Administration and Office of Coastal Zone Management. 1977. *Coastal zone management, annotated bibliography.* NTIS ≠ PB-265-270. Washington, D.C. 475 pp.

Wallach, Kate and Romaine Kupfer. 1977. *Comparative coastal zone management.* A selective partially annotated bibliography. Sea Grant Publication LSU-L-001. 1977. Baton Rouge, Louisiana: LSU Center for Wetlands Resources, Louisiana State University.

Periodicals

The following periodicals often include articles pertinent to coastal zone management:

American Institute of Planners Journal. Washington, D.C.: American Institute of Planners. (bimonthly)

Coastal Zone Management. Washington, D.C.: Nautilus Press, Inc. (weekly newsletter)

Coastal Zone Management Journal. New York: Crane Russak and Co. (quarterly)

Journal of Soil and Water Conservation. Ankeny, Iowa: Soil Conservation Society of America. (bimonthly)

Marine Technology Society Journal. Washington, D.C.: Marine Technology Society. (10/year.)

Water Resources Bulletin. Urbana, Illinois: American Water Resources Association. (bimonthly)

SELECTED BIBLIOGRAPHY ON PORTS

American Association of Port Authorities (AAPA). 1976. Public seaport considerations applying to coastal zone planning. Unpublished paper. Washington, D.C.: AAPA.

American Society of Civil Engineers, Committee on Port Structure Costs, Committee on Ports and Harbors, ASCE Waterways, Harbors and Coastal Engineering Division. 1974. *Port structure costs.* New York: ASCE. 171 pp.

Amundsen, Paul and Martin J. Schwimmer. 1973. *Management of a seaport.* Report No. COM 741178/AS. Springfield, Virginia: National Technical Information Service.

Amundsen, P.A., J.S. Smith and H.D. Bentley. eds. 1961. *Ports of the Americas—history and development.* Washington, D.C.: American Association of Port Authorities.

Baker, C.C.R. and R.B. Oram. 1971. *The efficient port.* Oxford: Pergamon Press.

Bird, James. 1971. *Seaports and seaport terminals.* London: Hutchinson and Co., Ltd.

Borland, Stewart and Martha Oliver. 1972. *Port expansion in the Puget Sound region 1970-2000.* Seattle: Washington Sea Grant. WSG-MP-72-1.

Brown, A.H.J. and C.A. Dove. 1960. *Port operations and administration.* Cambridge, Massachusetts: Cornell Maritime Press.

Brockel, C.H. 1971. *The modern challenge to port management.* A Sea Grant Reprint Wis-SG-72-321. The University of Wisconsin, Sea Grant Program.

Bruffey, T.A. 1967. Port planning in the United States: A study of port authority and municipal government interrelationships. An Unpublished Master's Thesis, University of Washington, Seattle.

Celleneri, Louis E. 1976. *Seaport dynamics.* New York: Heath & Co.

Cooper, Hal B.H., Jr. and Ghassan M. Mahdi. 1974. Air pollution impact of maritime shipping operations in the Port of Houston. *Coastal Zone Management Journal,* 1(4):415-432.

Frankel, Ernst. 1973. *Studies on the future of Atlantic ports.* No. MITSG-72-18. Cambridge, Massachusetts: Massachusetts Institute of Technology, Sea Grant Project Office.

Gross, R.O. 1968. *Studies in maritime economics.* Cambridge: Cambridge University Press.

Hanson, Melvin A. et al. 1969. *Great Lakes port and shipping systems,* (2 parts). No. PB-188-791 and PB 188-937, Report for U.S. Department of Commerce, Maritime Administration. Springfield, Virginia: National Technical Information Service.

Kearney, A.T. and Co., Inc. 1974. *Domestic waterborne shipping market analysis: Executive summary,* COM 74-10411/8. Springfield, Virginia: National Technical Information Service.

Manalytics, Inc. 1972. *The impact of maritime containerization on the U.S. transportation system,* (Volumes I and II), PB 72-10405/6, Report for U.S. Department of Commerce Maritime Administration. Springfield, Virginia: National Technical Information Service.

Matson Research Corporation. 1970. *The impact of containerization on the U.S. Economy, (Volumes I and II), COMM No. 71-00050/1,* Report for U.S. Department of Commerce, Maritime Administration. Springfield, Virginia: National Technical Information Service.

Marcus, Henry S., et al. 1976. *Federal port policy in the United States.* Cambridge, Massachusetts: MIT Press. 371 pp.

Mayer, H.M. 1975. *Wisconsin's Great Lakes ports: Background and future alternatives.* Milwaukee: Center for Great Lakes Studies, The University of Wisconsin.

Metcalfe, Vernon. 1959. *Principles of ocean transportation.* New York: Simmons-Boardman Publications Corporation.

Nathan, Robert R. Associates, Inc. 1972. *A study to determine U.S. port needs.* A Report for U.S. Army Corps of Engineers, Washington, D.C.

National Research Council. Panel on Future Port Requirements of the United States. 1976. *Port development in the United States.* Maritime Transportation Research Board, Commission on Socio-technical Systems, National Research Council. Washington: National Academy of Sciences.

Operations Research, Inc. 1964. *Federal policy for United States ports.* Report for U.S. Department of Commerce, Maritime Administration. Springfield, Virginia: National Technical Information Service.

Oran, R.B. 1965. *Cargo handling for the modern port.* Cambridge, Massachusetts: Cornell Maritime Press.

Schenker, Eric and Henry Brockel, eds. 1974. *Port planning and development as related to problems of U.S. ports and the U.S. coastal environment.* Cambridge, Massachusetts: Cornell Maritime Press.

Schumaier, C.P. 1975. *Utilizing the existing regulatory structure to influence port development.* Report for the Department of Transportation, Office of Systems Development and Technology. Cambridge, Massachusetts: Massachusetts Institute of Technology.

Takel, R.E. 1974. *Industrial port development.* Bristol, England: Scientechnica, Ltd.

Tulpule, A.H. et al. 1974. *An analysis of some world transport statistics.* Department of the Environment. Crowthrone Berkshire. Transport and Road Research Laboratory. NTIS PB 232 940. 48 pp.

United Nations Council on Trade and Development (UNCTAD). 1971. *Port statistics—selection, collection and presentation of port information and statistics.* Geneva, Switzerland: United Nations Office.

U.S. Department of Commerce, Maritime Administration. 1961. *Port series part 1, United States seaports—Alaska, Pacific Coast and Hawaii.* Washington, D.C.: Government Printing Office.

_____1963. *Port series part 1, United States seaports—Atlantic Coast.* Washington, D.C.: Government Printing office.

_____1965. *Port series part 1, United States seaports—Gulf Coast.* Washington, D.C.: Government Printing Office.

_____1966. *The economic impact of the United States ocean ports.* Washington, D.C.

_____1974. *Public port financing in the United States.* Washington, D.C.: Maritime Administration.

_____1974. *North American port development expenditure survey: 1966-1972' with projections 1973-77.* Washington, D.C.: Government Printing Office.

_____1975. *Trade outlook of the Northern California ports: Year 2000 and beyond.* Prepared by Policy Planning Consultants from U.S. Maritime Administration and the Northern California Ports and Terminals Bureau. Oakland, California.

_____1976. *Port requirements for the San Francisco Bay Area, Phase I summary report.* Prepared by Frank C. Boerger for U.S. Maritime Administration and The Northern California Ports and Terminals Bureau, Inc. Oakland, California.

_____1976. *Methodology for estimating capacity of marine terminals, Volume I, standardized methodology.* Prepared by Manalytics, Inc. for U.S. Maritime Administration and Northern California Ports and Terminals Bureau, Inc. Oakland, California.

_____1976. *Methodology for estimating capacity of marine terminals, Volume II NORCAL port capacities.* prepared by Manalytics, Inc. for U.S. Maritime Administration and Northern California Ports and Terminals Bureau, Inc. Oakland, California.

U.S. Department of Defense, Corps of Engineers. 1962-1974. *Port series—part 2* (50 Volumes on individual ports). Washington, D.C.: Government Printing Office.

_____ Annual. *Waterborne commerce of the United States* (5 Volumes) Washington, D.C.

U.S. Department of Transportation. 1977. *National transportation trends and choices* (to the year 2000). Washington, D.C.: Government Printing Office.

Van Lopik, Jack R. and James Stone. 1974. Environmental planning for future port development, in *Port planning and development,* eds. E. Schenker and H. Brockel. Cambridge, Massachusetts: Cornell Maritime Press. pp. 154-174.

Washington Public Ports Association. 1975. *Port system study for the public ports of Washington State and Portland, Oregon.* Volume I, Executive summary prepared by The Aerospace Corporation for Washington Public Ports Association, the Port of Portland, and the U.S. Maritime Administration. Olympia, Washington: WPPA.

_____1975. *Port system study for the public ports of Washington State and Portland, Oregon.* Volume II. Technical supplement/Part I. Study approach, commodity specifications, trend analysis, and domestic trade origin and destination data. Prepared by the Aerospace Corporation for Washington Public

Ports Association, Port of Portland, and U.S. Maritime Administration. Olympia, Washington: WPPA.

_____1975. *Port system study for the public ports of Washington State, and Portland, Oregon.* Volume II. Technical supplement/Part 2, Port facilities inventory. Prepared by Reid, Middleton and Associates, Inc. for Washington Public Ports Association, Port of Portland, and U.S. Maritime Administration. Olympia, Washington: WPPA.

_____1975. *Port system study for the public ports of Washington State and Portland, Oregon.* Volume II. Technical supplement/Part 3, Forest products analysis. Prepared by Greenacres Consulting Corporation for Washington Public Ports Association, Port of Portland and U.S. Maritime Administration. Olympia, Washington: WPPA.

_____1975. *Port system study for the public ports of Washington State and Portland, Oregon.* Volume II. Technical supplement/Part 4, Puget Sound and Lower Columbia subregion commodity forecasts. Prepared by EMSCO Engineering and Management Sciences Corporation for Washington Public Ports Association. Port of Portland, and U.S. Maritime Administration. Olympia, Washington: WPPA.

_____1975. *Port system study for the public ports of Washington State and Portland, Oregon.* Volume II. Technical supplement/Part 5, Marine-port technology forecasts and demand analyses. Prepared by F.J. Nickols for Washington Public Ports Association, Port of Portland and U.S. Maritime Administration. Olympia, Washington: WPPA.

_____1975. *Port system study for the public ports of Washington State and Portland, Oregon.* Volume II. Technical supplement/Part 6, Port capacity analysis and methodology. Prepared by Reid, Middleton & Associates, Inc. for Washington Public Ports Association, Port of Portland and U.S. Maritime Administration. Olympia, Washington: WPPA.

Periodicals

Container News. Container News, Inc., 150 East 52nd Street, New York, N.Y. 10022. (monthly)

Container International Yearbook 1977. London: National Magazine Company Ltd. Chestergate House, Vauxhall Bridge Road. (annual)

Handling and Shipping. Industrial Publishing Company, 60 East 42nd St., New York, N.Y. or 812 Huron Road, Cleveland, Ohio 44115. (monthly)

Marine Engineering Log. Published by Simmons-Boardman Publishing Corporation, 85 West Harrison Street, Chicago, Ill. 60605. (monthly)

Marine Journal. Primrose Publishing, New York, N.Y. (monthly)

National Defense Transportation Journal. The official publication of the National Defense Transportation Association. NDTA, Suite 706, 1612 K Street N.W., Washington, D.C. 20006. (bimonthly)

Ports and Harbors. Central Secretariat of the International Association of Ports and Harbors, Kotohira-Kaikan Building, I Kotochira-Cho, Minato-Ku, Tokyo, 105 Japan. (quarterly)

Transportation and Distribution Management. Traffic Service Corporation, Washington Building, Washington, D.C. 20005. (monthly)

World Ports. The official publication of the American Association of Port Authorities. Published by Amundsen Publication, Inc., P.O. Box 39092, Washington, D.C. 20016. (annual)

Bibliographies

Assembly Select Committee on Deepwater Ports, California. 1974. *Deepwater ports bibliography.* Sacramento, CA.

Harrison, E. A. 1973. *Supertankers and superports: a bibliography with abstracts.* Springfield, Va.: National Technical Information Service.

Hurd, B., and Passero, B. 1974. *Oceans of the world: The last frontier, an annotated bibliography of the law of the sea,* Report No. COM-74-10817. Springfield, Va.: National Technical Information Service.

Maritime Research Information Service, National Research Council, National Academy of Sciences. *MRIS abstracts.* Washington, D.C.: National Academy of Sciences. Monthly.

Oosterbaan, N. 1974. *An introductory bibliography on dredging and the environment.* The Hague, Netherlands: International Association of Dredging Companies.

Pollution Abstracts, Inc. *Pollution abstracts.* La Jolla, CA: Pollution Abstracts, Inc. Bimonthly.

U.S. Department of Commerce. Maritime Administration. 1975. *Port information sources.* Maritime Administration, Washington, D.C.

INDEX

Air, water quality, 51, 61-2

American Association of Port Authorities, 8

Ameriports, See Philadelphia Port Corp. South Jersey Port Corp.

Brownsville Navigation Dist.
  organization, 163
  permit procedure, 87-8
  state management program interaction, 96, 98
  water quality control, 62

Brownsville, Port of
  case study, (cargo characteristics, tonnages, location and facilities, maps, administration, planning and expansion programs, current issues), 158-64
  industrial development, 12, 108
  permit coordination, 106-7

Brunswick (Ga.) Port Authority, 154

California
  capital improvement program, 126-7
  coastal management program, 171-6
  port organization, 9
  South Coast Regional Commission, 100-1
  State Coastal Commission, 71, 171-5

California Assoc. of Port Authorities, 94-5, 101, 169

California Coastal Act of 1976
  air, water quality, 62
  development, 101
  dredging policy, 61
  energy facilities sites, 71-2
  environmental damage mitigation, 64
  GAPC determination, 37, 174
  generally, 41, 167-8
  landfill policy, 53-4, 57
  permit procedures, 86
  port development role, 104
  public access policy, 67
  regulatory agency coordination, 39
  small craft harbors, 75
  waterfront land conservation, 81

California Coastal Conservancy, 67

California Coastal Zone Conservation Act of 1972
  See also California Coastal Act of 1976
  environmental damage mitigation, 65

California LNG Terminal Act, 71

Camden, NJ
  See also South Jersey Port Corp.
  case study (cargo characteristics, tonnages, location and facilities, maps, administration, planning and expansion programs, current issues), 140-4

Capital improvements, 125-7

Case studies
  See also specific case studies
  cargo tonnage, 18
  criteria, 5
  information gathering, 128

Citizen involvement, 42

Clean Air Act, 61

Clean Water Act of 1977, 22

Coastal Area Facility Review Act, See New Jersey

Coastal energy impact, 49

Coastal Energy Impact Program, 126

Coastal management programs
  See also State management programs specific states
  definition for study, 7

Coastal Marshland Protection Act of 1970, See Georgia

Coastal zone
  boundary determination, 34-5
  definition interpretation, 15-6

Coastal Zone Management Act of 1972
  aesthetics considerations, 66, 68
  air, water quality, 61-2
  authority granted to states, 40
  GAPC, 36
  generally, 1-2, 7, 29
  public access, 66
  public-government involvement, 42
  purpose, objectives, 30
  state-federal interaction, 42-3, 46

Coastal Zone Management Office, 42-3, 46

Coastal Zone Management Advisory Committee, 8

Coastal Zone Task Force, 48

Coast Guard, 22

Columbia River Estuary Study Team
  dredged material disposal, 61
  environmental damage mitigation, 68
  interstate planning, 48, 106, 110

Commerce
  US waterborne, 19
  world seaborne, 17

Corps of Engineers
  channel maintenance, 15
  dredging, 58, 130
  environmental damage mitigation, 53, 68
  permit procedures, 86, 90
  regional development, 103-4
  regulatory powers, public works, 23-7

Deepwater Port Act of 1974, 22

Delaware River Basin Commission, 138-9, 149

Delaware River and Bay Region, 138-9

Delaware River Port Authority, 99, 110, 138-40, 146-9

Dredging
See also Environmental damage mitigation
estuary management, 105-6
generally, 51, 57-61

Economic development, 107-8

Economic Development Administration, 15

Energy facilities sites, 71-2

Environmental damage mitigation, 51, 53, 63-6, 124-5

Environmental Policy Act
See National Environmental Policy Act specific states

Environmental Protection Agency
environmental damage mitigation, 65
regulatory authority, 23, 26, 28

Estuaries
See also Columbia River Estuary Study Team
Grays Harbor
management, 105-6
national studies, 30
sanctuary establishment, funding, 49

Federal agency
See also specific agency
coordination of, 43-4

Federal Energy Regulatory Commission, 72

Federal Maritime Commission, 22-3

Federal regulations
See also specific acts
generally, 23-6

Fish and Wildlife Coordination Act, 25

Fish and Wildlife Service, See US Fish and Wildlife Service

Fish and Wildlife, state ownership, 27

Funds, funding, 8, 13-5, 47-8, 126

GAPC (Geographic Area of Particular Concern)
See also specific states
generally, 36-8

Georgia
Coastal Area Planning and Development Commission, 111
coastal management program, 156-8
Coastal Marshland Protection Act of 1970
dredging policy, 59
environmental damage mitigation, 64
landfill policy, 53
permit procedures, 85
Coastal Zone Advisory Council, 151, 157

Georgia Ports Authority
case study (cargo characteristics, tonnages, location and facilities, maps, administration, planning and expansion programs, current issues), 150-4
GAPC, 38
public-private relationship, 12
state program interaction, 96

Grays Harbor, Port of
case study (cargo characteristics, tonnages, location and facilities, maps, administration, planning and expansion programs, current issues), 176-81
dredging policy, 59-60, 103-4
estuary
as GAPC, 38
study, 111
task force, 60, 78, 105
industrial development, 12
landfill project, 54, 57
permit coordination, 107
planning, 15
shoreline alteration controls, 24
state program interaction, 98-9
waterfront land
allocation, 78
conservation, 79-80

Great Lakes Basin Commission, 48, 109-10, 137

Hazardous facilities, 51, 70-2

Hueneme, Port of, 41, 64

Information exchange, 121-2

Interstate coordination
See also Regional planning
generally, 48

Interstate Commerce Commission, 22-3

Interstate grants, 109

Landfill
See also Environmental damage management, 51-7

LNG terminals, 70-2

Long Beach, Ca., 41

Los Angeles, Port of
case study (cargo characteristics, tonnages, location and facilities, maps, administration, planning and expansion programs, current issues), 166, 169-72
growth, planning, 16-7
public-private ownership, 12
state program interaction, 98

McAteer-Petris Act (Ca.), 55

Maritime Administration, 22

Massachusetts
coastal management proposal, 92
energy facilities sites, 71-2
redevelopment, 91-2
small harbor development, 73
waterfront land allocation, 78-9, 83

Merchant Marine Act of 1920, 22

Mid-Atlantic Governor's Coastal
Resources Council, 110

Milwaukee, Port of
case study (cargo characteristics,
tonnages, location and facilities,
maps, planning and expansion
programs, current issues), 128-32
public input, 100
state program interaction, 96-8

Mitigation
See Environmental damage mitigation

National Academy of Science study, 8

National Environmental Policy Act, 23, 26,
28

National Estuarine Pollution Study, 30

National Estuary Study, 30

National interest considerations, 43-4, 46,
114-5

National Marine Fisheries Service
environmental damage mitigation, 53,
65
regulatory authority, 23, 25-6

National Research Council study, 4

Navigable waters, definition, 25

New England-New York Coastal Zone
Task Force, 109

New England River Basin Commission, 8,
48, 109

New Jersey
See also South Jersey Port Corp.
Coastal Area Facility Review Act, 36,
61, 88, 140, 144-6
coastal management program, 144-6
project review, 88-9
regulatory authority coordination, 39

New Orleans, waterfront access, 69

New York/New Jersey Port Authority, 15

Northern California Ports and Terminals
Bureau
port capacity study, 17, 103
regional planning, 103

Ocean Dumping Act, 49

Oceanographic Commission of
Washington, 111

Oregon
environmental damages mitigation, 64
port organization, 9

Pennsylvania
coastal management program, 148-50
waterfront land allocation, 79

Permits
coordination, 106-7
delay problems resolution, 120-1
procedure streamlining, 51, 83-7

Philadelphia Port Corp.
case study (cargo characteristics,
tonnages, location and facilities,
maps, administration, planning and
expansion programs, current issues),
146-8
facilities, 143

Philadelphia, Port of
dredged material disposal, 61
interstate participation, 110
redevelopment, 90-1
waterfront land use, 79

Port and Waterway Safety Act, 22

Portland, Or., Port of, 105

Ports
See also specific ports
administration
Brownsville, 162-3
Camden, 142
Georgia, 154-6
Grays Harbor, 179-80
Los Angeles, 171
Milwaukee, 132-4
Philadelphia, 147-8
capacity studies, 3
development, 13
economic impacts, 21
enabling legislation, 9, 11
growth statistics, 11-2
planning generally, 15-7
sizes of selected US, 6

Redevelopment of facilities, 51, 90-2, 108-
9, 122-3

Regional planning
see also Interstate coordination
allocation of facilities, 118-20
forecasting, 102-3
Great Lakes, 99
multijurisdictional problems, 109-11
study examples, 81-2

Research training and technical
assistance, 48

Rivers and Harbors Act of 1899, 25

San Diego Unified Port District, 41

San Francisco Bay
estuary management, 106
landfill, 55-7

regional planning, 81-2, 103
waterfront land allocation, 77-8

San Francisco Bay Conservation and
Development Commission, 55, 78-9,
128, 173

Savannah/Chatham County Metropolitan
Planning Commission, 111

Savannah Port Authority, 156

Savannah, Port of
See also Georgia Ports Authority
case study, 151-2, 156
facilities ownership, 12

Sea Grant studies, 8

Seattle, Port of
air, water quality, 62
environmental damage mitigation, 65
landfill management, 57
planning, 15
public access, 67-70
Shoreline Master Program, 62

Small craft harbors, 51, 73-5

South Coast Regional Commission, See
California

South Jersey Port Corp.
case study, 140-4
state program interaction, 96

State-federal conflicts, mediation, 42-3

State management programs
See also specific states
appeals boards, 42
approved, operational, 2
authority granted under federal act, 40
funding, 47-8
implementation, 31-4, 40-1, 47
interagency relationships, 38-41
port
development effects, 114
interaction, 93-9
participation in, 104-5, 116-7
public input, 100-1
review by Office of Coastal Zone
Management, 46-7

Stratton Commission, 7, 30

Tacoma, Port of, 46

Tampa, Port of
dredging, 106
environmental damage mitigation, 66

Texas
Coastal Coordination Act, 88
coastal management program, 164-6
Dredged Materials Act, 86
Natural Resources Council, 40-1, 86-7
permit procedures, 86
port organization, 9
project review, 88

Texas Coastal and Marine Council
program development, 111

public involvement, 100
regional planning, 103

Tonnage
handling growth, 17-20
port statistics, 6, 18

US Fish and Wildlife Service
environmental damage mitigation, 53, 65
federal interaction in state, 46
regulatory authority, 23, 25-6
water dependency determination, 79

US Marine Council, 7, 30

Vessel traffic-control systems, 22

Washington
coastal management program, 176-82
energy facilities sites, 71
environmental classifications, 82-3
Environmental Coordination
Procedures Act, 85-6
environmental damage mitigation, 64
Environmental Policy Act, 87
permit procedure, 85-7
port organization, 9
project review, 89
Shoreline Management Act
federal involvement, 44-6, 183-4
GAPC determination, 37, 183
management, 182-4
public access, 67
small craft harbors, 74
water-dependent uses, 34-5
waterfront land allocation, 76-8
Tanker Safety Act, 46

Washington Environmental Council, 101

Washington Public Ports Assoc.
data systems study, 17
Ports System Study, 81, 102
regional planning, 81, 102

Waterbottom management, 27

Waterfront land
access, aesthetics, 51, 66-70
allocation, 51, 75-83
preservation, 79-82
redevelopment, 108-9

Water Pollution Control Act, 25, 61

Water Resource Development Act, 65

West Coast Oil and Ports Group, 110

Wilmington, Del., Port of, 110

Wisconsin
Coastal Coordinating and
Advisory Council, 42, 129-30, 137

coastal management program, 129-30, 134-8
Environmental Policy Act, 87
GAPC determination, 38, 137
Shorelands Act, 137